Stafford Chronicles

Manahawkin Railroad Station looking south from Stafford Avenue, about 1914.

To the memory of
Lou Brescia
and
Jack Cervetto,
who dedicated themselves to
Stafford Township
and to its rich history.

Stafford Chronicles

A History of Manahawkin, New Jersey

The mood seems to be relaxed on a sunny day, as even the dog goes out for a stroll.

For information, address:
Down The Shore Publishing, Box 3100, Harvey Cedars, NJ 08008
www.down-the-shore.com

Down The Shore and its logos are registered U.S. Trademarks.
Manufactured in Spain. First printing, 2001.
10 9 8 7 6 5 4 3 2 1

Book design by Leslee Ganss.

Library of Congress Cataloging-in-Publication Data

Stafford chronicles : a history of Manahawkin, N.J.
    p. cm.
    Based, in part, on Lillias F. and Louis A. Brescia's Stafford Township, 1749-1964 : a
pictorial review, published in 1964.
    Includes index.
    ISBN 0-945582-72-2
    1. Stafford (N.J. : Township)--History. 2. Stafford (N.J. : Township)--History--Pictorial
works. 3. Stafford (N.J. : Township)--Biography.   I. Brescia, Lillias F. Stafford
Township, 1749-1964. II. Down the Shore Publishing.

F144-S84 S73 2001
974.9'48--dc21

                                     2001032455

The unpainted cedar home was common, as were the noted cedar boats that the area produced over the past 200 years.

Dock Road, Cedar Run, 1908. Note the shell piles along the edge of Cedar Run.

CONTENTS

Taken from the Methodist Church steeple in the early 1900s. The railroad station is on the left, and Manahawkin Lake is at the top right of the photograph.

CONTENTS

From the same vantage point as the facing page; the Beach Avenue school is on the right, and the Baptist church is visible at the top.

INTRODUCTION

The tales of a town emerge from many places. On a windy night, they whisper through the trees. From sepia-toned photographs, the eyes of ancestors seem to speak. From some prescient person in another century who saw that the words were worth something, another picture develops of their place in time. And when today's living legends turn the key to the treasure chest of their memories, yesterday tumbles out.

Stafford Chronicles is a collection of those old and new reflections, reaching into the storehouse of research and gathering newly archived experiences of longtime residents.

The stories are based in Stafford, but they range to high points of shore area history from the 1600s to surfing in the 1960s.

The book started out to be a reissue of some wonderful work done by local historians. When the Stafford Township Historical Society approached The SandPaper and Down The Shore Publishing prior to the township's 250th anniversary celebration, it was looking to republish a volume of historical essays and vintage photographs. The volume, *Stafford Township: A Pictorial Review,* had been compiled and edited by Lillias F. Brescia and Louis A. Brescia for the Stafford Township Tercentenary Committee, which was observing New Jersey's 300th year in 1964.

Indeed, it was time for those priceless photographs and historical sketches to be seen by a larger audience.

Stafford Chronicles includes and adapts much of that original volume. The Brescias' in-depth research encompasses history of the town's transportation, government, religion, education, Manahawkin Lake, and businesses "gone but not forgotten."

Warren Grove resident and four-time Stafford Township mayor Jack Cervetto gave the community a lasting contribution that appears in adapted form at the beginning of *Stafford Chronicles*. Cervetto's "A Brief History of Manahawkin" spans 300 years. It was one of the few compilations of township history when it was published in 1964, and remains so.

Cervetto wove a genuine appreciation of local history and folklore into his account. He found a lot to work with — Manahawkin had a Revolutionary War skirmish on its main street, and its outlying forges made iron for munitions to defeat the British. Cervetto's historical scrapbook of later eras details the growth of a rural town at the shore's edge. His wife, Pearl, adds her own wealth of information on early-day Warren Grove.

To this, the book adds profiles of township residents.

Several writers interviewed local folks to preserve a time "back in the day." From a vantage point at the turn of the 21st century, they glance back with wit and wisdom.

Some, like Perry Inman and Ed Hazelton, are the descendants of the whalers and the adventurous Englishmen who carved the land into a place of their own. Because this is the community that their families built, they feel its history in their bones.

In his own words we can learn what adventures led to Perry's timeless advice to "stay the heck off of salt ice." In another anecdote, we read about the time Perry's dad and uncle certainly saw a sea serpent.

We can relive young Ed Hazelton's days when kids scrambled to the train station on Stafford Avenue to ogle the huge sea turtles carried on flatcars from "The Beach."

Another of these descendants of pioneers, Harold Crane, had already passed away between the time the writer interviewed him and the book was published. So his genealogy of the Cranes of Revolutionary times and of the Life Saving Service lives on here.

Manahawkin's own big-league baseball legend, Roger "Doc" Cramer, recalls the days on the diamond in a rare retrospective two years before his death in 1990. This local boy played the game with Ty Cobb, Joe DiMaggio and Ted Williams, and at home, he gunned with Babe Ruth off Cedar Run.

Stafford Chronicles compiles stories for everyone. For sportsmen, there's Milton Cranmer's recall of gunmetal-gray days duck hunting from "Cream Puff Castle" on the Flat Creek meadows. For railroad buffs, it's "All aboard" to ride the "Yellow Jacket" back in time.

There are men who can tell the tales of ocean fishing at dawn in the now-defunct pound boat industry. Phil Hart lets us feel the salty spray that braced these

Another view from the Methodist church steeple, this one from 1964: the Beach Avenue school and railroad station are visible; Cavalry Cottage is at the bottom left of the photograph.

men on their way through the breakers toward a hard-earned living.

Others shaped some of the East Coast's first surfboards in our Manahawkin back yard. Earl Comfort and John Spodofora recount the beginnings of the Ron Jon Surf Shop, a wave that was later marketed worldwide by neighbor Ron DiMenna.

Huck Finn-type adventure? Stafford had it. Burrel Adams describes growing up in a house perched on the wooden causeway bridge — his father was a bridge tender from the 1920s on. His accounts of fishing from a house window and watching causeway comings and goings are a delight.

Catamounts in the swamps and sharks cutting capers around an eight-foot sailing garvey: they're in Charley Farley's chapter. The Manahawkin grocer had jotted down the tales told around the wood stove in the earlier part of the 20th century, and added his own yarns. His manuscript comes to readers years after his death.

From the book *Four Months in a Sneak-box* are excerpts of Nathaniel Bishop's trek down the Mississippi River in the 12-foot craft. One SandPaper writer was led to investigate Bishop's local ties after a nature hike at Oxycocus, the site of one of his 18th-century cranberry plantations. She found that the Bishop Building of the Ocean County Library was the repository of Bishop's letters and business accounts. (Bishop had endowed the first Ocean County Library).

Women made a mark in the local workplace. Some set out to do so; others simply did a good job earning a living. Louise Hannold, age 79 at the time of the interview, runs a landmark eatery that has kept the tourists and the locals returning to Manahawkin's Bay Avenue. It's easy to see why — she and Warren Grove's Lucille Bates-Wickward serve up their own snappy brand of repartee along with the good food.

Other enterprising women answered Bell Telephone's call in the 1940s. The money was good, though the hours were long. Meanwhile, candy was sweet to Barbara Eismann as she entered her husband's family business that continues as one of Stafford Township's most unusual industries.

Stafford Chronicles also shares the birth and growth of Southern Ocean County Hospital, the glory days of the old Manahawkin Airport and the rise of the Beach Haven West development from the marshes in the 1950s.

Readers can hear from folks like Ziggy Kalicki, happy at home in Mud City, despite the 1962 tide so high it swept eelgrass to the roof.

The book tells of everyday people whose impact on the people around them is not so ordinary, like fire company volunteers Dan and Barbara Soper. It takes us close-up into the clamming business with Charles "Chill" Paul and the obstacles to carrying on a tradition.

There is lingering pleasure to be found in the past. By chuckling at the resourceful exploits and marveling at the changes, today's residents might control where we want to go next.

This collection is meant to appeal both to the families of the founders, and to the newer-comers to the township, so that they may know more about the place they call home.

— *Maria Scandale*

A woman's matronly manner by the backyard arbor speaks of home.

A Brief History of Manahawkin

If we had lived in Manahawkin in 1755, we would have found about 20 well-organized farms. On the farms stood other buildings to house the hired help and slaves.

This 1964 period piece is adapted from Jack Cervetto's booklet by the same name published during the celebration of New Jersey's tercentenary. The longtime Warren Grove resident and four-time Stafford Township mayor wove a genuine appreciation of local history and folklore into his research. Today's readers can take a look at the past through the eyes of a chronicler who, in 1964, hadn't seen the changes that were yet to come.

The first known white men to land on New Jersey shores were Giovanni da Verrazano and his crew in the ship *Dolphin*. Sailing for France, they landed at Sandy Hook in the spring of 1524.

Verrazano's account to the king of France gives a detailed description of the waterway there. He traveled up the river in a small boat and reported to the king that "The people on the banks are like us," and that they were dressed with bird feathers of various colors.

In 1609, Sir Henry Hudson visited our coast in the ship *Half Moon*. There is in the log book of the *Half Moon* a good account of his passage through an inlet where he found himself entering a large lake, which no doubt was Barnegat Bay. He spent two days at the bay shore. Finding the Indians to be friendly, he exchanged gifts with them. His mate wrote in his log book, "It is a very good land to fall in with and a pleasant land to see."

The first deed to lands that white men acquired in what was then Monmouth County was conveyed from two Indian brothers, Sachem and Mishacoing Popomora, on January 25, 1664. James Hubbard, John Bowne, John Tilton, Jr., Richard Stout, William Goulding, and Samuel Spicer acquired the parcel called Nevesink. Articles exchanged for the land were "118 fathoms of seawamp (wampum), five coats, one gun, one clout capp, one shirt, 12 pounds of tobacco and one ankor wine."

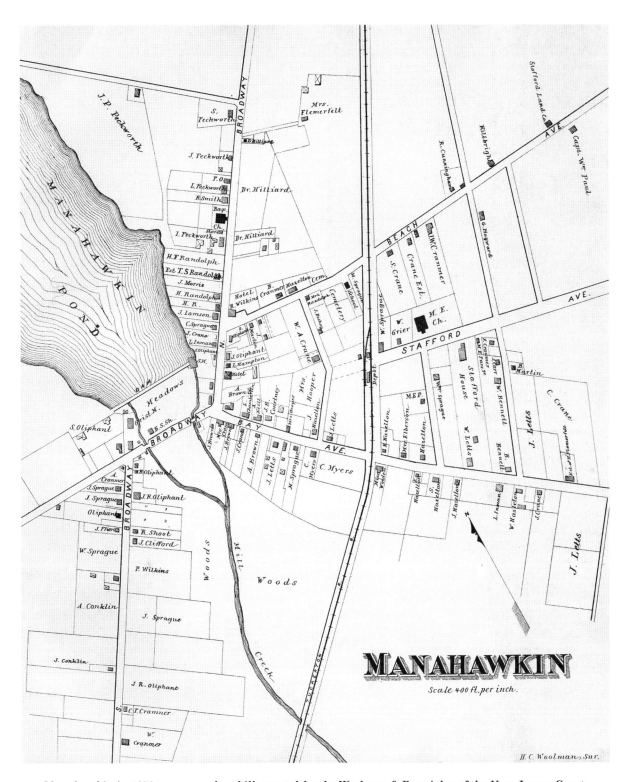

Manahawkin in 1878, as surveyed and illustrated for the Woolman & Rose Atlas of the New Jersey Coast.

"Bolton's Cottage" about 1924, looking northwest toward Main Street in Manahawkin.

This deed is recorded at Albany, New York; copies are in the Proprietors' Office in Perth Amboy and the Office of the Secretary of State in Trenton. Other transactions followed, and in a few years settlers stretched along the shores of Monmouth County and the land that would become Ocean County.

In 1664, when the white settlers took possession of their new land, about 2,100 Indians lived in the state. According to the census, in 1880 there were only 74 left. It is not known how many Indians then made their home in Stafford Township. We do know they left their villages in the forests of Central and West Jersey and came to our bay shores for the summer to live. They sun-dried clams and other bay foods for winter.

The last two Indians who were documented as living in Manahawkin were Cato and Lash. They lived at what was known as the Cato Place near Mill Creek Road. They are buried in the small cemetery at the corner of Beach Avenue and Division Street. The open well they used is still there.

I find no record as to the date of the first settlers in Stafford Township, but I find this statement:

"Brightly is the sun, lots of fertile land, bay full of clams, oysters, fish, plenty of wood, woods full of berries, marsh hens, rabbits, deer, and plenty more, all for the taking, and no taxes."

They settled near a creek on knolls as close to the bay as possible. Their only means of transportation was by boat. Clearing a piece of ground, they built huts of trees and covered them with sod and dirt. Some made log cabins and thatched their roofs with salt hay shingles that they bundled and fastened together.

Their main concern was clearing land for crops. The only fertilizers they had were leaves and fish. In the spring, shad came up the creeks to spawn. There were so many of them that it was no trouble to get what they wanted for their compost pile. Parts of three old fields can be found today along Cedar Run Dock Road, Mill Creek Road, Lower Beach Avenue and other places.

The first men to purchase lands in Stafford Township were Benjamin Paul, Levi Cranmer, Timothy Ridgway, James Haywood, Perry Paul and Luke Courtney. Records show that these men bought large tracts of land between 1735 and 1743. James Haywood, Perry Paul and Luke Courtney came from Staffordshire, England and settled in Manahawkin in 1743. They had purchased land here before they sailed from England.

That same year, 1743, the proprietors of the eastern part of what is now New Jersey hired their surveyor, John Lawrence, to draw a boundary from Little Egg Harbor Bay to the Delaware River at Fishkill. As more settlers came, it was thought that this boundary would serve to divide East Jersey and West Jersey, although the West Jersey proprietors would not agree to it. Lawrence marked the line with stones set along the way, finishing it in 1747. An original stone of the Lawrence Line remains on the west side of Route 9 north of West Creek.

Stafford Township, when it was created, started at Oyster Creek near Waretown and stretched southward to Eagleswood and the Little Egg Harbor line, across Long Beach Island and west to the Burlington County line.

Some towns were already settled when the new township was formed: Manahawkin (which included Cedar Run and Mayetta), Barnegat, Waretown, Wells Mills, Brookville, Cedar Bridge, Cedar Grove (now Warren Grove), West Creek, and towns on Long Beach Island.

Other family names that were established before or soon after Stafford came into being included Crane, Pangborn, Pearson, Randolph, Jennings, Hazelton, Brown, Lamson and Corlis.

A main attraction of the land around Manahawkin, besides the abundant seafood in the bay, was the vast cedar swamp. The virgin cedar averaged two to three feet in diameter and rose about 60 to 70 feet tall. Manahawkin was a site of one of the first sawmills in the area, along with those at Wells Mills and Cedar Bridge. Water wheels supplied the power. Anywhere today where there is a cedar swamp of any size, you will see the remains of a saw mill along its bank.

Mill Creek got its name from the sawmill that

Looking southwest from the Methodist Church steeple on Stafford Avenue, around 1910. The railroad tracks run diagonally across this view, crossing Bay Avenue at a location that is now near the center of town. The train station is at far right, and a railroad car can be seen sitting to the left. Cedar Run is in the distance.

The National Hotel around 1900. At this point the building had a fourth upper window and rear wing added to the original structure. Note the man with the shotgun, and the covered horse. One of these buggies was used for mail delivery.

known as the Manahawkin Tavern, on the corner of Beach Avenue and Route 9. During the American Revolution, the inn would serve as the meeting place of the Manahawkin Militia.

The Old Stone Store was also built about this time and was the first general store here. The road that goes by the store between Route 72 and Route 9 was called South Broadway.

The only stone hills I know of are west of Warren Grove, in a small area along Three-foot Branch. Is it possible that the stones were hauled 12 miles through the woods to construct this building?

Right from the beginning, people had to provide their own food. Most of them raised their own potatoes, beans and other vegetables. They stored them and canned them for year-round use. They raised their own corn and wheat and brought it to the grist mill at the Old Stone Store, where it was ground into flour. All families had chickens, a cow and a horse or mule, and most kept sheep. The women made clothes from the wool. The men tanned animal hides; then the women sewed work clothes and boots from the skins..

Those who did not follow the sea, with the exception of a few in business along the shore, spent the warm part of the year part-time in the bay clamming or oystering and part-time farming. In the cold weather, they chopped firewood and cut cedar by the cord for a sawmill operator. Working in the bay in summer and the woods in the winter is still a practice in this area, although there are only a few people left who are doing it.

Records show that a lumber company bought the Oswego Cedar Swamp in 1743, and it set up mills at Cedar Bridge and Warren Grove. These mills gave year-round work to the men. The old mill area at Cedar Bridge is called Candlewood. It was on the

operated by Manahawkin Lake. A dam was built across Mill Creek to have water deep enough to run the power wheel for the sawmill. These mills produced lumber which proved to be the best quality for houses and boats. The unpainted cedar home was common, as were the noted cedar boats that the area produced over the past 200 years.

A swamp in Cedar Run was cut out and its stream dammed. Macajas Willits built a grist mill there, and an old road along the Cedar Run Swamp to Cedar Bridge is called Macajas Road.

The quality of the area's cedar became known in the larger towns of North Jersey, New York and the towns west of us. Cedar was in demand, and boat building was a big business. Trading started about 1740 and increased as more boats were built. Many of the young men went to sea, and many eventually captained their own boats. Some of the homes honored in the tercentenary celebration are built partly or mostly of timber that grew around town.

The building on Hilliard Drive that became the Shinn Funeral Home was built in 1750 by Captain Reuben Randolph as his residence. Captain Randolph also owned and operated an inn, later

Manahawkin Tavern at the northeast corner of Beach Avenue and Main Street in the late 19th century. During the Revolutionary War, Capt. Reuben Randolph used his tavern as the headquarters of Monmouth Militia's Fifth Company, Second Regiment.

west side of Cedar Bridge-Warren Grove Road, which started along the west side of Cedar Bridge Hotel, then followed Oswego Swamp to Warren Grove. Along this road can be found holes in the ground where houses once stood. The Warren Grove Old Mill area was on this road just north of town.

Many years ago, when the Candlewood Sawmill was operating, there was a young man working there who was caught molesting a young girl. The men in the area went after him as he headed down Macajas Road toward Manahawkin. He turned off through the woods to a hollow. These men caught him there and mobbed him. This place is still called Mob Hollow. It is one of the starting points of Mill Creek.

A sad incident in Warren Grove that has been told through the years is the story of a five-year-old girl. Mrs. Mullin, mother of the girl, gave her a cup and sent her down to Mrs. Johnson at the next farm for some sugar. Between the two farms, an old road runs through the woods that she walked into. It was summer and little girls usually stopped along the way to pick huckleberries. She must have lost her sense of direction, and that night a hard thundershower came over the area. The family searched everywhere, but she could not be found. The following deer season, some hunters found the child's body about 50 feet off the old road, seated against a big pine tree with the cup in her hand and a few dried berries in it.

If we had lived in Manahawkin in 1755, we would have found about 20 well-organized farms. Some had good homes with a fireplace in each room. On the farms also stood other buildings to house the hired help and slaves.

We should give these first settlers a lot of credit in the manner they planned their town. The roads laid out by these men are still used today with proper width for traffic. It can be truly said that they planned for future progress.

About this time, the settlers were seriously thinking of building a house of worship. By 1758, they had acquired a deed for land and a building was finished. For about 12 years, the church on Main Street was open to all preachers who passed through Manahawkin. In 1779, nine members, under the leadership of the Rev. Benjamin Miller, organized the First Baptist Church Society in this house of worship. This society is still in existence, though the present structure dates from just before the Civil War. This is the first house of worship in what is now Ocean County.

The church doubled as the only school in Stafford Township until about 1800, and the only book was the Holy Bible. The children were given credit for the number of verses they memorized. They made red ink from poke berries and blue ink from indigo berries. They used crow quills for their pens, and they had only stone slabs and wood to write on.

In the Thick of Revolution

The discovery of bog ore in about 1760 opened up a new enterprise in South Jersey. Charles Read of Burlington built and operated iron furnaces at Atsion and Batsto. A little later, others bought his interests and built a furnace in Old Martha, west of Warren Grove, and at Stafford Forge, south of Warren Grove. Batsto and Atsion were in operation as early as 1765 and 1766. Martha Furnace and Stafford Forge were built during the Revolutionary War. These iron operations produced cannons and ammunitions which helped defeat the British. The enemy knew this and made many attempts to enter the Mullica River to destroy the furnaces. Our forces stopped them every time, several of these times by bloody battles along the Mullica shores.

The seeds of the Revolution were planted in the self-sufficient towns like those around Stafford. England, seeing the towns in the colonies prospering, imposed taxes on these people who worked so hard to establish their new homes. The colonists, who were not represented in England and derived no benefit from the taxes they paid, formed committees that united in one great force to free themselves of this burden. Independence came after many bitter battles and sacrifices.

In the midst of a revolution, the local men could not rest without having an organized guard unit on watch. Manahawkin had its own militia, whose principal job was to guard the shore and to capture any British ship sailing along the coast. The Manahawkin Militia was a part of the Second Regiment, Monmouth Militia. Its captain was Reuben F. Randolph and its adjutant, Nathan Crane. The men plotted by candlelight at Captain Randolph's inn on the corner of Beach Avenue and the road that is now Route 9. They built a stockade at the rear of their

headquarters to temporarily hold prisoners. Confiscated supplies became a source of income when they were used or sold. The men seized ships like the *Polly* and the *Dilly-Latta* along the coast of Long Beach Island. Taking the crew as prisoners, the militia searched the ships. Found on board were 202 barrels of flour, a very valuable item during this period, and 15 kegs of bread. In 1778, Captain Randolph and Adjutant Crane and their men captured another armed British vessel at Barnegat Inlet. The take was 60 prisoners and 5,000 pounds' worth of cargo. Privateering proved to be an invaluable way to capture the invaders and their goods before they could land on our shores.

One devastating blow fell against the Manahawkin Militia members October 25, 1782, after a ship bound for the British Virgin Islands grounded just south of Barnegat Inlet. Several militiamen answered a call by Cape May-based privateers to help raid the stranded vessel, and about a dozen men were left there to unload the ship. That night while they were sleeping, the notorious Loyalist John Bacon sneaked up and killed them and seized the goods.

Another incident occurred at Cedar Bridge, near Warren Grove, during that war. The Mount Holly Militia was after Bacon and his men between the Half-Way House and Cedar Bridge. When Bacon crossed the bridge at the Cedar Bridge Hotel, his pursuers blocked it with logs and started shooting. Several of the militiamen were killed, including an officer, but Bacon and his men got away. It seems that some of the Cedar Bridge residents were on Bacon's side, because later they were picked up and brought to Burlington, where they were tried and convicted. [This skirmish was the last battle of the Revolutionary War.]

The Half-Way House is where Mayo's Tavern on Route 72 is today. When the stage coach made the run, that spot was half way between Mount Holly and Manahawkin.

Just before the war, a gang of men called the Pine Pirates were under Bacon's leadership. He used a cave northwest of Warren Grove at a place called Bacon's Ridge. During the war, they joined the enemy. They would enter a town at night and steal what they wanted and then withdraw to the woods. One night while the men of the Manahawkin Militia were asleep at Captain Randolph's inn, they were awakened by the outside guard and told that

South Broadway, A Road Not Traveled

Varying views of South Broadway (now the Route 9 south exit from Route 72), which connected with present day Route 9 just south of the lake. Above, at the turn of the 20th century and below, in 1964, looking from about where the Old Stone Store stands, toward the still-nostalgic town center. Visible are the distinctive mansard roof of the Hall store (today, the site of the Diamond Mine), and the National Hotel (now a parking lot for Carroll's).

Standing approximately at the intersection of Bay Avenue and Route 9, looking northwest: At top, circa 1900, Shutes' blacksmith shop is on the left. A closer look, around the same time, shows the Old Stone Store (center) and the grist mill (right). The lake would be to the right of the mill.

A 1960 view of the National Hotel, on what is now Carrol's parking lot. The third story and enclosed porch were added under the ownership of William F. Taubel, who bought the hotel in 1887. The popularity of the hotel peaked after the railroad came to town in 1871, but it stood as a meeting place for another century.

the enemy was approaching from the north. It was Bacon and his men. The militiamen got out in time before Bacon's crew arrived, but became engaged in a battle outside between the inn and the Baptist church. The militia, seeking reinforcements, decided to retreat toward West Creek. In the battle, Lines Pangborn was killed and Sylvester Tilton was injured. Bacon's wounded men were placed in the church, which their leader made his headquarters for a while.

Not long after this battle, the militia was enlarged. The tavern became headquarters for the Fifth Company, Second Regiment, Monmouth Militia from 1776 to 1783. Bacon was shot and wounded in Manahawkin and later killed in a West Creek tavern in 1783.

The needs of the war opened many wagon roads. People moved into the woods to do business from the western part of the state and Philadelphia. Materials were in great demand at the foundries at Batsto, Atsion, Martha, Stafford Forge and others. Charcoal burning was an early industry because trees were so abundant. Charcoal was first used as a purifier of ore in the smelting process; later it was

applied to heating and cooking. For many years the Pine Barrens smoldered day and night. Meanwhile, men were looking everywhere for bog ore to fuel the furnaces. In Stafford Township, we find signs where ore was taken from the east side of Three-Foot Branch, Mob Hollow, Stone Hollow, Dry Branch, and the head of Cedar Run Branch.

From the Revolutionary War to about 1850, virtually every square mile of the Pine Barrens produced something for market. Saw and axe attacked the great cedar swamps. Sawmills buzzed everywhere. Pine was cut and stacked for charcoal pits. Oak was felled for firewood, for it was the only means of heating and cooking all year 'round. Although it seemed that every able-bodied man along the shore became a captain, still more goods were produced than the boats could transport. New roads were laid, soon trodden on by horse and wagon hauling goods to Mount Holly, Burlington, Trenton, Camden and other markets.

The bay was also attacked by hungry settlers, and as early as 1720, the first restrictive regulation on oystering was passed. It became illegal to disturb the oyster beds during the spawning season, from May 10 to September 1.

Travelers on the earliest developed roads would have encountered post riders on horseback, carrying news and communication to all parts of the state from the central post office at Trenton.

The first stagecoach route from New York to Tuckerton was established about 1800. The coaches stopped at Freehold, Lakewood, Toms River, Manahawkin, and Tuckerton. These stages carried the mail, leaving it at taverns where the stage would stop to pick up or let off passengers. These old coaches were covered Jersey Wagons that held 12 people and were drawn by four or six horses. The loose, white sand through the pines made for hard pulling.

The second stagecoach route made connections at Mount Holly to Ong's Hat, with stops at Cedar Bridge and Manahawkin Tavern. The Cedar Bridge stop was at the old Cedar Bridge Tavern, which was owned and operated by Luke Courtney, then later run by his son, John. The late Luke Courtney whom some of us remember was born in this tavern that was operated by his grandfather.

In 1790, there were two townships in what is now Ocean County. The first was Stafford, created in 1749, and Dover was created in 1767. The population of Old Stafford in 1790 was 883 and Old Dover, 910. In 1810, Old Stafford had 1,239 residents and Old Dover, 1,882. Union Township was the first township to separate from Stafford in 1846. Its towns were Barnegat and Cedar Bridge. Eagleswood Township separated from Old Stafford in 1874. Towns in its jurisdiction were West Creek, most of Staffordville, and Stafford Forge, as well as the communities on Long Beach Island. Ocean Township separated from Old Stafford in 1876 with its towns, Brookville, Wells Mills, and Waretown. There is a very good possibility that it was originally Waier's Mill. Abraham Waier, records show, had several mills. He founded Waretown in 1737 and became a prominent businessman in the area.

About 1790 when people were living almost normally again after the war, there was a stir of religious revivals caused by the influence of Bishop Asbury, the Rev. Waters and others who preached a powerful doctrine of Methodism. In a few years there was a Methodist church built in almost every town of fair size in New Jersey. About the turn of the 18th century, a group of people organized to build a Methodist church in Stafford Township. The men salvaged the lumber of wrecked ships to help it, and the church was finished in 1802. Although the church was altered and added to in later years, the lumber from these wrecked boats is still in that church on Stafford Avenue.

In the early 1930s, a Civilian Conservation Corps camp, under Army discipline and management for young men, was established in Manahawkin on the upper end of Oxycocus Road. The young men were put to work digging drainage ditches in the bayshore swamps and meadows. The trenches are commonly called mosquito ditches. Several of these young men married girls here and stayed in the area. Some of these men that I know are Frank Marini, Sr., Paul Vlcek and Daniel Tortoriello.

At the start of World War II, the CCC camp stopped operations, and all the buildings were sold and dismantled. A growth of pine covers the land where the camp stood.

Soon after the camp closed, the Ocean County Board of Freeholders formed a Mosquito Commission. Stephen Johnson of Manahawkin was put in charge of our area and continued the mosquito ditching along the bayshore area. Later it was mostly done by machine.

Some of the town's old businesses were improved in Manahawkin when Benjamin Oliphant moved here from Medford in 1813. The cedar around Manahawkin was his main interest at first. He bought a large acreage including the old sawmill on the dam, the old grist mill and the Old Stone Store.

He immediately brought to Manahawkin skilled help and laborers. His first project was to enlarge the sawmill with the most modern machinery of that day. After the mill was finished, he built homes for his men along present-day Route 9 on the lake side. His lumber business proved very successful, and most of the lumber was shipped to the New York market by boat. The Old Stone Store was attractive for a country store of those days. Mr. Oliphant carried a variety of items — food, clothing, hardware — most everything a family needed. He also enlarged the old grist mill, and it produced flour and animal feed for people from miles around.

Stafford Avenue, looking east from Division Street, about 1900. Look closely and see that a friendly dog seems to be begging for attention.

Benjamin Oliphant was elected to township office for many years and later was elected a freeholder of Monmouth County, to which Stafford still belonged.

A son, Samuel Oliphant, attended private school at Burlington. Along with tending to business, he also was elected to township office for several years, and like his father, became a county freeholder. Another son, Joseph, spent his life in charge of the mills. Benjamin Oliphant died in October 1873 at 83 years of age. After his father's death, Samuel retired and turned his share of the business to his son, Benjamin, who operated it to the end.

The Oliphants also ran a boat building yard and a large farm in Manahawkin. All these operations ceased about 1900. The only landmark that can be seen today is the remains of the Old Stone Store.

Another business establishment was the two-story blacksmith shop operated by Seymore Shutes east of Old Broadway, about opposite the Old Stone Store. About 200 feet south of the blacksmith shop on the same side of the road was a large sawmill operated by Gideon Giberson. The Giberson home was torn down in 1963, as it was feared that children playing or roaming there could get hurt. The Gibersons have a fine reputation of having been good sawmill men for several generations. Everett Giberson operates a sawmill west of the Old Stone Store.

The date that the Manahawkin Tavern ceased to operate is not known. The last man running a hardware store at the same location was Elmer Cranmer. His wife was principal of Manahawkin School for many years. In the mid-1940s, this building was remodeled and made into a private dwelling.

The National Hotel enjoyed its peak of business after the railroad came through Manahawkin in 1871. The big red barn behind it was a popular place for dances and other entertainment. The operator of this hotel was Dick Shafto. To satisfy the large number of men who stayed in his hotel in duck season, he built a pole road through Manahawkin Swamp to the meadows to make it easier for them to get to their duck blinds. The hotel was improved many times during the years. In 1964 it was being managed by Nicholas Visco.

Many other businesses have come and gone in our township. There was a blacksmith shop in Warren Grove, and the last blacksmith was Thomas Haywood. The only marking of the location today is the Haywood lot.

For years there was a fair business in salt hay, sphagnum moss, charcoal, oystering and farming. Now these types of operations are just about finished.

The first doctor in Manahawkin — the first in Ocean County — was Dr. G. Augustus Hankinson, who came here in 1825. He lived with Benjamin Oliphant for 10 years. In 1836, Dr. Hankinson bought Capt. Randolph's property on Hilliard Drive. Dr. Hankinson's nephew, Dr. William A. Newell of Allentown, New Jersey, came to live with his uncle. In 1848, Dr. Newell was elected to Congress. He is credited with sponsoring the first life saving stations along the coast.

The property was later purchased by Dr. Phineas Kirkbride Hilliard. He served the people well as a doctor in the area for many years. On February 1, 1873, Joshua Hilliard was born in Manahawkin. After studying at the Jefferson Medical College in Philadelphia and the University of Maryland, he started to practice in his father's office in 1901.

In 1950, at the observance of the 100th anniversary of Ocean County, Joshua Hilliard suggested that the time had come to start an Ocean County Historical Society. The society was soon created, with him as its first president.

In 1956, a couple of years after Dr. Hilliard died, a few of us in the township office were sold on the idea that with the background of the Hilliard property and its ideal location, it would be a good move to buy the property for municipal purposes and museums. The township at this date had no municipal building. But the people turned out in large groups to protest the township's purchasing the property for $10,000.

The property was bought by Thomas L. Shinn, funeral director, and made into a funeral home. This building is the same structure today as it was when it was built as Reuben Randolph's home in 1750, with some reinforcements and minor changes made outside.

The first postmaster in Manahawkin was appointed in 1819. The post office was located in various businesses in the early years. I am quite sure that after the first postmaster was appointed at Manahawkin, the post office was located at the place of business of every newly appointed postmaster. One of these places was the grocery and meat store on Stafford Avenue. This business was owned

Manahawkin's business section around the turn of the 20th century, when Main Street was still a dirt road. The building at right is the Hall store (today the Diamond Mine), operated by William R. Hall of Philadelphia as a boarding house and general store. Charles A. Sprague was the next owner, in the early 1900s. In the center of the photograph is the National Hotel.

and operated by Thomas Sprague. He was appointed postmaster at two different periods, in 1889 for three years and again in 1899 for 25 years.

The appointments made to date for postmaster in Manahawkin are as follows:

Edward Jennings, February 22, 1819; Samuel I. Jennings, October 24, 1832; Silas A. Crane, May 28, 1834; Samuel M. Oliphant, May 4, 1839; Charles M. Sloan, July 13, 1861; Jacob F. Allen, December 16, 1864; Joshua S. Lamson, March 18, 1868; Lewis B. Peckworth, October 1, 1869; William H. Flomerfelt, January 25, 1881; Jarvis H. Brown, June 20, 1881; Charles H. Cranmer, June 26, 1882; Uriah M. Adams, October 23, 1885; Edward E. Predmore, September 21, 1886; Thomas S. Sprague, April 3, 1889; Edward E. Predmore, July 12, 1893; John L. Lane, May 3, 1897; Thomas S. Sprague, April 2, 1899; Charles B. Sprague, March 27, 1926; Lucy M. Buckbee, August 29, 1934.

On July 1, 1921, post offices were set up in Manahawkin, Cedar Run and Mayetta, and the post office's rating was upgraded from fourth class to third class. In 1926, the post office moved from Sprague's store to a building at Stafford Avenue and Route 9, and to a new post office on Stafford Avenue in 1963. The Warren Grove Post Office was set up in 1910, with mail coming out of the Barnegat Post Office. Martha Cranmer was the postmaster at Warren Grove until about 1942, when it was closed and a rural route was established out of Barnegat. The post offices of Cedar Run and Mayetta were closed about 1950 and rural routes established to these towns out of the West Creek Post Office.

The first bank in Ocean County, The Ocean County National Bank, obtained its charter from the federal government in 1859. The bank in Toms River began business in the winter of 1862 and 1863. Before banks opened, the most important citizen of a community was the tavern keeper; he was the so-called banker. Business at the time of the Revolutionary War was conducted in taverns throughout the colonies.

During the Civil War period from 1860 to 1865, very little military action happened here. Those answering the call from this area were Joseph Cranmer, who carried a bullet wound on his forehead until he died; Thomas Hazelton, who was imprisoned by the Confederates; William Lowery; Samuel Corlis; William Throckmorton; George Pharo; Charles Smith; Alfred Johnson; Henry Allison; Joseph Bishop; Michael Bishop; Samuel Curtis; and Thomas Lamson. They all returned after the war. After the war a large number of families decided to pack wagons with their belongings and go west. This is the reason, I believe, that many of the old names are not here today. It was told that they traveled as far west as North Dakota and found a place that they liked there and made a settlement which they called Manahawkin.

The first train entered Ocean County at Toms River on July 3, 1866. The line was soon extended to Barnegat. At this time a group of businessmen formed the Tuckerton Railroad Association and laid a track from Tuckerton to Whitings and connected to a branch of the Pennsylvania Railroad. In 1871, the first train entered Manahawkin and went through to Tuckerton. Because of this train service, more people moved close to the shore. Cedar Run and Mayetta had an influx of new people and new homes in this period.

In 1883 and 1884, the Pennsylvania Railroad built the first railroad bridge from Manahawkin to Ship Bottom and then on down to Beach Haven and north to Barnegat City. This line connected with the Tuckerton Railroad at Manahawkin, and a railroad station was built here. There was also a spur, or side track, laid into Cedar Run starting at about the lower end of Jennings Road. It ran from the main track southwest on Manahawkin Avenue, then up Green Street, crossing Route 9 to a gravel pit. The railroad cars were pulled from the main track to the gravel pit by cables, then loaded with shovels by hand labor. When a car was full, the grade was sloped such that the load car rolled by itself to the main track. When the engine came along, it picked the car up and took it to the beach. For many years, car load after car load of fill and gravel went to the Island in this manner. This continued until trucks replaced the railroad cars.

The mainland residents became involved in lifesaving efforts during the many shipwrecks of the 19th century. One incident occurred in 1836, when Captain Stephen Willetts of Tuckerton was sailing up the coast of Long Beach Island during a heavy storm. The crew spotted an overturned hull of a ship. They went to it and soon heard tappings coming from underneath. They chopped away the

The schoolhouse on Beach Avenue. On the site today is the Stafford Township First Aid Squad building.

planks and found a young Spanish woman inside. She was the sole survivor of the wreck. This area is still called Ship Bottom.

Another terrible disaster took place on April 16, 1854. The ship *Powhattan*, on its way from Havre, France to New York with 300 on board, was driven ashore in a storm and all lives were lost. Of the dead, 250 were German immigrants. The ship wrecked along Long Beach Island off the Peahala shore. Manahawkin men and others found and picked up 128 bodies and laid them out in the Predmore barn behind the Predmore store on Stafford Avenue. They dug a long trench behind the Baptist church and buried the bodies there. A small monument was placed there by a relative of one man, and in 1904, the state of New Jersey erected a large monument in the church cemetery to memorialize "The Unknown from the Sea."

Congressman Newell of Manahawkin had been fighting hard in Washington to fund lifesaving stations. His efforts led to an agreement to build a station every five miles, but it called for only one watchman in each station. Finally, in 1886 a policy required each station to be manned by a paid crew, 24 hours a day.

Before this, volunteers stood watch for possible shipwrecks, especially during a northeasterly storm. Although they received no pay for this duty, some were rewarded by salvaging goods that floated ashore.

Progress Changes the Times

About this time, the Island began to experience a building boom, ushered in by the completion of the railroad to Beach Haven, which provided jobs for mainland residents. Most of the early industries were slowing down, and some were gone. The furnaces and forges that employed many of our people could not compete with the more plentiful Pennsylvania ore. The market for firewood and charcoal slowed as the demand for kerosene and Pennsylvania coal took over.

Cedar and pine lumber, though, jumped in demand when the Island developed. Every house had a cedar shingle roof and siding. The mainland woods could not produce the amount of lumber the Island boom required. Developers had to look elsewhere, so they shipped in lumber by railroad car. This gave rise to lumber yards. It seems strange that the area was one of the greatest lumber-producing areas in the past, shipping lumber everywhere. Now we go to a lumber yard to get the materials needed to build a small fence.

A wave of change had come. Many sea captains turned to carpentry and construction work. The railroad replaced boats for transport of foods. Farming was reduced to working backyard gardens. For years a very large number of our people depended on the Island for work from spring to late fall. One of the oldest building contractors in our township is Herbert Cranmer of Cedar Run. He is in his 80s and is still active in business. The houses he and his son Lawrence built would cover a large portion of the Island.

About 1912, some of the businessmen from the mainland and the Island created an authority to build a causeway across Manahawkin Bay and a road from the causeway to Beach Haven. The cost of this project was $93,000, which was raised by selling certificates to the general public. The project was completed in 1914.

In 1926, the state Highway Department accepted this bridge and made a wider causeway across the bay. It served the purpose until 1955, when work began on a new bridge with proper lighting. Building a four-lane highway through Manahawkin is being considered for the near future.

In the early days, the only lights people had in the evening were pitch pine knots. Later, tallow candles and fireplaces were used. Later still, the kerosene lamp came into use. In 1926 to 1928, electricity came to the shore. Soon after, we exchanged the old dripping ice box for an electric refrigerator. Later on, the kerosene stoves were replaced by gas or electric stoves. Many people kept their wood ranges in the kitchen for many years after coal and oil furnaces became practical.

Along with the hometown hardware and grocery stores, many businesses in town remain only in memory now. A cobbler shop was operated by Jessie Bishop next to the railroad on Stafford Avenue. On the southwest corner of Stafford and Letts avenues was a bakery shop. Delicious bread, pies and cinnamon buns were made and sold there in the railroad era.

On the opposite corner stood the Predmore Store. A variety of items, such as ice, groceries, hay, yard goods, etc., were sold here. The upper floor was used as a meeting place for the Ladies of the Golden Eagles, The Knights of the Golden Eagles and the Junior Order of American Mechanics. It was also the place where many a delicious church supper was served. Aunt Libby Crane and Aunt Hattie Willetts once had a candy store where Frank Marini built his new Firestone store.

On the west side of the railroad, northside and adjacent to Stafford Avenue, was the Atlantic Flour and Feed Co. It was owned and operated by Lee Hazelton and David Corliss. It did a good business in grains, flour, fertilizers, seed, wood, coal, hardware and many items used in homes and farms. On one side of the main entrance room stood a large potbelly stove. Here is where the men gathered. It was a favorite place for seafaring men, baymen, gunners, farmers and others who would sit for a spell and talk of bygone days and experiences. They would also spin a tall tale or two once in a while, and of course, the pleasant subject of women was discussed. This favorite spot is just a memory now. All gone.

Charles Cranmer and his father from Cedar Run were about the only surveyors in our township in the past. Their works are of great help today when trying to survey properties.

In our township today [1964] we have one medical doctor, Dr. Robert Irvin, who has his office and residence on the corner of Union Street and Bay Avenue. We have one dentist, Dr. Aaron Powitz on Selma Drive, Beach Haven West; two lawyers, John E. Selser of Manahawkin and John D. Crowley of Ship Bottom. Their offices are on Bay Avenue next to the drug store.

Roy Simmons is the first lawyer from Manahawkin. He attended schools here and lived in Manahawkin until he became a law partner with Judge Percy Camp. He then moved to Toms River. The offices of Camp and Simmons represent our township in all legal matters.

There was a time at the end of the 19th century when people in their new homes on Long Beach Island would get on the train and come to Manahawkin to get their groceries and other supplies. Thomas Sprague, being close to the station, had an extensive business. Many boxes of groceries and meats were loaded on the train in Manahawkin from Thomas Sprague's store and sent to the Island folks.

Another grocery was on the corner of Stafford Av-

Bessie and George McElvin's service station on Route 9 and Cedar Run Dock Road in the late 1920s. The business eventually became Love's Deli; today the building survives as Luv's Deli.

enue and Route 9. This store was owned and operated by Clark Cranmer. In the mid-1920s, this store was rented to the American Stores Co. with the agreement that it would sell the grocery line only. William Soper operated a butcher shop next door in the same building. American Stores went out of business here in the early 1950s. Charles Boltner bought the building from Charles Sprague and operated a grocery and meat line until abut 1960. Felix DiMenna now operates the same business here today.

Mainlanders picked cranberries on the Island at Cranberry Hill, now called Spray Beach. The Warren Grove and Cedar Bridge families picked their wild cranberries in open marshes along the Oswego River. Wild cranberries still grow in these same areas along the river.

About 1880, a man by the name of Webb experimented with cranberry plants and set out a small patch along the edge of a cedar swamp that was cut off. These plants produced so well that by 1900, there were thousands of acres of cedar swamps converted into cranberry bogs. Dams were built across cedar swamps with water-controlling trunks on both ends of bogs to feed water to the bog or release the water. Cranberry bogs had to be flooded with water in the winter to protect the vines from freezing. They were drained off in the latter part of April for the year's crop. Cranberry bogs in our township are found west of Manahawkin, in Cedar Run and Warren Grove. There are only five states in the United States that produce cranberries, and New Jersey

ranks third in production.

About the same time men started to cultivate cranberries in the cedar swamps where the cedar was cut off, the rich peat bottom produced a fungus called sphagnum moss. This moss was soon in demand by florists and nursery men. It would absorb water and hold it for a long period of time if properly wrapped. Florists made wreath designs with it on wire frames, then covered them with special paper. Fresh flower stems would be pushed through the paper into the moss to keep them fresh.

The nurserymen used moss to pack roots of trees and shrubs for shipping. Strawberries and other plants are still shipped in moss. During World War II, men who had gathered moss turned to defense jobs, and the florists and nurseries had to look for substitutes. Before that war, every man in Warren Grove and a number of men in Manahawkin, Cedar Run and Mayetta gathered moss for a living for many years. After the summer season, baymen would turn to the gathering of moss in fall and winter when it was not frozen. Some of the dealers in the past were Joe Paul of Manahawkin, Calvin Conklin and sons, Stanley and Marshall of Cedar Run, and myself.

Huckleberries grow wild most everywhere in the woods and swamps. The swamp blues are the most popular for pies. There are 18 different varieties of these berries. Some ripen early and some late. The small swamp blues and small swamp blacks start to ripen in mid-June. The large swamp blues and swamp

The Cranmer Building in Cedar Run

Cramner Building. Cedar Run, N. J.

Around 1925, W. S. Cranmer (who also served as justice of the peace and notary public, among other duties) and his wife operated a multi-service business on Route 9 (then called New York Road), at the intersection with Oak Avenue in Cedar Run. After standing empty and falling into decay (above, left), the 28-room building burned on Halloween night, 1964. The town once went by the name of Cranmertown, due to the large number of Cranmers in the community.

blacks, as well as all the upland berries, start to ripen the first of July. The bill berries and grouse berries are the last berries to ripen. They grow in low, moist bottom and start to ripen about the middle of August, and on through to September. Many of our people in the past picked these berries in the summer and shipped them to New York markets by rail express. Later there were dealers in the area with trucks who bought all they could get. The crop was sold in New York City and stored in freezers.

In the early 1920s, men started to cultivate the big swamp blues in the low moist bottom. This was so successful that today South Jersey produces more cultivated blueberries than any other state in the union.

In Stafford Township we have only one blueberry plantation, and that is at the lower east side of Cedar Run. It was started by Frank Reeder, who still operates it with his son Gene. This patch produces the largest berries in South Jersey. I am told they have some berries that will cover a quarter. The average large size will cover a nickel.

The first telephone lines ran through our township about 1905. Phones were only installed in business places, and the owner of the business was responsible for all calls made. The first telephone exchange in Manahawkin was in a small building on Stafford Avenue opposite Division Street. It was recently sold by the Hazeltons to the owners of Smith-

An advertising cart displayed by W. S. Cranmer.

ville Inn, who are collecting historic buildings. The phone company at the time was the Delaware and Atlantic Telephone Co. People called telephones the howlers, as they made a lot of howling when not used and off the hook. A few years later, the Bell Telephone Company had control of all phone service in the area, and a central office was set up in Barnegat. In about the mid-1950s, a new central building was constructed on Stafford Avenue in Manahawkin. Miss Bessie Ellis and Mrs. Alice Johnson, living in Manahawkin today, have seen many changes in the phone systems as they are the older phone operators in our township.

The telephone and electric service was brought into the Warren Grove area in 1940. This was made possible by the government, which installed a radio communication system here.

It was in this period that the Tuckerton Railroad Co. had to stop operations. The Pennsylvania Railroad was slowing down, and in 1935 it stopped operations from Manahawkin to Long Beach Island. The visible signs of tracks and right of ways which stood out proudly, and the colorful stations with the movement of people and goods are an operation of the past.

Three men who lived in Manahawkin and operated and managed these last stations were George Bowen at Beach Haven, Franklin B. Southgate at Manahawkin and George Magee at Barnegat.

Although the passenger service by the Jersey Central Railroad stopped about 20 years ago, the freight station in Barnegat remained open and was operated until December1962.

There is an area between Warren Grove and Manahawkin called the Head of Dry Branch. It is considered the humpback of New Jersey. This is where some of our main streams start and water travels in four directions. It is the start of Mill Creek, which flows into Manahawkin Lake and travels east. A branch of West Creek begins in this area and travels south. Dry Branch starts here and travels west into Oswego River, and Turpentine Branch starts near this area and travels north into Brookville, Wells Mills and Oyster Creek.

The oldest roads going east and west from shore towns are: the Old Stone Store Road from Old Broadway at the store to Warren Grove; the Macajas Road from along Cedar Run Branch to Warren Grove and Cedar Bridge; the Mayetta Road from Lamson Road to Warren Grove; and the Old Country Road from Cedar Bridge Hotel to the entrance of Hilliard Boulevard on Route 9. Warren Grove is the hub of all the old roads leading everywhere in all directions. The old road leading from Warren Grove to Barnegat by way of Cedar Bridge was improved in 1926. The old road to Tuckerton was improved in 1930, then widened in 1936. The old road to Whitings was improved in 1942. The old road to Sim Place was improved in 1945.

The first travel on wheels was by the velocipede, a forerunner of the bicycle. It was introduced in our township in 1860. It had a large wheel in the front and a small wheel in the rear. The day they were brought into Manahawkin for a demonstration, most everyone in the township was there to view the performance. People were charged 10 cents a lesson to learn how to ride them. Only a few people could afford to own these expensive velocipedes, and they required skill to ride.

By 1880, the chain and sprocket bicycle with ball bearings in wheels was introduced. These bicycles became very popular in later years. For about 10 years, only the rich could afford to buy one. They sold for $150, almost as much as the first Model T Ford. By 1895, the price was lowered and the bicycle became very popular. It was the cheapest and fastest means of transportation in our area until the automobile became popular about 1920.

The first dealers in bicycles and automobiles in our township were W. S. Cranmer of Cedar Run, who later sold automobile licenses and insurance; the late Howard King, who had the dealership of the early Fords on the corner of Bay Avenue and Route 9; and the late M. L. Cranmer, who had the dealership of the first Chevrolet on Route 9 at Mayetta. These men went out of business in the early 1940s.

Another prominent man in Poplar Neck, now Cedar Run, was George Thomas Cranmer. He was a descendant of Levi Cranmer, who was the first Cranmer to own land in Stafford Township. In 1879,

Mr. Cranmer was appointed collector of customs in the District of Little Egg Harbor by President Hayes. In 1882, he was elected to the House of Assembly. In 1883, he was elected to the state Senate, and again elected in 1886 to the Senate. He was also appointed to high office in the Coast Guard for 25 years. He married Tacy Margaret Conrad of Barnegat in 1893.

The first summer resort areas in our township were Hilliards, or Mud City, Bonnet Island, and the lower end of Cedar Run Dock Road. In the mid-1950s, Jerry and Herb Shapiro started a lagoon resort development along the Manahawkin Bay, called Beach Haven West. The location and the superb planning of this development have attracted many people to buy homes here. There are more than 900 homes sold to date, and at present the construction of more new homes is at its peak. An attractive approach to Beach Haven West is delayed on a promise by the New Jersey Highway Department to construct a new road to the bridge.

A major development in a wooded area of our township is Ocean Acres, headed by Roy Riker of Burlington. It was started in the spring of 1963, and in about one year, more than 2,000 lots were sold. There are several new homes being built at this writing.

Beach View is a small settlement northwest of Manahawkin. Several chicken farms operated here in the past. The noted farm there was the Sylvester farm. Sylvester Jablonski and his sons Charles and Enoch operated a large farm with cattle, hogs and chickens for many years. They also carried on a salt hay business.

The First and Second World Wars have called many of our young men, and some have lost their lives for our freedom. In the Second World War, several of our women answered the call. On the corner of Route 9 and Route 72 stands a memorial monument with the names of the gallant men who served in World War II. [This monument has been relocated to a courtyard behind the Stafford Municipal Complex.]

Now, since the white man settled in parts of our state, we honor those of the past who paved the way for us. We know and realize this was not easy. I am sure we are all thankful for their work.

— Jack Cervetto

Ed Hazelton

Edward Hazelton's ancestral connection with Manahawkin goes back 250 years, to Stafford Township's founding.

Stafford Township's earliest days go back to the 1700s when James Haywood of Staffordshire, England, named the area for his homeland.

Haywood was a home-rule kind of man and saw to it that Stafford broke off from Monmouth County. He had a 2,000-acre plantation in Manahawkin where his son, James, married Ann Hazelton.

Edward Hazelton, born in 1914, is Haywood's "greaty-great grandson — six or seven greats going back," and has a copy of James Haywood's will. He also has the perfect timing and re-call of a natural-born storyteller. When it comes to Stafford Township, he knows the cultural details that conjure up what a place was and who gave it breath and life. His love for his town makes his narratives glow.

Ed Hazelton's Stafford Avenue home is less than a minute's walk from his birthplace, where his son now lives.

His is a Manahawkin of the past, when children called adults aunt and uncle, not because they were related but as a sign of respect born of intimacy: This was a small town where every-one knew everyone else, where those "aunts" would call small children to their back door for some freshly made cookies, where Aunt Fanny Bennett would call in little "Ned" Hazelton as he trailed small game with his dog, Prince.

"I talk about Uncle Tom Cranmer; he's not my uncle. I talk about Uncle Frank Haywood; he's not my uncle. That was the respect we had for them as we grew up."

Baymen tied up their boats at Manahawkin Creek, docking at the spot that was later Zefutie's old Ranch House on East Bay Avenue. Bay Avenue was called Eel Street then, testimony to the burlap sacks of eels the baymen carried up the street for packing off on the train to Camden and Philadelphia.

"They would tie the top of the bag shut, so the eels couldn't get out. Then they'd tie the bag in the middle," Ed recalled, "so

At the junction of Main Street, Bay Avenue and South Broadway. Go straight and you are heading up South Broadway (the Old Stone Store and grist mill are on the right); turn left and you are on Bay Avenue, eventually to end up crossing the causeway to Beach Haven and on to the Engleside Hotel, according to the sign. Turn right and you are heading north on Main Street (Route 9). The farm on the left is where Route 9 south will eventually join Main Street.

they could hang that bag over their shoulder."

Salt hay farmers would wait for a good westerly breeze in the early spring before they burned off last year's browned hay. The clouds of smoke rolled out over the bay, but few mallard or black duck hens and broods were killed: The burning was timed just before nesting season.

Baymen and guides built their own boats or commissioned them from builders at a local yard. Just southeast of the landing dock on Manahawkin Creek there was a boatyard where cedar boards from Mill Creek sawmills became smooth-riding sneakboxes and garveys under skilled hands. Harvested from nearby swamps, those trees measured two to three feet in diameter.

"Now, this story was told to me," Ed began. "Those boat builders would lay on their backs under the boats and caulk (the seams) with oakum. They had that coiled up on their chests and would work it into the seams. Well, this one man had a long beard. When he was finished with his coil of oakum, he tried to get out from under the boat and couldn't. He had worked his beard right into the caulking."

A Community in All Seasons

Neat fields were laid out right next to homes, and farmers took their workhorses to the horse hole, a deep spot just south of the pavilion on Manahawkin Lake.

"Granddad — Charles H. Cranmer, my mother's father — built a pavilion on the lake, where the parking lot is now. On the Fourth of July, folks of early times would row out on the lake with Chinese lanterns. We also played a game, my friends and I, where we would swim underwater from one cedar tree stump to another.

"Manahawkin Lake was a cedar swamp at one time, you know. Reuben Randolph — he was one of Stafford's founders — he built a dam and the swamp filled up."

Before electricity and refrigeration, ice houses on the lake stored blocks skillfully cut during winter and insulated with layers of cedar sawdust. "Granddad had a big icebox with a spigot. As the ice melted, we had ice water which always tasted of sawdust."

You could buy a Maxwell and get a haircut at the Triangle Garage on the triangle, both from Earl McAnney. Ed Hazelton, in fact, can recite the lay of the landscape of the whole town as if he was standing there 50 or a hundred years ago.

"Speaking about the corner up here — when you came down Route 9 and you came to the intersection of Bay Avenue and what we call Main Street, that was a dead end," Ed pointed out. "There was a dairy farm there, so you went around, past the Stone Store and on down, and came out where the telephone yard is now.

"Earl McAnney, he was from New Gretna, married a local girl, and they built the Triangle Garage. Earl did the barber work in there; there was a little room off it, on the end toward Carroll's, and that was the barber shop. That must have been when I was 10 years old, and the Fredricksons had the National Hotel."

The National Hotel is gone now, a parking lot on the south side of Carroll's, a building C. H. Cranmer owned when it was called The Lake House.

"As far back as I can remember, The Lake House was a little restaurant, an ice cream parlor. A man by the name of Al Adams lived there and had an ice cream parlor, and a man by the name of Charley Farley had a snack bar. He served clam chowder, oyster stew, hamburgers in there. Cora Schroder had a millinery shop there in the same building. When the Mascolos took it over, they put in pool tables and a bowling alley. The bowling alleys are still under the main dining room at Carroll's."

Kids ran up to the train station on Stafford Avenue to ogle the huge sea turtles carried on flatcars from the Island, on their backs, tied down with ropes. In 1884, the Pennsylvania Railroad had built a line to Long Beach Island, not called the Island, but the Beach. Running south from Barnegat, the line passed Ed Hazelton's grandfather's home.

"Where Jack Gardner's Cadillac (Pine Belt Nissan) agency is now, there was a Y (of tracks). You

Ed Hazelton and "Musket" on the meadows after a morning of duck hunting.

went straight down to Tuckerton or you went to the Beach.

"I can tell if you're new around here," Ed revealed, "because you say 'I'm going to the Island' instead of 'I'm going to the Beach.' The Y broke off just the other side of Cumberland Farms, just in back of my Uncle Henry's house, and it went to the beach.

"It came right down to Mud City and right across in front of Tonneson's and just north of Margo's and right across by the Bonnet Club, which is now the Duck Inn marina. That was built by Humphrey Martin, who married one of my cousins. Humphrey sold clams and oysters, and he had fishing parties and gunning parties stay there. It was listed on the railroad schedule as a stop: Martins.

"Margo's was built by Uncle Tommy Cranmer and his sister, Mabel, about 1917 as a fishing and gunning party retreat. Aunt Mabel served meals, and later on she built a restaurant out in front. It was called The Bay Side Inn. He sold clams and oys-

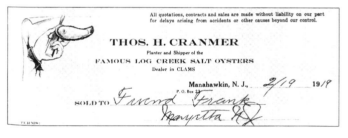
Bay Side Inn was built by Thomas Cranmer about 1914, in the area known as "Hilliards." Margo's Marina at the Causeway now occupies the same building. Cranmer was the "planter and shipper of the famous Log Creek salt oysters;" his sister Mabel served meals to the fishermen and gunners who stayed at the inn.

ters, too. He had the best oysters in the world. He kept them up in Log Creek Pond."

And where was Log Creek Pond?

"You go up Cedar Creek and through Log Creek Canal into Log Creek Pond before you come out to Dragging Cross Place. Between the North Pond and the main bay there was a little spit of meadows. Later on, they cut a notch in it, but it got its name because you had to drag your boat across it."

The trains to the Island on Fridays and Saturdays were excursion trains that, unlike the local runs, came barreling through Manahawkin without stopping. If there was a message for the train, it would have been received in the switchman's tiny shack, marked with an "MU."

Once the message was written down, it was stuck on the end of a long-handled bamboo pole bent in the shape of a nine. For young Ned, it was a big thrill to hold out the pole as the train approached, stretching to position the nine's loop right at the track. As the train thundered past, the fireman leaned out a window, hooked his arm through the loop, retrieved the message and dropped the pole.

His is a Manahawkin of the past, a Manahawkin where little Ned stepped carefully into the imprints left by his father in the snow while the two hunted fox, a Manahawkin where everyone gathered to watch the Stafford Orioles or, in later years, the Stafford Bears play, a Manahawkin where busy sawmills turned out boards of the long-grained, non-splintering cedar shipped out by train, but it is a past that becomes alive and vibrant again with Ed Hazelton's remembrances.

— *Marion Figley*

Two Boys of Summer

"I always felt out of place a little, coming from so small a town. I remember when I first walked into Yankee Stadium, with 80,000 people there. I didn't know whether to go back down into the dugout or keep going right out through the stadium. But I played."

I t's just a ball and a bat, after all, a leather and horsehair sphere stitched together and hit with a polished wooden stick, or today by a tapered metal club.

But on the fields that dot the landscape in every hometown from Sacramento to Manahawkin, boys and girls put all they've got into throwing that ball and running the bases, pursuing one common dream — making it to the big leagues.

At least one local boy did just that. He played the game so well that manager Connie Mack picked him to join the Philadelphia Athletics professional baseball team in 1928.

In the 1920s and '30s, baseball was an all-consuming passion for the boys of those summers long ago. This is the story of two of those boys, one who made it to the big leagues and starred for 20 seasons while batting a lifetime .296, and the other who might have made it had family and religious commitments not stepped in.

Roger "Doc" Cramer and Ed Hazelton played baseball at the shore for many years, where teams became whistle stops for big league scouts. Both men loved playing the game so much in those early years that they literally played for nothing. And that was all they ever wanted.

Edward Hazelton, born in 1914, is a leathery old salt who knows the bay and the history of Manahawkin perhaps better than anyone. There are several names synonymous with that part of the Jersey Shore's past: Sprague, Inman, Cramer and, of course, Hazelton, and any line of work that made the world go round in those parts was probably done by the Hazeltons.

"My dad had a coal, feed, and lumber yard, and I grew up working all those things for him," Ed said. "We had a big tree in the corner of our lot, and I would climb the tree on Saturday afternoon and look up toward the ball field. Dad would say, 'Are they there yet?' and I'd say, 'Yeah, there's three or four of them there,' and he'd say, 'Come on down, you're done for the day. Go and get your glove and get yourself up there.'

"Work stopped when it was time for playing ball."

Ed and his fellow players hit the ball for a team called the Manahawkin Bears, made up, as he said, mostly of local boys, but they occasionally imported players from nearby small towns when they played the big teams from other counties. Atlantic, Burlington, Monmouth, they all lined up to play the boys from Ocean County, and there were always Manahawkin or Long Beach Island players running the bases for the Ocean team.

Roger Maxwell Cramer played for both the Manahawkin and Beach Haven teams, too, a few years ahead of Ed. Roger was called "Doc" by the townsfolk because he liked to ride in the horse and wagon of old Dr. Joshua Hilliard, a local fixture who "brought about 2,000 of us into the world back then," as Ed put it.

The nickname stuck, even when he was in the big leagues. They had another name for him there, too; they called Doc "Flit" because of his ability to catch fly balls.

It seemed that good base running, good fielding and good hitting were trademarks of the boys from the Jersey Shore. The scouts from the "bigs" knew all about that when they went down there to look them over.

Ed Hazelton had a chance to make it in the bigs on his own. He pitched and played center field, and was known for his strong arm. "When I was 17 or 18, in high school, according to my coach and manager, I probably could have gone on, if my parents had permitted me," Ed said.

His dad, Leon W. Hazelton, was a force behind Manahawkin and Stafford Township baseball around the turn of the century, and Ed must have inherited his gifted throwing arm from his dad.

"I remember the old boys talking about my dad, how he threw a man out at home plate from deep center field one time," Ed said. "Dad was picked up and scouted by the Phillies, but we had the religious situation where we were not allowed to play baseball on Sundays, and you know, you have to play baseball on Sunday, so Dad never played pro ball."

Those same religious convictions entered Ed's life when the time came for him to think about playing

pro ball. He was offered the chance to play for a team in Asbury Park, a solid club made up mostly of college boys, and a real proving ground for the big leagues. But he chose not to play for religious reasons.

"My dad said I would never know what I could have done if I had played pro ball, but if it made him happy that I didn't play, that was all right," Ed decided. "I was in the Navy Air Corps during World War II, and after I was discharged I had a month to make up my mind whether to re-enlist. If I went back in I'd be made an officer, but my grandmother did not want me to go, and I didn't do that, either. I was successful at doing both, as far as I was permitted to go, but I was successful in other things in life, too."

Part of the success of the leagues at the Jersey Shore was the quality and intensity of the play, and most of it was self-taught.

"Doc would tell me that the boys would play, and they really had no one to teach them anything," Ed said. "We'd go out and do this, or do that, but no one ever showed us how to slide, so we learned from each other. I would pick up something from one player, or I'd get something from my dad. Doc's brother, Paul, my older sister's husband, was as good a player as Doc. We all had the instincts to play the game; we all knew something about baseball, and we grew up right into the sport."

He said each team had a coach or manager, but the players themselves would coach the bases. All the manager did was change pitchers or make some defensive changes and put together the lineup, but the players mostly handled their own strategies on the field.

"Doc always said that a baseball team really doesn't need a manager," Ed related. "He felt the manager was just a tenth man, because if you know, really know baseball, you know all the moves and what to do and where to throw the ball."

After the war, while Doc was still hanging around the big leagues coaching after he retired from playing, Ed Hazelton had a chance to play a little more ball, if only for fun and charitable causes.

Baseball the way we played it started to die off after the 1950s and early 1960s, and by now none of the old fields are still around," he said. "We had a chance to play some ball with the Lions Club, and we played the high school team in a pickup game. I remember we had a little guy from the old days, Bill Flynn, and I told him if he could get on base, I'd try to hit him home. Sure enough, Bill got on with a walk, and I hit a liner between second base and shortstop, and got a two-bagger, driving him home. You know, that's the last time I played, and I was in my 50s then."

Ed Hazelton gets a faraway look in his eyes when he talks about his playing days, and even though he did not follow his close friend to the big leagues, he has a gloveful of memories from those seashore sandlots.

"I remember the first time I saw Babe Ruth hit a home run in Shibe Park. I was a kid, maybe 13, 14 years old, from down here in Manahawkin, watching Babe Ruth hit a home run ... my God, I couldn't believe it. I met Mickey Cochrane, Jimmy Foxx, Lefty Grove, and several others. What more could I ask for?"

Still, sometimes he wonders what if ...

"But when I do, I remember that I had success in my life, and if what I did made my father happy, that was all I wanted. I have no regrets."

It was left for Ed Hazelton to live out his baseball days vicariously in the person of Doc Cramer, who was plucked off the sandlots by Connie Mack and his scout Cy Perkins.

Home Boy Becomes Legend

In an interview given two years before his death in September 1990, Doc Cramer reminisced about a broad range of baseball topics, told of how his hometown of Manahawkin had changed over the years, and shared impressions of his life.

Doc, who worked equally well with a hammer or a baseball bat in his hand, was lucky enough to see much of the United States from 1929 to 1948, using baseball as his ticket. But even though Cramer took the baseball ride as a 24-year-old, he said he never lost his small-town roots, nor did he ever feel at home in the big city.

"I always felt out of place a little, coming from so small a town," he said. "I remember when I first walked into Yankee Stadium, with 80,000 people there. I didn't know whether to go back down into the dugout or keep going right out through the stadium. But I played."

Cramer said he never got used to the big crowds, no matter how many times he encountered them.

"One day when we played in New York, there were 83,500 people in the stadium; that's the biggest crowd they ever had. I'd never seen anything like that. With all the smoke coming out of the stands, you could lose the ball in that smoke when you were trying to catch it. That was some crowd."

Playing the Yankees brought unexpected benefits for Cramer, such as the friendship he struck up with Babe Ruth. Doc would invite Ruth down to hunt on the marsh, and both would go down to Cedar Run and gun for ducks.

"Babe was really something. He would pass himself off as a real swinger, but he was a country boy, just like me," Doc said. "He'd eat four or five hot dogs before a game, end-ways, from both ends. I've never seen anything like it."

Once Babe gave Doc his gun, a gift Cramer cherished. Doc kept it until the day he died.

He became buddies with other players, too. "We went out on the field to win, and so did they, but after the game, we would all go out together; everybody was friends."

Doc told of the time he went out with Johnny Allen, a notorious fastball pitcher. Doc told Allen that he'd never had a fastball thrown completely by him, that he'd always be able to foul it off or something. "Well, Johnny was just as ornery as he could be, and he told me that he'd be pitching tomorrow, and that he would throw one by me or through me, one or the other. First time up, he hit me right in the thigh with a fastball. We always went out to win," Doc said.

Good pitching wins its share of games, and Doc had seen the best. "Lefty Grove won 31 games one year and lost four, and three of the four losses were one-run games. He was some pitcher," Doc said.

His memories of Ty Cobb were equally positive. "Cobb was a good guy; there was nothing wrong with him. He just went out to beat you, and he didn't care how he did it."

Doc's big league career began in 1928 and ended in 1949, with stops at Philadelphia, playing for the Athletics; at Boston, where he played on the Red Sox with Ted Williams; at Washington, where he played with the Senators, and finally with the Tigers at Detroit. He was also a player-coach for the

White Sox. Doc held a special place of reverence for some of the greats of the game, and he cherished the games he played against Joe DiMaggio. But of all the players he remembered, Ted Williams stands out as a favorite.

"You couldn't beat Ted Williams," Doc said. "He was as good as you ever want to see. Of course, he didn't get along with the sports writers, but in fact he was right a lot of the times. What they said either was not true, or they put things in their stories they claimed he said but he never said them. But Ted was a good boy all the way around."

Looking Back on the Way It Was

Take the professional career out of his life, and Doc's story would be just like any boy's growing up near the bay. Born in Beach Haven, Doc moved to Manahawkin when he was a year old.

He remembered a gravel road that eventually became Route 9, and another that was Bay Avenue, which was gravel for a long time. He remembered that he worked on Bay Avenue when it was built.

"There were 100 teams of horses going down that gravel path. Route 72 was not even there then."

Playing ball since he was 10, he gained most of his early baseball experience in pickup games, since there was no organized league. "I played on every field there was," he said. Beach Haven's team was Doc's first organized experience, but he liked playing for Manahawkin's team, too.

In between his amateur days and his pro career, and even after his pro days were over, Doc Cramer did whatever he had to do to live. He resided in Manahawkin for 80 years on and off, and worked at an unusual and varied number of jobs during those years.

"I had to work to keep from starving," Doc said. "I was in heavy construction most of the time, and I helped build that power plant (the Oyster Creek Nuclear Generating Station at Forked River) up there. I farmed; I did what I had to do. I worked right around here in Manahawkin most of the time, building houses."

Doc also worked on the houses built in the late 1960s in what is now Beach Haven West.

Doc retired when he was 62, after both his wife and daughter got sick. "I had to quit," he said. He spent his days puttering around, working on this or building that.

As Ed Hazelton said, "There was always something to do, if anyone wanted to do something. Doc, for example, would go out into the shop and make something, or he worked on his house, or went fishing. He would go visit, or go gunning." Doc had few hobbies, and did not like to carve, as many of his contemporaries did, but he did like to work with his hands. "He made really nice furniture," Ed said.

Doc Cramer Boulevard was named for Roger; it intersects with Route 72 just east of the Garden State Parkway. Doc knew the area well; he passed through the intersection hundreds of times on his way west to Philadelphia or when he went fox hunting in the pines.

One of the things Doc loved best was gunning for ducks, something as familiar to those old-time boys of the bay as was that well-oiled glove and stealing second. It was, as he said, practically automatic.

"It was a way of life," Doc declared. "I'd come home from playing ball, and I'd go right out fox hunting or duck hunting. We'd go out on the bay gunning; we didn't even think about it. We'd get right into our sneakbox and row right over to Surf City if that's where we had to go. That was no problem."

Doc Cramer: Legacy of a Local Boy

Doc Cramer played 20 years in the major leagues, from 1929 to 1948. He played with the Philadelphia Athletics from 1929 to 1935, with the Boston Red Sox from 1936 to 1940, the Washington Senators in 1941 and the Detroit Tigers from 1942 to 1948.

He batted .296 lifetime with 2,705 hits. Doc had more hits than anyone else who played under the old 154-game schedule and is not in the Hall of Fame.

He hit .300 or better eight times, and another four years hit over .290. In 1935, his last year with the Athletics, Doc hit .332 with a career high 214 hits as well as a career high 37 doubles. Doc seemed to have his best years just before he was traded. In 1940, his last year with the Red Sox, he hit .303, his fourth straight year over 300, with a league-leading 200 hits and a career high 12 triples.

Doc was an all-star when the other All-Star outfielders were named DiMaggio and Williams, playing in five All-Star games: 1935 as a member of the Philadelphia Athletics, and 1937-1940 as a member of the Boston Red Sox. His best overall years were probably with the Red Sox.

He played in two World Series, first in 1931 with the Athletics. They lost the series, four games to three, to the Cardinals. Doc had a two-out, bases-loaded pinch single in the bottom of the ninth in game seven, and the A's almost pulled it out. In 1945 he led the Tigers to the world championship with a team-high .379 average and a team-high 11 hits, including three hits and a stolen base in the decisive game seven over the Cubs. His overall World Series average was .387.

Doc scored over 100 runs in a season three times and on six other occasions scored over 90 runs. He is known for getting six hits in a game twice, one of only two players in history to do so.

He was a hitting instructor for Nellie Fox

Free Press Photo

Roger Cramer, whom the Tigers obtained from the Washington Senators, appears in his new uniform at the Detroit training camp at Lakeland. Cramer, who signed his Tiger contract Saturday, is expected to take over a regular position in the outfield.

Signed by the Detroit Tigers in 1942 (above), Doc later installed gold tigers by the front steps at his home on Hilliard Drive, in honor of his days with Detroit. They still guard the entrance today. At the time of his death he lived in a house to the west, at the corner of Route 9.

while a coach for the White Sox in the 50s. Fox credited Doc for teaching him how to hit — Fox was named to the Hall of Fame, which can be considered a tribute of sorts to Doc.

— *Jim Estelle*

There would be a problem today, he said, with all the boats on the bay.

"Those boats would cut you in two if you tried to go over there today," Doc asserted.

Doc witnessed more than 80 years of change in his native area; he was not happy with all the changes he'd seen.

"The cost of living is too high; the taxes tripled since I've been here; there's a lot of crime in the area," Doc said in 1990. "The old local people were never involved in crime. Just the other day I had to run a couple of kids off my lawn; they were throwing stones at my house. They don't even know the meaning of the word respect ..."

His voice trailed off. He'd talked enough. Then the conversation turned again to baseball, and Doc was interested in giving his opinion of the players today.

"I watch the game today until I get mad; then I turn it off," he said. "These ball players today are real show boats. If you watch the game and a guy goes up there and hits a single, if he makes it home, all the players go out there giving high fives like he won the World Series. When I played, if you do your job, drive a runner over or score a run, you came back into the dugout and sat down. We all played like that. Today, if a player hits a home run, I half expect him to go up into the stands and give the fans high fives."

He also thinks the game today is much different, especially during the little dramas that occur each at-bat between the pitcher and the hitter. Today, he said, the pitcher will throw this far (indicating a distance with his hands outspread as far as they could go) from the batter and still the batter will jump back or go flat on the ground.

"When they threw at you when I played, they didn't throw at you to hit you; they threw at you to kill you."

Doc expressed no regrets over his 20-year career. In addition to his lifetime .296 batting average, he appeared in two World Series, once for Philadelphia in 1931, and the other for Detroit in 1945, and had a combined .387 batting average for both. He coached for seven years after he retired from playing, for Detroit and teams in Chicago, Buffalo, and Seattle.

"Baseball didn't owe me anything, and I didn't owe baseball," he said. "Coaching was a bad deal, though. Once you get there, you're just hanging on."

He had no plans to manage, even though he did, but just once.

"I did not want any of that," Doc said. "I managed while in Chicago for a month, and I found out right then I didn't want to manage. There was too much second-guessing. All your players second-guessed you; the other coaches, the general manager and the owners all second-guessed you, every damn one of them."

No one has yet named a road for Ed Hazelton, and he probably likes it better that way. For Ed and Doc the game was what mattered, the oiled glove, the crack of the bat. After all, it's all about the ball and the bat.

And there's nothing like the game for teaching the concept of teamwork.

Ed Hazelton could not agree more. "When we played, we all wanted to play. And we always played our hardest. Oh, there were some who didn't play as hard, and that made the rest of us mad, but most of us gave it our all."

Today, somewhere above center field, Doc Cramer would probably nod in agreement, and couldn't help but smile.

— *Bill Geiger*

Doc Hilliard: Old-Time Physician

Old-timers recall that when they needed a doctor, they'd hang a cloth on a tree and Doc Hilliard would know to come around.

Manahawkin's Joshua "Doc" Hilliard embodied the very definition of the old-time family doctor. At the turn of the 20th century and almost until he died in 1952, Hilliard was there for the community members at the time of birth, sickness and death.

Arriving by horse and buggy in the early years, he delivered more than 3,000 babies, mostly at the patients' homes, in his 50 years of practice from 1901 to 1951.

Old-timers recall that when they needed a doctor, they'd hang a cloth on a tree and Doc Hilliard would know to come around. More-remote residents would send word or come to get him, and Doc would travel to a bay island to deliver a baby.

Upon his retirement, the president of the New Jersey Medical Society lauded Hilliard's life as "the perfect example of what a physician should be."

Hilliard himself simply urged other aspiring doctors to "put service to mankind first and monetary benefits to yourself second."

Hilliard had continued the tradition of his father, Dr. Phineas Kirkbride Hilliard, a physician in Manahawkin who was highly esteemed throughout the state. P. K. Hilliard bought the Reuben Randolph home, which had been built in 1750 and in the mid-1800s had housed the first doctor in town, G. Augustus Hankinson.

Greatly interested in the genealogy of the shore pioneer families from which he was descended, Joshua Hilliard was instrumental in founding the Ocean County Historical Society. He was the society's first president, in 1950.

His mother was Elizabeth C. Jones Hilliard, of a Jones family that settled in Monmouth County in 1670, and also of direct lineage to the "Great John Mathis," Revolutionary wartime patriot, money lender and magistrate.

The first Hilliards (later Hillyards) to live in England were French Huguenots who fled there during the reign of Louis XIII.

The home of Dr. Joshua Hilliard on Hilliard Drive had housed other Manahawkin doctors. In the mid-1800s, the homestead built by Capt. Reuben Randolph was purchased by Dr. G. Augustus Hankinson. His nephew, Dr. William A. Newell, founder of the U.S. Life Saving Service, also occupied the house when he came to Manahawkin as a young physician. Hilliard's father, Dr. Phineas Kirkbride Hilliard, later bought the home. The landmark is in service today as the Thos. L. Shinn Funeral Home, where parts of the original building remain within renovations and additions.

They were established in America by the time the first provincial council under William Penn convened in Philadelphia in 1683. "The Hilliard family of New Jersey is the offspring of two of the most distinguished blueblooded families of early Colonial days," notes *Salter's History of Monmouth and Ocean Counties*.

Joshua Hilliard attended the State Normal and Model School at Trenton, and after choosing his profession, he earned the money for his own education by teaching for five years in Ocean County schools. He studied at Jefferson Medical College in Philadelphia and finished his preparation at the University of Maryland.

He served as tax commissioner of Ocean County and as jury commissioner of the county, and ran as a candidate for the New Jersey Assembly and state Senate, but his affiliation with the Democratic Party left him with a minority of votes.

Salter's History recalls him as "one of the foremost physicians of South Jersey." In 1953, the Ocean County Board of Freeholders named Hilliard Boulevard in his honor.

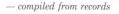

— compiled from records

Dr. Joshua Hilliard

Doc Lane and Lane's Pharmacy

John Lewis Lane was know as "Doc Lane" in Manahawkin, where he made his rounds accompanied by his little daughter, as the above photograph shows. A native of Tuckerton, Lane graduated from Jefferson Medical College in Philadelphia in 1888. Residing in Manahawkin, he set up an apothecary on Stafford Avenue, where the prescribed medications were dispensed. The structure was at one time the post office and polling place for Stafford Township. In 1964, the building was prepared for transport (right) to the Historic Village of Smithville.

In the early 1900s, the house in the background belonged to W.S. Cranmer. Known as the Cranmer-Hazelton house, it was once the home of Ed Hazelton, and still stands today.

Lane's Pharmacy in its active days at the turn of the century, above, with the C. H. Cranmer family on their neighboring lawn and a man relaxing on the pharmacy porch. Cranmer was a prominent businessman in town. Dr. Lane's house (below, left) was moved in the 1890s from the south side of Stafford Avenue to the north side (pictured below, right, in 1964).

Aerial view of the intersection of Route 9 and Bay Avenue in 1958. The old ice house is visible by the lake, top right, and on the far right is the National Hotel. The rectangular building in the center is the location of today's Dunkin' Donuts plaza, and the Esso station by the lake is now a modern office building.

Getting Around

At each watercourse, travelers had to risk fording the stream, or submit to delays while waiting for ferriage. They faced, in addition, the torments inflicted by a formidable foe, the mosquito.

During colonial times this shore area was off the beaten track of the established "post roads" that crisscrossed New Jersey. These byways from New York to Philadelphia were completed in 1765. The only avenues of rural transportation were sandy Indian trails or foot paths which wound through the swamps and woods, connecting the many villages. Thus, very few — if indeed any — carriages or stagecoaches ventured to what is today Stafford Township.

Anyone wishing to travel or transport could go by way of the rivers and streams that emptied into Barnegat Bay. Water transportation was virtually the only practical means of carrying commodities. Travelers often preferred to journey by land to avoid the constantly changing moods of tide, wind and weather that could turn a trip into a disaster.

Left with this choice, travelers complained constantly about the condition of the highways. The main roads were either privately owned, requiring tolls, or they were built and maintained by local labor. Overseers of roads in each township supervised the labor, but the roads were usually ungraded, poorly drained and unsurfaced. They often became quagmires in the spring and frozen ruts in winter, a menace to both man and beast. At each watercourse, travelers had to risk fording the stream, or submit to delays while waiting for ferriage. They faced, in addition, the torments inflicted by a formidable foe, the mosquito.

At this time "stages" were springless farm wagons with sides. Passengers sat packed together as tightly as possible on crude benches as the wagon bumped unceremoniously over the paths. Drawn by four or six horses, these jolting vehicles made it possible to go from New York to Philadelphia in three days. By 1775, when some refinements had been introduced and a few of the stages had been replaced by coaches, the trip could be made in two days, with a stopover at Princeton. In the early days of the 19th century, a two-day stage trip transported visitors between Philadelphia and Tuckerton, where small boats afforded passage to Long Beach Island. The luxury of one-day travel arrived in 1820.

The main highways then became liberally dotted with taverns or inns, which provided indifferent accommodations for travelers. Picturesque signboards, reminders of an age when literacy was far from universal, beckoned visitors to the King's Arms, the White Hart, the Red Lion, the Bamber Inn, or the Bell. The innkeeper was frequently a citizen of considerable prominence. In addition to serving the weary traveler, the tavern was a social and political center of each community.

Stagecoach lines began expanding. The first widely documented stage line to Manahawkin began in 1821 to carry vacationers from inland areas. Samuel C. Gray and James Bodine inaugurated a Burlington-Manahawkin stage that operated two days a week. The coach left Burlington upon the arrival of the Philadelphia steamboat *Bristol*, stopping overnight at Mount Holly and arriving in Manahawkin early the next afternoon. Here a "wagon connection" departed to Tuckerton, and several ferry operators carried travelers to Long Beach Island. In fact, an advertisement by one owner, Seth Crane, appeared in a Philadelphia newspaper dated July 12, 1823.

The next stage line to operate here seems to be one from Tuckerton to Toms River and then on to Freehold, continuing to a point on the coast where boats sailed for New York. According to an account of an Ocean Grove resident in the *New Jersey Courier*: "In 1825, White, Dobbins & Co., proprietors of the 'Great Swamp Long Beach Company,' had completed their elegant establishment opposite Manahawkin, which now consists of a new mansion 90 x 28 feet in addition to the one built a few years since by Mr. Cranmer. The distance in crossing the bay is short, and can be effected with large or small boats at any time with perfect safety." The fares were quite high compared with the purchasing

Butcher selling his meats over muddy Manahawkin streets.

power of the dollar then. The fare from Freehold to Toms River was 75 cents and from Freehold to Manahawkin, $1.50. From New York to Manahawkin, the cost was a prohibitive $2.50.

It was not until after the Civil War that roads, other than town roads, were built to replace the network of meandering Indian trails. At first this challenge was principally undertaken by "turnpike" companies, which then charged tolls of all travelers who used the roads and bridges. These toll roads finally connected many of the shore towns to the inland towns by straight, direct routes.

Towns were expanding, meanwhile, and increasing the number of roads within them. When the Stafford Land Company came to town in 1870, General Grier plowed a road from the rail line (Letts Avenue) eastward to the company's new land holdings. He made it a very wide road in order to accommodate the wagons and stagecoaches used to squire his clientele from the train to the various parcels of land. In 1875, a Mr. Sprague bought land from a Mrs. Wilkins to extend Stafford Avenue to the west and join the main shore road (now Route 9). This road was not opened until 1877 because of an obstruction by Allen Neill, who kept erecting a fence across it. He was taken to court and he lost, but the delay was already accomplished.

A ride to the beach was taken any way one could get it. Tourists in from the stagecoach hopped aboard the wagon to the docks to board a Long Beach Island-bound ferry. Until the railroad crossed the bay in 1886, boat travel to the island was the only way to go.

Thomas Sampson, the contractor on the southern portion of the township turnpike (now Route 9), completed his contract using very durable material for the roadway. Joseph Carr was the contractor on the northern portion of the turnpike and the road from Manahawkin to Barnegat. He had cleared all the stumps to the width of two roads, grading down the hills and filling in the lower portion of the road in July 1882. These "overseers" of the roads built and maintained them and reported to the freeholders.

In March 1891, a new law made null and void the election of numerous road overseers in the townships all over the state. The bill transferred to the township committees the full supervision of the roads.

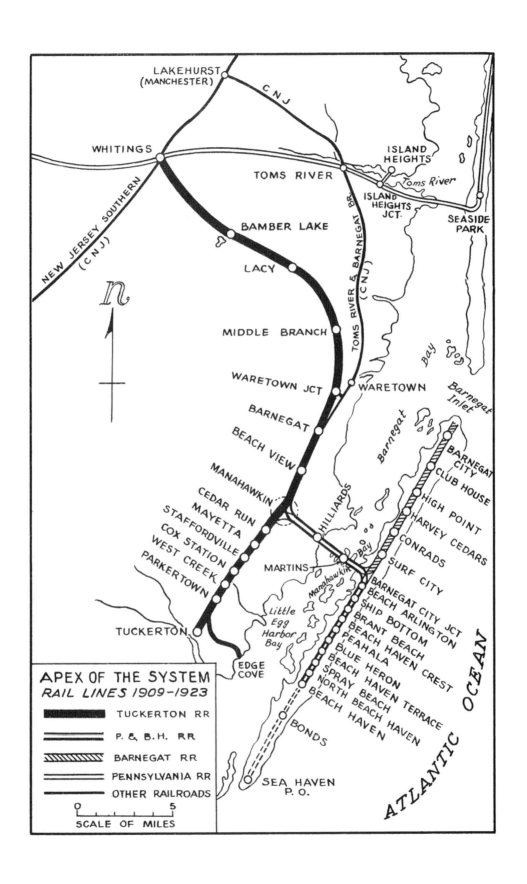

APEX OF THE SYSTEM
RAIL LINES 1909-1923

- TUCKERTON RR
- P. & B.H. RR
- BARNEGAT RR
- PENNSYLVANIA RR
- OTHER RAILROADS

0   5
SCALE OF MILES

All aboard the Seashore Express! Pennsylvania Railroad No. 2513 carried beach-bound passengers from Camden through the pines to Manahawkin and on to Beach Haven. The coal-burning locomotive pulled seven passenger cars.

Under the old law, the township committees had been able to do nothing but distribute the money appropriated for road purposes among the township's various road districts. When the party primaries were held for the nomination of the township officers, they had to agree on the amount of money that should be spent for roads during the coming year, and that was placed on the ticket with the candidates' names. This amount could not be exceeded. Residents had no way of knowing how much money it was advisable to expend. Often the amount was insufficient and the consequence was poor roads.

However, under this new act, the township committee had full management of road construction and repairs. They were authorized to appoint, an-

nually, a competent person or persons to superintend the work. The committee could buy gravel pits and stone quarries and take title to them in the name of the township. The township committee, instead of the voters in general, set an advisable amount of money to expend in making or repairing roads for the ensuing year. Taxes assessed could not exceed that amount.

The Railroads

A group of sea captains from Toms River, Forked River, Barnegat and Manahawkin, after organizing a bank in Toms River called the Ocean County National Bank, turned its attention to the erratic means of transportation which was stifling the

Engine No. 1, above, known as the "Yellow Jacket" for the color of its coaches, began operation by the Manahawkin and Long Beach Transportation Co. on March 17, 1894. Engine No. 2 and crew, below, Alfred Brown, Clarence Bennett, Alex Inman and Morton Crane.

Manahawkin Railroad station force (from left) George Bowen, Lewis Asmus, Ernest Stiles and George Pharo.

area's growth. They organized a railroad system, called the Toms River and Waretown Railroad. The first section was built between Manchester and Toms River, with the first train pulling into Toms River on July 3, 1866. Work on the tracks progressed to Waretown and then to Barnegat.

Several capitalists from Tuckerton joined others from Philadelphia to fund a venture to the south. The Tuckerton Railroad was developed by nine directors: John Rutherfurd, Archelaus R. Pharo, Rutherfurd Stuyvesant, Theophilus T. Price, John A. Brown, Samuel Ashhurst, Thomas D. Armstrong, H. C. Smith, Charles T. Parry. The Tuckerton Railroad grew to have a direct influence on Stafford Township. This single-track line started at Whitings, as the town of Whiting was known by railroaders. There it connected with the existing Pennsylvania line and proceeded to Tuckerton via

Bamber, Barnegat, Manahawkin, West Creek and Parkertown. October 18, 1871 marked the day that the first train clattered from Whitings through Manahawkin to Tuckerton.

Curious travelers were anxious to hop aboard this new mode of transportation. It soon became clear that a connection should be made all the way to the beach. The Long Beach Transportation Company built a one-track trestle bridge to link Manahawkin to the island at Ship Bottom. A hand-operated swing bridge to cross the main channel was completed in June 1886.

As the locomotive approached the shore, "A touch of salt air drew deep inhalations while cool sea breezes filtered through open windows, providing natural air conditioning difficult to match elsewhere those days," wrote John Brinkmann in his chronicle *The Tuckerton Railroad*.

"Brakeshoes gently arrested our pace as the hollow sounding rumble and anguish of groaning timbers divulged entry upon the long low bay trestle," Brinkmann wrote. "Minutes multiplied while land receded to the rear, causing one to speculate on the possibility of the railroad having put to sea. However, Long Beach Turnpike's wooden bridge and the sight of many dinghys and garveys manned by patient anglers assured us that we were not alone above the sparkling aqua. Wheels echoed once more to solid land, followed by a succession of shorter trestles until our slow-moving express cautiously inched over Cedar Bonnet drawbridge and joined the sandy terra firma of Long Beach."

The rail line had been laid north to Barnegat City in 1886 and then completed later the same summer to Beach Haven. It was primarily a result of these railroad connections that the southern and northern ends of Long Beach Island began to develop, since they eliminated the tedious ferry ride up and down the bay.

"No more crossing of the great bay on a raft; no more sneaking about for sneak boxes — in fact, no more poke alongs; no more risk of life upon the ice in mid-winter in order to go and come to this old isle of the sea," acclaimed a Philadelphia lawyer, William H. Bird, in an account in *The Tuckerton Railroad*.

Beach Haven organized itself and became politically detached from the mainland township in 1890. Harvey Cedars, once the site of a whale fishery, separated itself from the mainland in 1894. One of the chief reasons for withdrawal was to independently raise funds to develop the seaside area through local taxation. The town fathers saw a great opportunity. The railroad lines offered the very latest in transportation, and the communities were proud of their accommodations.

The railroads drew a more comfortable line from the city to the shore. In 1902 it took five hours and 18 minutes to travel from New York to Manahawkin on an evening run, but only four

Self-propelled railroad car of Manahawkin and Long Beach Transportation Co. It ran a route between Barnegat City Junction (now Ship Bottom) and the north end of Long Beach Island.

Waiting for the train at the Manahawkin station, top, 1914. The couple at left is enjoying each other's conversation, and the boys at right aren't missing any of the day's excitement, which may or may not include a visit to the Mount Holly Fair. Left, the switchman's house at the junction south of the Bay Avenue crossing.

R. R. Station, Manahawkin, N. J.

Manahawkin Railroad Station, top, looking north about 1910. In 1964, above, buildings and weeds have altered the same scene. Today, the parking lot for Larry's Hair Styling occupies the spot. The abandoned station was eventually moved to its present site near the Old Stone Store and restored.

hours and three minutes to go from Manahawkin to New York in the morning.

A number of different railroad companies became involved in the ownership of the various lines, but the Pennsylvania Railroad, through reorganizations and foreclosures, absorbed the lines from Whitings to Tuckerton and the spurs to the island.

In 1909, County Engineer Isaiah H. Cranmer of Mayetta surveyed the site for a proposed bridge from Manahawkin to the beach just south of the P.R.R. Bridge. Questions arose over the cost. Freeholder Cranmer pointed out that the people on Long Beach Island were building a road the length of the beach without asking any help from the county, and that Stafford Township could build the route from the Main Shore road to the bay to connect such a bridge. The county would then take charge of the road after it was built, he proposed.

Some of the men — and one woman — who worked on these railroads in our area in the past are:

• **Station Agents at Manahawkin:** Oscar F. Brown, George S. Ware, Wm. A. Simpson, Edward Inman, Alexander H. Inman, Harris Corlis, Morton Crane, Ernest Reeves, Wm. B. Sprague, Russell Sprague, Benjamin Martin, Josephine Paul Cox, J. Henry Paul, Napoleon Cranmer, Erving Cranmer, Norman Corliss

The Methodist church as seen from the railroad depot (top). Above, servicing an engine; year unknown.

• **Train Crews:** Frank L. Sprague, James V. Jones, Clarence Bennett, Harry Carver, Jason L. Fennimore, Lawrence Elberson, Hugh Bolton, Charles Marshall, William C. Maulsbury, William B. Paul, Frank Paul, Rudolph Cranmer, William

Construction crew on early drawbridge, top, predating the 1904 railroad drawbridge and trestle below.

Storage houses and loading platforms on the meadows near the bay, left, in 1904. The building in the foreground held clams and oysters, and the hay house in the rear was used for storing salt hay. Below, Milt Paul seems to be enjoying the ride on a handcar delivering milk to clubhouses on the bay about 1900.

Burnham, Albert S. Cranmer, Earl Ford, Roy Jackaway

• **Track Force:** Frank Paul, Sr., Walter C. Paul, George Cranmer, Charles Allison, William Conklin, Walter Rossell, Wm. Paul, Haywood Abbott, Jacob Peer, James Upton, Gilbert Peer, Tobe Bennett, Charles Conklin, George Fauser

• **Stations Force:** Lewis Asmus, Brooks Asmus, Ernest Stiles, George F. Pharo, Le Francis Groene

• **Drawbridge Force:** John Paul, Alvin Paul, Milton Paul, Birdsall Paul, Howard K. Conklin, Daniel Johnson

The Automobile

Within just a few years came the automobile, which ushered in the construction of the causeway in 1914. With the motor car also came better road surfaces, paved with gravel. When the causeway opened, it was only 18 feet wide. It was widened to 30 feet in 1928 and stayed that size until the present bridge across the bay was completed in 1959.

Cedars take hold along the old railroad right-of-way in 1964. The station can be seen at left, and in the background at right is the Methodist Church.

As the automobile caught on, the clamor for better roads grew, and the traffic on the railroads declined. The railroad companies gradually cut back the number of scheduled runs, then began shortening the runs, and finally the Tuckerton line came to a halt. In November 1935 the crowning blow fell on the seashore line when a fierce northeast storm washed away the trestle bridge. The very last train from Beach Haven managed to make it across at the beginning of the storm in what must have been a white-knuckle ride. Since that time the rails and ties have been removed, and very few signs remain that a railroad ever ran through the area.

A roadway had been completed to Barnegat City in 1920 so cars could travel north on the island. This development marked the end of the line for the rail route to the north.

By 1936 the tracks and ties had been removed from the beach, and the southern road to Beach Haven was widened and straightened since it no longer had to go around the sidings set up for slow-moving trains to move off the main line.

It was only the beginning of road-building to accommodate autos that would caravan more and more visitors to the shore. The state and the county took over the supervision, maintenance and construction of main arteries in 1904. Manahawkin saw its first paved roads in 1904, when the main arteries were paved in sections starting in town and a mile beyond. Route S-40 was completed in 1935 from the Four Mile Circle into the western end of Manahawkin; it was renamed Route 72 in 1950. With the completion of this southerly spur from Route 40 (now known as Route 70), Long Beach Island became the closest seashore to Philadelphia and more accessible from Trenton.

MANAHAWKEN AND LONG BEACH BRIDGE OVER BARNEGAT RIVER, N. J.

THE CAUSEWAY ACROSS BARNEGAT BAY

Access to Long Beach Island has come a long way since the days of dirt road approaches and rickety planks. In 1930 (bottom), though the ride was slow and low to the water, one no longer had to pay a bridge toll. In the photograph, the remains of the old railroad bridge can be seen just beyond the wooden causeway.

Circa 1957: Steel girders are lifted into place 60 feet above Manahawkin Bay during construction of the main bridge in the channel span. Below, the causeway opened a new era of transportation to Long Beach Island when it was dedicated on Memorial Day weekend in 1959. At the time, peak summer traffic numbered 20,000 cars per day. The cost was $8.5 million. An engineer's design of the flourescent lighting mounts, which affectionately became known as the "string of pearls," led to the bridge's re-naming in 2000 as the Dorland J. Henderson Memorial Bridge.

The great span of causeway bridges, heading east to Long Beach Island. Mud City is the cluster of homes in the lower left corner; the new, developing Beach Haven West on the right gives a mere hint of its present sprawl. Note the railroad bed still visible on the bottom left, heading through Mud City and disappearing over the bay. The old causeway pilings can be seen in the center, just north of the current bridge.

Manahawkin Airport

Manahawkin Airport was dedicated on Memorial Day, May 30, 1957. During the ceremony, all eyes turned upward as Major Leland Cranmer executed a flyby in an Air Force jet.

The original airport was built by Edward Brown of Monmouth County. The first airport manager was a young college graduate, Charlie Harvin. A contest was held in the local school to name the airport; the winning name was Manahawkin Airport, submitted by Eddie Marini.

The gravel runway had a large mound in the middle that obstructed the view to the other end of the runway. For nighttime operations, smudge pots (kerosene lamps) glowed along the runway. Therefore, pilots landing at night had to call ahead when they filed their flight plans.

Lou Brescia flew sightseeing rides to the Island and back. He used a Piper Tripacer, which had four seats, a high wing for visibility of the ground, and a tricycle gear. The plane was fabric-covered. A fly-in/drive-in theater, the Manahawkin Drive-In, had opened the same year as the airport. Brescia's flights took off before the movie and then again during the intermission. The drive-in operated on a limited basis the second summer, but the airport was officially closed for the next 10 years.

The theater screen sat next to the airport hangar, which was located behind a realty office and Perk's Electric store. At that time the projection booth and the refreshment stand were housed in the same building as the airport office. The building burned to the ground a few years later. A rear hangar, to the south of the main airport hangar, was erected by a group of small-plane owners, Joseph Bennett, Frank Muth, Maurice Perkins and Bob Heinrichs. They used a slab foundation from the burned building as a foundation for the hangar. The airport operating area and parking for aircraft were

Lou Brescia removing windsock when the Manahawkin Airport was sold in 1992. The airplane on the sign at the Wal-Mart plaza was placed there at the request of the township planning board to mark the former airport site.

farther south in a clearing beyond the old office. A gravel taxiway ran perpendicular to the middle of the runway from the parking area.

Ray Eick, a former Navy and airlines pilot, bought an old PT-19 Navy trainer and stored it at the airport. He and Lou Brescia ran the first aviation ground school in the evening in the Southern Regional High School library. They also attempted to organize a small flying club. Within a year or two, though, the aircraft was vandalized and rendered unflyable.

During the 10 years in which the airport was officially closed, a few adventurous pilots flew in and out, usually during the summer months. The pilots, to protect their planes from possible vandalism, taxied to park close to a nearby diner, which stood where the Exxon station now stands on Route 72.

About 1966, the Island municipalities and Stafford Township formed a joint Airport Feasibility Study Committee. Joe Bennett and Lou Brescia

Stagecoach Stops for Seashore Travelers

Travelers have always found a path to the seaside. Getting there in the 1700s and 1800s could take a day or two, so the hostelries along the way gave welcome rest. Manahawkin offered the Landing House and the Ferry House on the edge of town.

The Ferry House was built on the meadows east of Manahawkin in about 1785. Seashore visitors could stop there for refreshment while waiting for the sailing ferry that carried them to the beach. Others used it as a rendezvous point toward their daily excursions to the fishing and gunning grounds.

The Ferry House's first host in the memory of older residents was Hud-

THE FERRY HOUSE

THE LANDING HOUSE, MANAHAWKEN N.J.

The Cedar Bridge Inn as it looked in 1964, 244 years after it was built. The bridge locates the site of the last battle of the Revolutionary War.

son Busbee. Following him were Joseph Wilkins, Silas Crane and Adolphus Crane.

The Landing House stood on Bay Avenue at the head of Brown's Creek that flowed into the bay. It was built in 1812 and enlarged and partially rebuilt in 1832.

By 1833, access to "Long Beach" had improved. An excursion was recommended that year to the resort "opposite the little village of Manahawkin," to which "a good stage with four horses runs every Monday, Wednesday and Friday from Burlington."

The Landing House served visitors well as a place of entertainment, as well as a stopping place for travelers before they set sail for the beach.

None can remember hearing the name of the first proprietor, but in the early part of the century, it was the property of Nathan Crane, and a few years later it was kept by Seth Crane, his brother. The last known proprietor was a Philadelphia sailmaker, "Major" Flomerfelt, who installed various caretakers.

With the advent of the railroad and the growth of hotels on Long Beach Island, the popularity of these two houses gradually declined. All evidence of the inns has vanished with time and encroaching vegetation.

Before travelers reached Manahawkin along one stagecoach line, they could stop at the Cedar Bridge Inn, also known as the Cedar Bridge Hotel or Cedar Bridge Tavern. Built in 1740, it was owned and operated by Luke Courtney, one of Stafford Township's founding landowners, and later by his son, John.

Travelers opened the door of taverns such as the Cedar Bridge Inn to find a warm fireplace along one wall, food and drink at the other end, and beds upstairs.

It was the site of the last skirmish of the Revolutionary War in December 1782, when Captain John Bacon, leader of a group of loyalists know as the "Pine Robbers", clashed with militia at the bridge.

Aerial of Manahawkin in the early 1970s as construction begins on Route 72. South Broadway is soon to become part of the ramp for the Route 9 south exit.

were appointed as Stafford's representatives. Representatives from Long Beach Island were Brian Engelsen, John Gould, Fran Puskas and Henry Reed.

The committee decided to put its efforts on hold after Lou Haslbeck of Little Ferry explained that he was interested in purchasing and developing the airport as a privately owned general aviation facility. He had heavy earth-moving equipment brought in to cut the hump out of the runway by moving the dirt to both ends. He converted a mobile home trailer into a temporary operations center in the summer of 1968. He also paved the runway, put in a gas pump, and built a hangar. Lou Brescia, having obtained FAA Certified Flight Instruction certification, was hired for the summer to operate the airport. He also taught an aviation ground school

in the evenings.

Bud Burroughs, owner of Bud's Flying Service, ran his banner towing business from the airport during the summer months. His wife set up a sewing machine in a hangar loft to sew and repair banners. To hoist a banner, the pilot swung the plane low over the meadows to catch the waiting banner with a hook.

On September 4, 1968, Lou Haslbeck died in a plane crash, along with a photographer who was his passenger. The crash occurred in the bogs on the final approach to runway 22, so named because 22 indicated the direction on the compass. The runway approach also took the plane over Route 72. The airport was once again closed, but with the help of her son, Ethel Haslbeck reopened it and continued its operation until 1992. The National Realty and Development Corporation of Purchase, New York, bought the 58-acre property, on which it sited a Wal-Mart and a Pathmark store. The last plane to leave was a Piper Cherokee belonging to Frank Muth, on June 2, 1992. Now the airport, like the railroad, has disappeared with little trace left of either.

Garden State Parkway

The Garden State Parkway took shape in the 1950s as a series of roads that bypassed towns in three parts of the state. The 17-mile section between Toms River and Route 72 in Manahawkin opened to traffic July 15, 1954, three months before the parkway's official debut celebration that October. By 1957, all 173 miles of the parkway stretched from Route 9 in Cape May to the New York line at Montvale. The access it provided opened the floodgates to a new wave of tourists, many of whom could now buy houses at the shore and still commute to jobs and second homes in the more populated areas.

To accommodate the traffic increase, Route 72 was extended and widened to bypass Bay Avenue in Manahawkin, using the old railroad right-of-way over the meadows. A new bay bridge, with its unique "string of pearls" lighting, was built south of the old causeway and opened in 1959. In June 1997, the Stafford Township master plan called for construction of two additional ramps to the Garden State Parkway and a third lane on Route 72 to ease the volume of through traffic between the Parkway and Route 9. Work begun in 1999 converted Exit 63 to a full interchange, with both ramps filling the need for motorists to go north on the Parkway from Route 72, as well as east or west on Route 72 from the Parkway south. The work was also intended to improve response time of emergency vehicles trying to reach Southern Ocean County Hospital.

'How People Lived on the Shore'

"I remember when I was a kid of 14, that was in 1866, that all the youngsters in the neighborhood and the grown-ups as well went to the home of John Peterson, a great hunter, to see two bears he had killed in the Manahawkin Swamp."

Joseph R. Steelman, born in 1852, was a preacher and the superintendent of schools in Manahawkin until his retirement in 1912. His essay leads readers into life in Manahawkin in the mid-19th century, and even before, as he includes tales that the older generations told him. His story "How People Lived on the Shore Eighty or More Years Gone By" appeared in the New Jersey Courier in 1934, reprinted that year from the Asbury Park Press.

"I can see that old church at Manahawkin yet, dim with the light of its tallow candles, which were the only illuminant, the worshippers silent and indistinct, as they listened to the voice of the minister, whose shadow, of huge proportions, wavered to and fro upon the wall in back of him, as though it were a spectral figure there to lend emphasis to his words.

"Yes, they were what we would call primitive days along the bay shore section of Ocean County. But we didn't think so then, or believe we were suffering any hardships. We didn't know any better. The heart of man doesn't pine for the things he knows nothing of. The church is now lighted with electric lamps, and one can see from end to end, but I doubt worshippers are any the more fervent."

And as thoughts of other days crowded in upon him, the thin, intellectual face of Joseph Steelman brightened, but in the flood of reminiscence there was lacking that thought so many of an earlier era express, that the "good old days" were far to be preferred to modern times. "No, sir," says he, "the world is no worse today, as some seem to believe. It is better. And as far as depressions go, I've lived through others and the nation will live through this and be the better for it. Around 1872, I remember seeing people on the roads, begging their way. They didn't seem to know where they were going, just animated by an impulse to keep turning corners around which prosperity might be hiding.

"I was born at Manahawkin in 1852, September 13 to be exact. My father was Andrew J. of Pleasantville, a descendent of Swedish emigrants who settled in Salem about 1682. He was a veteran of the Civil War, enlisting twice, first in the 29th New Jersey and again in the 9th New Jersey, an organization of veterans. He was with Grant before Richmond, but when the war ended he was with Sherman.

"My mother was Martha Randolph of Manahawkin, of a family that took a prominent part in the Revolution and with which Governor Theodore F. Randolph of New Jersey was connected, a second cousin of my grandfather Joseph. As I recall it, the family was of Scotch origin, originally calling themselves Fitz Randolph. But the Fitz has been lost, somewhere along the years. But all those old families have disappeared or are disappearing. The Randolphs are practically gone.

"I never had much opportunity to go to school, but I went whenever it was possible and studied to better myself. As I grew up, my folks decided to make a schoolteacher of me. I studied every minute of the time and finally got a county certificate. I taught for 36 years, first at Wheatland, now called Pasadena; Whiting, Manchester (now Lakehurst) and Manahawkin, where I taught for 26 years. Part of this time I was supervising principal and county examiner as well.

"While at Whiting, in 1876, I met Mary E. Aker, and we were married. We both belonged to the same church and Sunday school, of which I was superintendent. I also was superintendent at Manahawkin and a local preacher as well. Four of our children are still living — Howard R., a ranchman at Exeter, California; Frederick, principal of schools at Eatontown; Mrs. Harriet Cranmer, wife of W. D. Cranmer of Cedar Run, a former Ocean County assemblyman; and Mrs. Marion Borden, wife of Howard Borden of Cedar Run."

Indians Leave Shell Heaps

"As far as I have been able to learn, the first settlers in the region of Manahawkin sailed down from Long Island to Barnegat Bay in their small vessels for the fine cedar that grew in a big stretch of lowlands that was known later as Hawkins Swamp.

"Of course, before them were the Indians. But very few of them lived along the shore the year 'round. They would come during the summer from West Jersey, Pennsylvania and other places, principally, I think, for the clams and oysters. These they gathered by the thousands, stringing them up and drying them for winter consumption. I've seen vast heaps of shells, thousands of loads of them, along the banks of creeks, where the Indians had operated their drying factories, as you might call them. Lots of relics have been found among the shells.

"As far as money went, we were poor in those days. But we didn't need money and there wasn't much in circulation. We lived on the land and the bay, were well fed and contented. Each family had a hog or two, often a spare cow or steer. We'd put up a barrel of fish, and how we'd wade into the mossbunkers when they were fat in the fall! We all had good appetites.

"Everybody who had land raised potatoes, of course. My father usually put away 40 bushels for the winter, as well as a barrel of fish and a barrel of pork. Now I don't believe the whole shore from Tuckerton to Toms River raises 500 bushels of potatoes a year.

"The people were all of one kind like one big family. There were no classes. And they were proud. It was a terrible thing to be compelled to ask for help. People are different nowadays.

"It was considered a disgrace to apply for aid to the overseer of the poor, but sometimes through sickness, death or other misfortune assistance was desperately needed by some families. To save feelings from being wounded, we organized what were called 'giving parties.' We would assemble at the homes of those in need, each bringing food of some kind. Then the evening would be spent in a social way and the recipients would feel in no way belittled.

"And that reminds me of an interesting story told of a family named Symes, consisting of an old man and his aging wife. It was known that they were in need, and a 'giving' visit was arranged. A large quantity of pork, flour, vegetables and groceries was heaped upon the table. The old man was not present when the visitors arrived. Coming in later, he went to the table, and after pawing over the articles, he gave a snort of disgust and in a very disagreeable tone roared out, 'You ain't brought no bread. How do you expect us to eat without no bread?' Of course, that was an exceptional case.

"The people were somewhat clannish, it is true. They felt free to criticize one another but would not allow an outsider to interfere. The residents of the section in those days were mainly descended from the 15 or more original setters. They had mostly intermarried to an extent that perhaps was not altogether desirable and were cousins several times removed.

"They had no such warm houses as we have today. There were no continuous fires day and night. They could not be kept up with wood as fuel, and there was then no 'stone coal,' as we first called it. I never saw it until I went to Toms River. No, the houses were cold, for fireplaces alone could not keep them warm. We got our supply of water from a well and the old oaken bucket. Many's the morning I've broken the ice to get water in which to wash."

Afraid of Kerosene Lamps

"Present-day conditions have everywhere caused a return to more or less simpler ways of living, but I wonder what people would do if they had to return to primitive ways such as lighting the church and homes with candles. In the church the tallow dips stood on shelves along the wall. The sexton made frequent rounds to snuff them, and when the lights flared a bit, it sometimes caught us young people holding hands.

"When the first kerosene lamps appeared, the people were about as much afraid of them as we are of dynamite. They had some cause to be, for there were accidents. I think perhaps the kerosene of those days was not so well cracked as it is today and some of the gasoline remained.

"It was a big thing for any family to get a lamp. At first the people would gather at the home that had purchased one of the newfangled contraptions and stand around at a safe distance as it was lighted, waiting for it to explode. But then they gradually became accustomed to the new method.

"Then along came the electric light. I remember the first one I ever saw was at the Centennial Exposition in Philadelphia in 1876. I thought it was wonderful, and I still think so. Another thing I saw there for the first time was an electric trolley car. It ran on a little circular track, and it was quite a dare-

devil treat to make the trip. I and my girl took a trip, and it was quite an experience. Later I saw them flourish, and now I am witnessing their passing.

"In those days the people in the lower section of Ocean County had three principal means of support. First was the income from sailing vessels principally concerned in the trade with Virginia and the Carolinas. Almost every small town along the shore had one or more of these vessels carrying charcoal and wood from ports of these states to New York, Boston, etc. On their return trip southward, these vessels would bring back from the large cities almost all the goods supplied the people by merchants of the bay and coast towns. The charcoal was needed by the cities for fuel as anthracite coal was hardly used at all and there were no stoves suitable for it.

"Many of the young men of the territory commenced their lives as sailors on these small vessels. Every community had some who wanted to go to sea, and the schoolteachers taught navigation and surveying. I don't know just why the latter was considered necessary. Some taught Latin and mathematics as well.

"Well, the lads who followed the sea often never would return or never more be heard of. There was no steam then and the vessels were small, and a storm would often pile them up on the beach. I recall when a boy that I wandered along the beach one day after a storm, and so many wrecks were uncovered in the sand that I could almost throw a stone from one hulk to another for a long distance.

"Yes, there have been tragedies of the sea off here. There was the *Adelaid*, a little sloop that was turned over in a heavy blow. Two or three men on board were washed overboard and drowned, and the hulk drifted up on the beach, still upside down. Two or three days later, some men heard knocking from the inside. They ran for axes and saws and soon had a hole through the hull. There they found a woman nearly dead from exhaustion and hunger. She had been in the cabin when the boat capsized, and an air bubble had formed, thus saving her from drowning. I think she was a resident of Waretown.

"Many shore residents used to make a trip to New York by way of the vessels. It was a great thing in those days to go to the big city. We could go by land, too, for there was a line of stages between Tuckerton, Toms River, Freehold and Keyport. From

Professor Joseph R. Steelman (top row) and his students in 1898.

the latter place a small steamer made the trip up the bay. When I was a boy of 12, one of the girls made the trip and she was a popular heroine. She told and retold the story of it, and we were never tired of listening. We considered her another Christopher Columbus. Yes, we were simple folk then, but I guess we lived as happily as people do now. Each family was a little state, and what they couldn't get, they did without.

"But to return to the sea. The business of ship building was carried on by most of the shore towns. The vessels were built along the banks of some deep creek or river, and when the hull was completed, then came the great day of the launching. It was made a gala occasion. The boss builder gave a general invitation to all the men of the locality to be on hand, and they came often accompanied by the children, for it was an occasion the kids wouldn't have missed for anything in the world.

"Then, when all was ready, the ways or sliding planks were greased and the word given to the men to heave, and heave they did, stimulated by a generous allowance of New England rum or Jersey applejack. After the vessel was launched, she was speedily fitted with masts, spars, rigging, cabin and everything needed to make her a thing of use and beauty, for the bay vessels were neat and good sailers.

"The second means of support for the seashore dwellers was Barnegat Bay itself. It had its creeks, and salt ponds teemed with fish, oysters and clams. During the gunning season, it afforded an inexhaustible supply of wild fowl, making probably the finest game section of its kind in the United States. There was no time of the year but what one could secure a bountiful supply of food from this body of water with little effort.

"The third source of support for these early settlers was, of course, farming. The first dwellers came about 250 years ago. As soon as they had prepared shelter for their families, they proceeded to clear a corn patch and garden for vegetables and potatoes. With an abundance of wild fowl and bay food, there was little more that a man could ask. Soon cattle, hogs and other domestic animals were brought, and thus there was an ample supply of the best food. The land along the shore in the lower part of Ocean County is much more fertile than in the pine barrens to the westward.

"The whole shore was closely cultivated. At Tuckerton, Forked River, Manahawkin and Toms River there were grist mills for grinding grain raised locally. The bay was full of mossbunkers. I remember the time when from 400 to 500 bushels would be gathered in one haul. These would be plowed under for fertilizer. In fertilizing corn, we'd place one in the furrows on each side of the hill. We also used black mussels for fertilizer.

"We then raised some of the finest corn the United States ever produced. I remember Joe Carr once raised a crop of 109 bushels and four quarts to the acre. They don't raise anything much now, and they get no mossbunkers. They're all scooped up at sea by menhaden fishermen, I guess. Of course, when I was a boy I did all the things a boy was expected to do. When I was 16 the family moved to Manchester, now Lakehurst. Raising cranberries was a big industry then, and my father took several contracts to lay out bogs and I helped him.

"I can remember when there were thousands of sheep along the shore. Everyone had them, and lots of old women spun wool and wove material for suits and dresses. At Manahawkin there was a mill to clean the wool. Now they are practically all gone. I took my daughter on a western trip once. She saw a sheep and wanted to know what it was. She had never seen one before. That is the difference between the old and the new."

A Visit to an Oldtime Home

"Shall we visit one of the houses of these people 75 to 100 years ago? It is in the late afternoon. The boys have been down to the meadows after the cows, and they are driving them into the milking shed. Every family, except the very thriftless, possessed at least two cows. It was arranged that one of these should freshen in the spring, the other in the fall, thus assuring the family of a supply of milk the entire year. In addition, many families had large droves of cattle which they sold to drovers from the agricultural regions of New Jersey and Pennsylvania.

"But to return to our family. The mother is probably preparing the evening meal. Probably she has no stove, or if she has, it is a crude, wood-burning affair. But whether she has a stove or only a fireplace, she has a large pot in which water is boiling merrily, and into this she throws handfuls of yellow corn meal. It is not such corn meal as we would buy at the present time from some grocer who has had it in stock for months. It is meal that has been ground a day or two ago from corn that has been recently shelled, perfectly dry cured.

"The mush, stirred by one of the larger children, must be well cooked. Then the hungry children and parents, and maybe visitors, gather around the plain plank table, each supplied with a large bowl of cool milk, and the perfect food is served. Soon shades of night enfold the happy family. Perhaps they sit awhile, the candles extinguished and the room cheerful in the light of blazing pine knots. It had been an easy matter to gather them. One might drive a team into the woods and, not moving after the first stop, load the wagon with resinous knots and the hearts of decayed pines. But sleep would soon claim the members of the hard-working family.

"Morning comes and again the family is gathered around the same rude table. There has been prepared a big pan of salt pork, fried to a crisp, a pot of the old-time 'Peach Blow' potatoes boiled in their skins. The mother, probably using the 'Dutch' oven, has prepared a bountiful supply of rye shortcakes, and all are ready with immense appetites for the morning meal.

"There was coffee in those days but it was green, the people burning or roasting and grinding it. It was not plentiful, however. Sometimes sweet potatoes were used as a substitute. Small ones would be cut into pieces the size of the end of a thumb, and these would be dried and roasted and then crushed. The concoction had the color and something of the taste of coffee. When not even sweet potatoes were available, slices of bread would be toasted until they were charred, and the crumbled pieces would be brewed.

"But back to the hungry family at the table. Each member would peel two or more of the bursting potatoes, and these they would mash and season with salt and a generous spoonful of fat or, as they called it, sop. That probably was the best way potatoes were ever prepared for food. Then, as an added dainty, slices of the mush left over from last night's meal, fried to a golden brown and covered with molasses, finished a meal fit for a king or, better still, a young, growing American."

"There were bears, too, in those days in Ocean County. I remember when I was a kid of 14, that was in 1866, that all the youngsters in the neighborhood and the grown-ups as well went to the home of John Peterson, a great hunter, to see two he had killed in the Manahawkin Swamp. One was a big female, weighing about 300 pounds, and the other was a cub weighing about 100. I think they were brown bears. Peterson said they lived on the seed pods of wild roses of which there were countless thousands in the swamp.

"There was considerable drinking in those days. Each town had its tavern, sometimes two. Joseph Wilkins operated one old place at Manahawkin that was built before the Revolution. I wasn't very familiar with them. My father was a strong teetotaler, and I was brought up the same way. When I was a boy, most of the stores had a barrel of apple whiskey, that famous old Jersey beverage, in a back room, and when a man paid his bill, he went back and dipped himself a drink from a tin cup. One day on my way to school, I passed the tavern. A drunken man ran out, pursued by another. The pursuer rain full tilt into a heavy cedar post and nearly killed himself. But he sobered up instantly and began to cry.

"Horse racing was a favorite sport then. A lot of the residents had good horses and bragged a lot about them. Taproom arguments would be followed by the posting of wagers, and there would be a race over a measured mile on the sandy road toward Barnegat.

"One of the popular means of enjoyment then was what we called the 'protracted meeting.' They correspond to what later came to be called 'revival meetings.' Every winter one was held in one of the churches, and sometimes there would be meetings in both churches. There were no motion pictures then, and everybody went, for there was lots of noise and excitement. Every year the same sinners would repent and go to the altar.

"They used to tell the story of a descendant of one of the early families. We'll call him Jim Jones, because that wasn't his name. Jim had a nephew named Bill and he was one of those who was converted each year but who always promptly backslid. At one of the meetings Jim prayed for his nephew just about as follows: 'Dear Lord, here's Bill again. He's sorry for what he's done. He's been drinking and fighting and carousing but he's sorry for it now. Dear Lord, convert him soundly and then kill him, for if you don't get him the short time he stays converted, you'll never get him at all.'

"There have been some gruesome tales told of the residents of South Jersey, known as 'Pineys.' I have lived there for years, and I think some of the yarns about their depravity are much exaggerated. Undoubtedly, though, many of them lived in primitive fashion and were shiftless, and also they were not always quick of wit. But you find that type everywhere. I remember one family at Whitings which lived in a forlorn cabin on land that had been 'coaled off' — that is, denuded for charcoal.

"The sill had rotted off on one side and allowed the cabin to tilt until it actually had a hanging doorway. It was a big family, and all slept in the one big room and all were consumptive. There was a big fireplace and lots of wood, but the place was always cold for the heat all went up the chimney. Still, they were contented. They didn't know there was any other way to live.

"The Pineys, however, were more religious than the people who live in the towns. At least they made more of a show of it. But they were primitive to the last word. Some of them never knew what a stove was, cooking all their meals over a fire.

"I don't know what the future of that section is. I guess it hasn't any unless they strike oil or gold, and that is mighty unlikely.

"Not nearly so many live in the woods as formerly. There is little or no timber there now. As soon as it gets two or three feet high, along comes a forest fire and burns it off. There have been a lot more fires since the railroads were built. Charcoal burners, however, used to be responsible for some of the fires. They'd start them so they could buy the wood cheap.

"And those were the 'good old days' that a lot of people think they would like to return to. Maybe they really would, but I doubt it. A week or a month of it and they'd be howling to get back to their 'effete civilization.' "

— *Joseph R. Steelman*

Nathaniel Holmes Bishop III

"It is admitted by old cranberry growers that Bishop's berries are the finest and largest in the state."

Nathaniel Holmes Bishop III was a Victorian-era adventurer and author who not only crossed South America on foot when he was 17, but in 1869 wrote a book about it, *The Pampas and the Andes: A Thousand Mile Walk Across South America*. In his 30s, he paddled a canoe made of paper down the Ohio and Mississippi rivers to the Gulf of Mexico, and repeated this same exploit in a Barnegat sneakbox a few years later. But he also spent part of his middle years cultivating the cranberry on his Manahawkin plantation, "Oxycocus."

It's hard to know just how much time Nathaniel Bishop spent in Manahawkin, because he kept houses on Lake George, New York, and in Lake Worth, Florida, as well as lands in Texas and Santa Monica, California. He spent time in Boston, Philadelphia and New York in addition to his South American travels. He also lived the later part of his life on Captains Row in Toms River, was a prominent citizen in that town and, upon his death in 1902 at age 64, left an endowment to establish the Toms River Library.

The Bishop Building that houses the historical collection of the Ocean County Library was the whole of the library system when it was built in 1941.

In 1983, Bishop's ancestors gave his archives, consisting of three cartons of papers, to the Ocean County Library. These book galleys, letters, and documents pertaining to his cranberry business allow today's readers a look into an earlier time.

The Mayeta Cranberry Co. was incorporated in 1846. Its trustees were Nathaniel H. Bishop, Samuel Shreve, John Gifford Jr. and Josiah Sprague.

Our adventurer, Bishop III, moved to Ocean County before 1864 and started growing cranberries near Hanover. He then moved to Manahawkin around 1871 or 1872. In 1873, he received a patent for a trademark, the words "Growers Own" around a star with the grade A, B or C in the middle.

His part in the cranberry business apparently established, Bishop set out for broader horizons. He became enamored of the wooden canoes gaining popularity in Great Britain and named his first canoe, an 18-footer built by J.S. Lamson of Bordentown, the *Mayeta*. In 1874, Bishop paddled the *Mayeta* from Quebec, Canada to Plattsburgh, New York, via the St. Lawrence and Richelieu rivers. But on a stop in Plattsburgh, his love affair with *Mayeta* paled when he heard about a new type of craft, a paper canoe being manufactured in nearby Troy.

Paper canoes were made of three to five layers of manila paper bonded and waterproofed with shellac and laid over a solid wood mold.

Perhaps sensing the increased publicity he would receive for his trip if he made it in a paper canoe, or perhaps because the paper canoe weighed only 57 pounds and he had to portage his boat in some places, he replaced the *Mayeta* with the *Maria Theresa*, a paper canoe built by Elisha Waters of Troy.

He paddled her all the way to Florida. It took him a year, and three years to write and publish *Voyage of the Paper Canoe,* which came out in 1878.

But it is his third and last book, *Four Months in a Sneak-box, Down the Ohio and Mississippi Rivers and Along the Gulf of Mexico*, published in 1879 by Lee and Shepard of Boston, that brought Manahawkin and the Barnegat Bay sneakbox to the public eye.

The introduction reads: "The author procured one of the smallest and most comfortable of boats, a purely American model, developed by the baymen of the New Jersey Coast of the U.S. and recently introduced to the gunning fraternity as the Barnegat Sneak-box. This curious and staunch

When not traveling the world or rowing down rivers, Nathaniel Holmes Bishop III (shown here at age 23 in 1860) spent part of his life in Manahawkin cultivating the cranberry.

little craft, though only 12 feet in length, proved a most comfortable and serviceable home while the author rowed it more than 2,600 miles down the Ohio and Mississippi Rivers and along the coast of the Gulf of Mexico, until he reached the goal of his voyage, the mouth of the wild Suwanee River which was the terminus of his Voyage of the Paper Canoe."

He announced that the craft, made of white cedar and named the *Centennial Republic*, did not leak the entire 2,600 miles.

In *Four Months in a Sneak-Box,* Bishop explained why he exchanged his graceful paper craft for the "comical looking but more commodious and comfortable" Barnegat sneakbox.

He learned from eight thousand miles of navigating North American waters that while the canoe is indispensable for exploring shallow streams, for shooting rapids and for making long portages, he was looking for a stronger and heavier boat to traverse the deeper waters.

"To find such a boat — one that possessed many desirable points in a small hull — had been with me a study of years. I commenced to search for it in my boyhood — twenty-five years ago; and though I have carefully examined numerous small boats while traveling in several foreign countries and have studied the models of miniature craft in museums and at exhibitions of marine architecture, I failed to discover the object of my desire, until, on the sea-shore of New Jersey I saw for the first time what is known among gunners as the Barnegat Sneak-box.

"The sneak-box offered ample stowage capacity, while canoes built to hold one person were not large enough to carry the amount of baggage necessary for the voyage; for I was to avoid hotels and towns, to live in my boat day and night, to carry an ample stock of provisions and to travel in as comfortable a manner as possible. In fact I adopted a very home-like boat which, though only twelve feet long, four feet wide and thirteen inches deep was strong, stiff, dry and safe; a craft that could be sailed or rowed, as wind, weather or inclination might dictate — the weight of which hardly exceeded two hundred pounds and could be conveniently transported from one stream to another in an ordinary wagon."

A big advantage over the canoe, Bishop said, was to be able to sleep in the sneakbox.

"Light indeed must be the weight and slender and elastic the form of the man who can sleep many nights comfortably in a seventy-pound canoe without injuring it. Cedar canoes, after being subjected to such use for some time, generally become leaky; so to avoid this disaster, the canoeist, when threatened with wet weather, is forced to the disagreeable task of troubling some private householder for a shelter, or run the risk of injuring the boat by packing himself away in its narrow, coffin-like quarters and dreaming that he is a sardine, while his restless weight is every moment straining his delicate canoe, and visions of future leaks arise to disturb his tranquility."

Captivated by the attributes of the sneakbox, Bishop delved into its history. He sought the help of William Errickson of Barnegat and William P. Haywood of West Creek. With their assistance, Bishop was confident that "I have been able to rescue from oblivion and bring to light of day a correct history of the Barnegat sneak-box."

"Captain Hazelton Seaman of West Creek village, a boat builder and an expert shooter of wildfowl, about the year 1836, conceived the idea of constructing for his own use a low-decked boat, or gunning punt, in which when its deck was covered with sedge, he could secret himself from the wildfowl while gunning in Barnegat and Little Egg Harbor bays.

"It was important that the boat should be sufficiently light to enable a single sportsman to pull her from the water onto the low points of the bay shores. During the winter months, when the great marshes were at times encrusted with snow, and the shallow creeks covered with ice — obstacles which must be crossed to reach the open waters of the sound — it would be necessary to use her as a sled, to effect which end a pair of light oaken strips were screwed to the bottom of the sneak-box, when she could be easily pushed by the gunner, and the transportation of the oars, sail, blankets, guns, ammunition and provisions (all of which stowed under the hatch and locked up snugly as if in a strong chest) became a very simple matter. While secreted in his boat, on the watch for fowl, with his craft hidden by a covering of grass or sedge, the gunner could approach within shooting-distance of a flock of unsuspicious ducks; and this being done in a sneaking manner (though Mr. Seaman named the result of his first effort the 'Devil's Coffin') the bay-men gave her the sobriquet of 'sneak-box'; and this is the name she has retained to the present day."

A simple device protected the boat against rough seas. Local craftsmen also added their touches to the construction.

"The first sneak-box built by Captain Seaman had a piece of canvas stretched upon an oaken hoop, so fastened to the deck that when a head sea struck the bow, the hoop and canvas were forced upward so as to throw the water off its sides, thus effectually preventing its ingress into the hold of the craft. The improved apron originated with Mr. John Crammer, Jr. a short time after Captain Seaman built the first sneak-box. The second sneak-box was constructed by Mr. Crammer; and afterwards Mr. Samuel Perrine, an old and much respected bayman, of Barnegat, built the third one."

Bayside Street Leads to Boat Builder

One bright morning in the early part of the fall of 1875, Bishop trudged down a road from Manahawkin through the swamps to the edge of the salt marshes that fringed the bayshore. Following this road named Eel Street about halfway to its end, he turned off to the right. He followed a wooded lane "to the house of an honest surf-man Captain George Bogart, who had recently left his home on the beach, beside the restless waves of the Atlantic, and had resumed his avocation as a sneak-box builder." Bishop found the setting picturesque, but the mosquitoes voracious.

"The house and its small field of low, arable land were environed on three sides by dense cedar and whortleberry swamps, but on the eastern boundary of the farm the broad salt marshes opened to the view, and beyond their limit were the salt waters of the bay, which were shut in from the ocean by a long narrow, sandy island known to the fishermen and wreckers as Long Beach, the low, white sand dunes of which were lifted above the horizon, and seemed suspended in the air as by a mirage. Across the wide, savanna-like plains came in gentle breezes the tonic breath of the sea while hundreds, aye, thousands of mosquitoes settled quietly upon me, and quickly presented their bills.

"In this sequestered nook, far from the bustle of the town, I found 'Honest George,' so much occupied in the construction of the sneak-box, under the shade of spreading willows, as to be wholly unconscious of the presence of the myriads of phlebotomists which covered every available inch of his person exposed to their attacks.

"The appropriate surroundings of a surf-man's house were here scattered on every side in delightful confusion. There were piles of old rigging, iron bolts and rings, tarred parceling, and cabin-doors — in fact, all the spoils that a treacherous sea had thrown upon the beach; a sea so disastrous to many, but so friendly to the Barnegat wrecker — who, by the way, is not so black a character as Mistress Rumor paints him.

"A tar-like odor everywhere prevailed, and I wondered, while breathing this wholesome air, why this surf-man of daring and renown had left his proper place upon the beach near the life-saving station, where his valuable experience, brave heart, and strong, brawny arms were needed to rescue from the ocean's grasp the poor victims of misfortune whose dead bodies are washed upon the hard strand of the Jersey shore every year from the wrecks of the many vessels which pound out their existence upon the dreaded coast of Barnegat? A question easily answered — political preferment. His place had been filled by a man who had never pulled an oar in the surf, but had followed the occupation of a tradesman.

"Thus Honest George, rejected by 'the service,' had left the beach, and crossing the wide bays to the main land, had taken up his abode under the willows by the marshes, but not too far from his natural element, for he could even now, while he hammered away on his sneak-boxes, hear the ceaseless moaning of the sea."

Bishop went on to say that a verbal contract was soon made and the boatbuilder charged $25 to build the best boat that had ever left his shop. Bishop was to supply the materials at his own cost. The oars and sail were not included in the contract; they would be made by other parties. In all, the cost came to $75. Bishop concluded that the little craft constructed by the surf-man was "the best investment I had ever made in things that float upon the water."

Outsiders Praise Bishop's Berries

Bishop had a penchant for clipping newspapers, especially those that mentioned him by name. Thankfully, it is through this streak of vanity that we can read about life around his Manahawkin cranberry bogs.

This clipping is from The Evening Post, *New York, dated October 25, 1873.*

Near the little hamlet of Manahawkin, in Stafford Township, Ocean County, are several of the

The Stafford Forge Cranberry Plantation in West Creek, as pictured in the 1878 Woolman & Rose Atlas of New Jersey Coast. Property owner Daniel R. Gowdy cultivated 73 acres here. The 22-acre Oxycocus plantation was located at the headwaters of Manahawkin Lake, between the lake and the Garden State Parkway.

largest cranberry plantations in southeastern New Jersey, and it is here, probably, that the culture is brought to the greatest perfection. The Eagleswood plantation contains eighty-four acres and is owned by ex-President Hill of Harvard University, Professor Knapp and several Quaker gentlemen from Salem County, New Jersey. Daniel Gowdy has seventy-three and a half acres of cedar swamp bottoms in cultivation (Stafford Forge) and Mr. Nathaniel H. Bishop about thirty-two acres.

Mr. Bishop is the owner also of two large tracts of swamp bottoms, each of which are about half a mile wide and one mile and a half in length and from year to year he proposes to bring a certain number of acres into cultivation.

Oxycocus and Mayeta Plantations

These two plantations are owned by Mr. Bishop and in some respects are models in their way. In laying out these plantations every fourth ditch which divides the beds is cut five feet wide and three feet deep and serves as a canal as well for draining and irrigating purposes. During the picking season a scow four feet wide by twenty feet long is run on these canals and is used to carry the filled crates to the packing houses. By this system there is a great saving of labor and little or no trampling on the vines as the berries have only to be carried by hand over one bed and a half instead of perhaps a half mile as formerly.

The Mayeta plantation is new and not yet under full cultivation. The packing house for this plantation that has just been erected is a two-story structure, the first floor of which is used as a saw mill and as a manufacture of crates, as well as for preparing the berries for market. The upper story has been finished off very nearly for a mission school and has been named by its owner "Cranberry Hall." During the picking season Mr. Bishop intends to give a series of interesting entertainments in this hall for the amusement of his pickers.

There are twenty acres in the Oxycocus plantation in bearing and the yield of cranberries to the uninitiated appears almost incredible. Last year the so-called premium acre yielded one hundred and fifty-one crates, of thirty quarts each, which were sold by the Mssrs. Knight of Philadelphia for $1,809.

The yield from this plantation during the past six years is as follows: First year, sixty-six crates; second year, two hundred and fifty-seven crates; third year, nine hundred and thirty-three crates; fifth year, twenty-seven hundred crates, and the present year, thirty-five hundred crates.

Manahawkin

This little village is situated on the Tuckerton Railroad, about eighty-two miles from New York. In addition to its cranberry plantations, it possesses many local attractions. Its situation is on a level plain and when reached after passing through a country but one removed from a desert, it appears like a veritable paradise.

The village proper is situated west of the railroad and is about one mile and a half from the shore of Barnegat Bay. Several hundred acres of fine land between the railroad and bay have lately been purchased by the Stafford Improvement Company, of which G.W. Campbell and G.W. Campbell Jr. of this city are the leading members. The area of territory has been laid out into blocks and two main avenues have been graded to the shore of the bay. A large church and several villas and other structures are in progress and the settlement bids fair soon to become a village of considerable importance. The soil is of a sandy loam and is very productive. The health of the section is remarkably good and malarial diseases are unknown. For a place of summer residence the neighborhood presents unusual attractions and its nearness to both New York and Philadelphia is also a consideration in its favor.

In Bishop's day, large newspapers would run columns of local doings along the shore. Unfortunately, Bishop left off the name and date of this newspaper he clipped with this column on West Creek.

"As there is a dearth of local news, no fires, nobody hurt much, no recent weddings, no one hung lately, and as the railroad has been flowed on so much, the engine has exhausted her steam, and cranberries — yes they are still fresh and not quite all picked; so with your permission and your patrons' forbearance I will endeavor to give a short sketch of "Half a Day on a Cranberry Plantation."

Having a little leisure and a pretty widow on our hands one day last week, we concluded to visit a cranberry plantation, and as I had seen all the noted ones except Oxycocus and had a standing invitation by the owner of that one to pay it a visit, we concluded to take a drive in that direction. In due course, we arrived in sight of one of the finest and best finished cranberry fields we ever saw. We were very graciously (at least the young widow was) received by the owner, Nathaniel H. Bishop Esq., and kindly conducted over and around about twelve acres of cranberry ground dotted over with men, women, children and boxes. Everything is conducted quietly and systematically, not an oath nor abusive language allowed on the premises. The owner, in speaking to the pickers, was as polite in manners and speech as he would be in a ballroom.

There are only six acres of vines in full bearing this year: they will yield eighteen hundred bushels fully. It is admitted by old cranberry growers that Bishop's berries are the finest and largest in the state, taking the whole crop together. We were surprised to see such large berries on the six-year-old vines, as they are apt to be small on vines of this age. We were curious to know the reason of these being so much larger than the others. Mr. Bishop informed me that it was due to heavy sanding; 15 inches is the depth over the whole plantation and we saw now lands just being sanded that fully came up to that depth. The vines were short, stiff and harsh to the touch, showing a large percentage of silica in their tissues and filled from top to bottom with the finest fruit our eyes ever rested upon.

Mr. Bishop is a young man of large experience, has not only traveled over nearly all the cranberry growing states in the United States but foreign lands also.

Bishop's books were a success among both armchair and outdoor adventurers, and his canoe, the Mayeta, and his sneakbox, the Centennial Republic, were shown at the 1876 Centennial Exhibition in Philadelphia. He spent his later years in an exhaustive genealogy search funded by his brother, Heber, to try to find a link to British aristocracy.

— *Pat Johnson*

Harold Crane

"I remember a lot of good times around here. You could swim in the lake all summer and skate on it all winter. I can remember having good thick ice by Thanksgiving and it would last and last and last."

L ike many of his ancestors, Harold Crane spent his lifetime in Stafford — within blocks, in fact, of his family homestead, the old Crane house on the northwest corner of Stafford Avenue and Division Street.

When he married, he purchased some of his father's garden and built a fine house on Union Avenue for himself and his new wife, Bernice. When he retired after many years as a lineman for the telephone company, Harold began using his carpentry skills to pay homage to Stafford's history by carving miniatures of local historical landmarks, and miniature sneakboxes. Some are displayed in the Barnegat Bay Decoy and Baymen's Museum in Tuckerton. His painstaking detail of Stafford's General Grier House, also known as Cavalry Cottage, was on view for many years in the Stafford Branch of the Ocean County Library before it became a family keepsake.

"I started it as a doll house for my granddaughter, but then I got so involved in it that people told me never to let the child get ahold of it. So then I took it more serious. Cavalry Cottage was built in 1760. General Grier lived there and he was a cavalry officer in the Civil War. It's supposed to be the oldest residence in town."

Harold's own roots in Stafford predate the Revolutionary War. Many of his ancestors played important parts in our young country's history.

"Nathan Crane and his son Silas both served in the militia and were both in the Battle of Monmouth, as I understand it. Nathan Crane was an adjutant in the state militia and was present at the first prayer in Congress (1776) in Carpenter's Hall in Philadelphia.

"Nathan Crane had 17 or 18 children by two wives," Harold said, adding that Nathan is something of a family mystery.

"They don't know what happened to him. He left Manahawkin and was headed for North Carolina, and nobody's ever been able to find out anything about him since. His last child, Mary, was born in 1789 so it must have been soon after that," Harold surmised. "They never found out what happened to him. People really delved into it, too.

"One of Nathan's sons, Silas, was born in 1759 and he had 10 kids," he continued.

Harold held up a copy of a document, dated 1802, from the office of President Thomas Jefferson. It was signed by Secretary of State James Madison, appointing Silas Crane as collector of customs duties at the Port of Little Egg Harbor.

"Whereas the office of the sector of the Revenue for the Port of Little Egg Harbor is at present vacant, now know ye that with the special truth and confidence in the integrity, diligence and discretion of Silas Crane of New Jersey, I do appoint him as secretary of the revenue for the set Port of Little Egg Harbor," the document states.

"I think he was appointed right after Ebenezer Tucker," Harold offered. "Ebenezer was the first collector, and I think he might have served two terms, and that would bring it down to the date of Silas.

"People have said, 'I wonder how he got down there?' and I said, 'I don't know.' Maybe he was one of the few around that could read and write at that time. A lot of them couldn't. He never lived in Tuckerton, that I know of."

Harold speculated that the customs house might have been open only on certain days because the trip to Tuckerton was a long one by horse or horse and buggy.

Besides being customs collector, Silas Crane was one of the judges of the court of Monmouth County and a member of the New Jersey Council of Trenton.

"Silas had 10 children. The youngest of those was

Harold Crane reflects upon his craftsmanship.

a Silas A., and he was my great-grandfather. Then Silas A. had eight children and the youngest of those was Charles G., born May 4, 1848. He was my grandfather. He died in 1933."

Next Harold pulled out a lined piece of paper with brown script on it, dated February 6, 1886. It is from the Office of the Life Saving Service, to the 4th U.S. Life Saving District, Captain Charles G. Crane, Keeper, Harvey Cedars Life Saving Station.

"Sir, Herewith is transmitted your commission as the keeper of the Harvey Cedars Life Saving Station.

You had better go before the collector of customs and take your official oath," reads the letter in part.

"They used to stay over there (on the Island) the biggest part of the year. Some seasons, in the summer I guess, they weren't active. Granddaddy was active in a lot of the rescues over there.

"Now, I remember reading in one of the books around here about Captain Bond down in Beach Haven way. They had a bad wreck and some of the lifeboats had got away, and he sent a runner up the beach to inform Captain Crane to be on the lookout for some of these lifeboats to come ashore. I think it was Granddaddy that he was referring to.

"Despite the long times apart from his wife, Charles G. had five children. One of those was Harry E., who was my father. He was born August 1876."

Harold remembered just one family story about his grandfather Crane. "This always sticks in my mind. My father, when he was young, had a dog named Pudd. When Granddaddy would come off the life saving station for a few days, Pudd would go back with him. At that time, there were no bridges, no nothin'. The dog would stay over there for a few days and then he'd show up back home. He'd swim home. They figured he must have gone from island to island to do it."

Harold was given a plain duck decoy that his grandfather carved to remember him by. "It never was painted. It's a hundred years old, at least. He wasn't known as a decoy carver, but I suppose all those fellows on the life saving service, they did the same thing to kill time. They were there all alone."

Another family treasure, from his mother's side of the family, is a model of a sailing ship. The model of a two-masted schooner stands two feet high and about the same length. It has the original rigging both fore and aft.

"My grandfather, Alfred S. Cranmer, built it. It's a model of the ship he used to work on, sailing up and down the coast. It was named after my grandmother, Rhoda. It's a well-done piece of work. It would sail if it was in the water, because the rudder, block and tackle all work."

Harold didn't know where the *Rhoda* was berthed. He only knew that his grandfather Cranmer was a sailor on the merchant vessel. "At that time, they would be a deck hand, a cook or what-

ever, all at once."

The model was in the possession of his aunt Mabel Cranmer Aller, who had it for "years and years." It's the only model his grandfather Cranmer made that he knows of. "That was the only one ever came down the line.

"Granddaddy went to sea when he was 14 years old. They started them out young then. His home was down where they call the ferry farm. It was down here on the meadows just at the edge of the woods where evidently they used to ferry people across the bay to get to the Island. There were a couple of farms down there, but I don't remember when they were active. I remember that old building there, the Ferry House."

A Hometown Near the Beach

In 1919, Harold Crane was born the youngest of five children. The oldest, Mary, was born in 1909.

"At one time, there were a lot of Cranes around here, awful lot. They had things populated for quite a while.

"I remember a lot of good times around here. You could swim in the lake all summer and skate on it all winter. I can remember having good, thick ice by Thanksgiving and it would last and last and last.

"Summers, I worked for my father. He was a builder on the Island. The first houses over there that he built, you wouldn't believe it: they sold for $299. They were just shacks, not much to them, two rooms. I can remember we had one for years and years. It was in Ship Bottom on 18th Street. The house still stands, but it was moved to Route 9 up near Beachview Avenue. It's been added to a couple of times, but the original part's still standing.

"When we had it, it was but two rooms. The front room was the kitchen, living room and everything else. The back room was the bedroom with two beds in it. It would be Mother, Dad, five children, a dog with pups and a cat with kittens, and the chickens would all go over there to stay for short periods during the summer.

"We'd go over on the truck. By the time we'd get all the dogs, cats, chickens and kids there, then we'd have company on top of it," Harold laughed. "We'd have big bonfires, marshmallow roasts, watermelon parties. At that time, there wasn't much but sand dunes and poison ivy in Ship Bottom."

Most of the other families vacationing in Ship Bottom were from outside the area. They started coming from Philadelphia once the automobile bridge was built in 1912.

"The first bridge to the island was a mile long, unbroken. I can still hear the planks rattling as the cars go over it.

"My Uncle Tommy had a place right down there on the bay which is now Margo's. Uncle Tommy built that in 1917, and he had hunting and fishing parties. At that time, when it was built, it was built right out over the bay, that you could run a boat underneath and get out of the boat and come up the steps into the center of the building."

Harold never was much of a bayman, he admitted.

"I never caught enough clams to make a chowder with. Later on I did some duck hunting in the bay, but nothing big.

"We used to crab and fish a lot off the old railroad bridge. That was when all you needed was a basket and a net. You'd scoop the crabs up as they went through (the channel)."

The Tuckerton Railroad connected Manahawkin with the Island before the causeway made it obsolete.

"I heard my folks talk about the old Yellow Jacket. That's what they called the (excursion) train that used to run over to the Island. It was just one car. That was before my time.

"I remember when the train used to run through town here over to the Island. I used to hop a ride on it once in a while; they would let you ride. You go down to what they called the 'Y,' where a train could turn around and branch off and go to the Island. They'd let us hop on as kids for that little ride — to get a big kick out of it.

"The train station was at Stafford Avenue. There was a main track and there was another siding and a place we called the hay bank. People would cut salt hay and bale it and bring it up there and ship it by rail to wherever it was going to go.

"When the train would deliver mail, that was great! That was the big time. That was when the train delivered everything from newspapers, mail, automobiles, oil, gas — all of that.

"My Uncle George Bowen was general manager of the Tuckerton Railroad when it folded up finally. That was during the Depression, in the '30s."

Harold looked at two photos of coal-fired steam engines he had framed with some original tickets. Some are signed by his uncle and some by T.R.R. co-founder Theophilus Price.

"I laugh at some of the old tickets," he said. *"From Manahawkin to Cedar Run or Mayetta or West Creek, one continuous passage — No stops."*

Doctor Lane was the doctor in Tuckerton, but he had a pharmacy and a home on Stafford Avenue.

"Back in those days, the doctors used to make their own medications. You know, black salve, ointments, witch hazel ... all that stuff," Harold recalled.

"The only doctor we had here for years and years was Old Doc Hilliard. He was the family doctor for everybody. He borned more kids than you can shake a stick at.

"If you wanted a birth certificate, you had to go to him and tell him when you was born and he would write down the information. He didn't keep many records."

Doc Hilliard lived in the house that is now Shinn's Funeral Home on Hilliard Drive. The structure of part of the house is older than Cavalry Cottage.

"If you was sick, you went there or he'd come to the house."

But if you needed a hospital, you had a long way to go.

"One of my older brothers, Edward, had a bad eye injury when he was a little kid and they had to go to Philadelphia. They had to load on the train, go to Whitings, get transferred there and go to Camden. Maybe you could cross on their train, I don't know. Chances are you had to take the ferry over. Took him to Wills Eye Hospital.

"In fact, when I was first on the first aid squad, you had to go to Atlantic City or Lakewood. I was on the squad for 10 or so years. I had the first life membership ever given."

Stager's Music Hall on Main Street was the first movie theater in Manahawkin.

"I remember the old silent movies there. They also used to put on medicine shows (outside). Traveling shows would come through town and recruit some local actors and actresses. Some of their own people, too. They'd try and sell all kinds of elixirs, medications. Inside the theater, the chairs were collapsible so they could hold dances after the movie.

"All through the movie, Sue Hadsell would play the player piano. It probably cost a nickel or so. And they had a little ice cream parlor alongside of it, too. You could get a dish of ice cream or whatever.

"I don't remember it being open during the day much. There were other ice cream places in town. Where the Diamond Mine is now used to be an ice cream parlor in there. In fact, old Clark Cranmer, he had the building at that time. He had the butcher shop, the ice cream parlor, the barber shop all in the same room.

"Have you ever seen these old wooden ice boxes with the sliding lids on the top? They're about six feet or so long. Used to keep sodas or whatever to keep cold. They say he used to sleep in that.

"Where Carroll's is now used to be the Old National Hotel at the time. My uncle, Elmer Cranmer, built a house on the corner of Beach Avenue. Now it's an ice cream parlor. The old general store was across from it and Johnson's Luncheonette.

"Across Beach Avenue was the old tavern. At that time, Prohibition was in, so the taverns folded up for a while. Rum running used to be a big thing. That was before my time. I remember when it was, but I was too young to get involved."

Harold's family was also involved with the local Methodist church, still standing on Stafford Avenue.

"My grandmother Crane burned the first mortgage of the Methodist church here in town. That was the practice when the mortgage was paid off. I don't know what she was in the church, but she was a good member."

Back then there were still times when a kid could run out of things to do on a summer day.

"Everybody had a bicycle. One family would have one bicycle and two or three kids would have to use it.

"The old Triangle Garage (on the corner of Bay Avenue and Route 9) ... I can remember as a kid sitting on the curb there with a bunch of other kids and one of the state troopers. Here comes Castle's

Elmer Cranmer, Crane's uncle, built this house on the corner of Beach Avenue and Route 9 in 1900, on the site of the Manahawkin Tavern. The building has served as a Baptist parsonage and various businesses, and is currently an ice cream parlor.

ice cream truck down Route 9 going towards the Island. And he stepped out and flagged him down and got in the back of the truck and got Popsicles for all hands. It was hot and us kids didn't know what to do right then; we weren't swimming, at least.

"We didn't have any locks on the windows for years. If anybody wanted to have their door locked, they'd use a skeleton key. But everybody in town had a skeleton key. [They all worked the same on all the locks.]

"If anything was missing you always knew right where to go, who was guilty. There weren't many crooks around.

"Years ago, used to be a constable in town. All you had to hear was 'I'm going to get the constable after you!' That would slow you down. And as a kid, there always was the threat of reform school.

"It was a bustling town, bustling enough. Today there is too many people around, too many developments. When I got married in '46, I think it was 900 people, and I'm not sure but that was the whole township.

"Stafford has always been a nice town. It's just too big now. Too big for me, anyway. It's lost all its old qualities now. But you can't do anything about it."

— Pat Johnson

General Grier and the Cavalry Cottage

Built about 1760, the little house on Stafford Avenue known as Cavalry Cottage is said to be the oldest residence still standing in Manahawkin.

The house got its name more than a century later, when Brigadier General Grier, a cavalry officer in the Civil War, so labeled his home. Grier, shown above in a portrait from 1872, was head of the "Stafford Land Company" and instrumental in carving some of the township's roads in the 1870s.

The home saw a revival of appreciation when lifelong Stafford resident Harold Crane re-created it in miniature. From later owner Bob Mesterton, Crane had learned that, evidently, another general had built the house, although his name has escaped documentation.

When first built, the cottage had two stories, but only two rooms, both of those on the first floor. (The pencil sketch of the cottage was drawn for Grier in 1872, by M.S. Bloodgool.)

"There was a ladder up the middle of what would have been the kitchen to the loft and it stayed that way for about 100 years," Crane observed. "Then, as I understand, the front porch, a stairway inside, and the dormer windows and the back section were added.

"It really is what they call brick pane construction, built after the old English style of wooden uprights, and then everything filled in with brickwork," Crane documented.

For the first hundred years, the original exterior brickwork showed. With renovation and expansion came the clapboard siding that covers the structure now.

The building still stands, but not with the National Historic Site designation that some in town had strived for. Its porch covered by purple wisteria in the spring (as shown in the photograph, above, taken in 1999), it is a favorite subject for local artists.

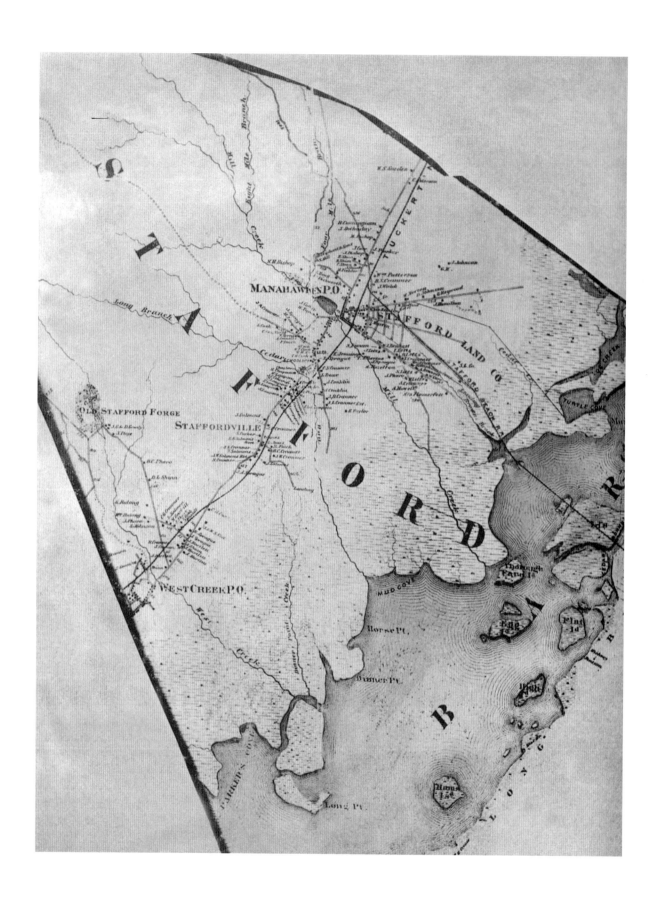

Government

Since the town did not have a "Town Hall," the group agreed upon a meeting place. In 1877 they convened in the hotel on the north corner of Stafford Avenue and Route 9.

Stafford Township officially came into its own on March 3, 1749. King George II of Great Britain, France and Ireland signed the patent, or charter, to set Stafford Township apart from Shrewsbury Township.

The patent gave the inhabitants directions by which to govern themselves. They were to annually choose two Commissioners of the Highways, one Overseer of the Poor, one Assessor, a Collector and a Constable for the town. They were also to "have, hold, and enjoy all the privileges, rights, liberties and immunities that any other townships in the province do or may enjoy."

A commission of three people would conduct the township's business and collect money for improvement of roads, lights and public areas. Each year one commission member was selected as mayor. For many years the mayoral post was rotated so each served as mayor at least once within the elected term of three years.

Since the town did not have a "Town Hall," the group agreed upon a meeting place. In 1877 they convened in the hotel on the north corner of Stafford Avenue and Route 9. The meeting dates recorded seem to show that they met whenever there was business to transact. The meeting place depended on who was on the committee. In 1879, when William Sprague was a member, they met in the Stone Store. When C. H. Cranmer was on the committee, in 1889, they met in a building then known as Cranmer Hall on Route 9. This building was later moved across the road. In 1964, the structure then housed Johnson's Luncheonette, but has since been torn down.

In 1932 the committee meetings moved to the Stafford Hall on Stafford Avenue. It was not until 1959 that the township had a municipal hall, when brothers Herbert and Jerome Shapiro donated a building and grounds to the township in honor of their father, Morris Shapiro. It was located at 775 East Bay Avenue.

By 1964, the town hall had already become overcrowded as

Mayors of Stafford Township

Walter H. Cranmer	1877
William S. Sprague	1878, 1879
Joseph E. Hazelton	1880, 1882
Lewis A. Cranmer	1881, 1889, 1893
William Flomerfelt	1883
Joseph R. Oliphant	1884
Edgar J. Cook	1885, 1886
John Letts	1887, 1888
Charles H. Cranmer	1890-1892, 1894-1899, 1902-1907, 1921-1922
Edward E. Predmore	1900-1901, 1903-1905
Benjamin Oliphant	1906
George F. Pharo	1908
William B. Sprague	1909-1914
George E. Bennett	1915-1920
Charles G. Crane	1923, 1924
Woodburn S. Cranmer	1925-1930
Harry E. Crane	1931, 1932, 1934-1936, 1940
Chester Cranmer	1933
Stanley Seaman	1937-1939, 1961
Lester Johnson	1941, 1942
Leslie Cranmer	1943, 1944, 1949, 1953
Russell Horner	1945, 1950-1952
Gilbert Garrison	1946, 1947
Calvin Conklin	1948
Howard King	1954
Milton H. Cranmer	1955, 1958
William S. Burnham	1956, 1959
Jack Cervetto	1957, 1963, 1966, 1969
Amos Michel	1960
Robert Holms	1962, 1965, 1968, 1971
Alden Corlis	1964
Charles W. Boltner	1970
Wesley K. Bell	1972, 1973, 1975, 1980, 1981, 1983
Charles E. Knight	1974, 1976, 1978
Louis Novotny Jr.	1977
Dolores Barnes	1979
Joseph Sorrentino	1982
Carl W. Block	1984- present

a result of the township's rapid growth. Trailers were brought in to relieve congestion and provide more office space, and in 1979 an addition was made to town hall. In 1981, the police department relocated to a former Hallmark card shop on Bay Avenue. But the moves fragmented the location of government offices, and officials looked for a larger site.

A new 42,000-square-foot municipal complex was planned on a site that held the police department, two older homes, and a nursery. This complex, completed in 1998, has incorporated all the governmental branches in one building at 260 East Bay Avenue.

In 1963 and then again in 1973, a move surfaced to change the form of government from a three-member committee to that of mayor-council, but voters rejected the proposal in each special election.

Voters did approve a referendum in November 1979 to change the constitution of the governing body from a three-person to a five-person committee. The request to change the government to the mayor-council form arose again on the November 1981 ballot. Voters approved the change, and the first election under the new charter was held in May 1982. The year 1983 marked the only recall election in Stafford Township history when voters recalled Mayor Wesley K. Bell on December 7, 1983, by a margin of more than two to one.

Another charter change, in 1987, brought the inclusion of the runoff provision, whereby mayoral and council contenders must obtain a vote majority of "fifty percent plus one" to win a seat on the governing body. If that majority is not gained in the initial election, a runoff election will be held that June as set by statute to determine the victor.

Milton Cranmer

As ducks and geese began to migrate, so did the gunners — right to the flats in the worst of weather.

In his younger days, Milton Cranmer was the foreman for the Manahawkin Bay Bridge and general foreman on the Atlantic City Expressway, a union carpenter by trade. But when he heard the call of the wild, it was time to go gunning on the bay.

Known throughout the East as gunning guides, Milt and friend Bill Inman led city dwellers and professional ballplayers to "sportsmen's paradise." That's what they billed their gunning club, "Cream Puff Castle," on the Flat Creek meadows.

As a boy, following his father, Milton learned the outdoors. He rode atop bales of salt hay piled on a scow as it made its way from the meadows down to the train siding at "Hilliards" where the railroad bridge ran across the bay. He speared eels with an old man named Johnny Johnson and hauled them to the rail yard by hundred-pound sacks. He stayed with his uncle, Frank Thompson, the lighthouse keeper in Barnegat Light. In the wintertime, the migratory birds flying south would be blinded by the lighthouse beacon. "They'd fly right into the lighthouse. You could go down there and pick yourself up a mess of ducks."

Born in 1911, Milton grew up in a Manahawkin of 500 to 800 people. From his papers, he pulled out a tax bill from 1883, a year when a town resident would pay his great-grandfather, tax collector Isaiah Cranmer, $6.

His father, Rufus, delivered mail to Barnegat Light in a motorized handcar, later in a Model T Ford. Rufus Cranmer earned part of his living as a bayman. Aquatic life abounded — even oysters, rare today.

"We always had plenty of food," Milton remembered. "When I went clamming, there was always plenty of clams, and the water was always pure enough that you didn't have to worry about whether they were fit to eat." In the Depression, clams sold for $3 a thousand, and Milton treaded 1,800 to 2,000 a day.

The bounty of the bay's surroundings extended to the sky. As ducks and geese began to migrate from October through January, so did the gunners — right to the flats in the worst of weather.

The gunning shack the locals called Cream Puff Castle was once a shanty for oystermen. "It was over 100 years old. My dad and some of the old-timers who are gone now built it," Milton said.

"My dad's half-brother, a fellow by the name of Joe Budd, was in the oyster business up there. A lot of these little shanties were oyster houses where they used to go up and stay and take care of the oysters."

Below Graveling Point, the state ran an operation where it "planted" oysters — dropped shells overboard so that young oysters, called "spats," would catch onto them.

"They would open it up a certain time of the year for water farmers, you might call them, and they would go down there with their garveys and pick these spats up with their tongs and bring them up and plant them up around Barnegat. In, say, about three or four years, they'd grow to be good-sized oysters. You could harvest them and sell them."

Milton Cranmer, former Stafford Township mayor, in 1998.

Milton's friend Willard "Bill" Inman loved to gun, so the two went into business in 1943 guiding hunting parties. Ballplayers such as George Case, local hero Roger "Doc" Cramer, Walt Masterson and Ray Scarborough paid $50 a day to soak up the cold salt air from a ground-level "box" that held five men staring at the sky.

Case was awed enough to write about it later. The date was January 1, 1945.

"Out of the muck, heading straight for the stools, came the biggest flock of broadbills that I have ever seen — I think I am being conservative in saying there were 5,000 of them. They were stretched out across the bay for a quarter of a mile and looked like a low-hanging cloud as they kept coming on. I began to shake and shiver, not because I was soaked to the skin and half frozen to death, but because of the realization that I was seeing a sight that few have ever seen. I have had many exciting things happen to me on the ball field and have had my share of thrills hunting and fishing, but I will always remember New Year's Day 1945 as the one that brought me the biggest thrill of them all."

"We killed a lot of ducks," Milton related. "You

couldn't get away now with what we used to. We also had a pond that had an artesian well that would stay open no matter how hard it froze. If there weren't gunning parties, we would go gunning anyway."

For 14 years, that's the way it was. "They were great days, I'll tell you.

"We had five kids in all, but at that time we had three — this gunning business made our Christmas for us," Milton said. "We was working away a lot of times — Bill and I doing carpentry work. When it got near gunning season, we quit; didn't make no difference how good the job was. We liked to gun."

Some of the guys from the city "didn't hardly know one end of the gun from the other," as the experts used to say.

"It was funny; Bill put these guys in the box and we wouldn't get in the gunning box with 'em. They'd start shooting at these ducks and wouldn't be hitting 'em, and Bill and I'd say, 'well ...' We'd get in there, and of course they'd start killing ducks: 'I got that one! I got that one!' "

Milton remembered Bill Inman as "one of the best wing shots I ever saw in my life."

Certain pursuits stand out in a gunner's memory. For Milton, one is a time he out-shot his buddy. They were gunning in the Upper Thorofare near the open bay.

"Three ducks came along. I shot one and killed one. Bill missed his. Another one came by and I killed that. Bill shot his and missed that. Three ducks I killed and he never opened his mouth for two hours. That's the only time I ever wiped his eyes.

"We had some good times together, and we had some rough times."

The good times: "We used to kill black ducks in that pond as the sun went down, and sometimes in the moonlight."

The hard times: "We seen a lot of storms, and cut our way through ice."

The Hurricane of 1944 caught the men on the Flat Creek meadows, determined to stay. "It came to the eye of the storm when it was all quieted down, so we decided, 'Well, this thing must be over, so we'll go across the bay,' " Milton remembers. "So we went over ... it started storming real hard. We decided we can't go home, we don't want to go back across the bay in this mess. So we stayed.

"Bill's wife didn't know where he was at and Martha didn't know where I was at," Milton continued. Most of the time, however, "she knew I'd be all right; she knew I could take care of myself.

"We stayed all night. We didn't have anything there; there was a can of sardines."

One of the boats was gone. The men went looking for it and found it, the bow ground up from where it had run against a bulkhead. Rube Corlies had it fixed in time to finish the gunning season.

The storm did claim three dozen Rowley Horner decoys that Milton had bought for $35. Certain Rowley Horner decoys now go for tens of thousands of dollars. "I'd like to have them now; they'd be worth some money," Milton acknowledged.

Of all the ducks the gunners winged from the air, "none of them went to waste," Milton said. "Whatever we killed, we ate. I filled the freezer up, and we had duck all winter."

A hurricane "took," but it might give back. Families were able to enlarge their houses or gunning shacks with found material. "After the '44 hurricane, we went over to the beach and gathered up a lot of material."

Milton surveyed Route 72 before it sped new families to the shore and changed things around Manahawkin. But in some ways, past residents could have used better transportation than they had in his childhood.

His mother, Bertha Ridgway Cranmer, died in 1922 when he was 11 years old.

"My mother was only 33. She died of a busted appendix. We didn't have any hospitals or anything nearby; they had to put her on a train and take her to Philadelphia. By the time they got there for an operation, it was too late."

Later in Milton's life, work as foreman on the Manahawkin Bay Bridge was one of several formidable jobs. But the bridge's construction took only one year. Working from the bottom up, men poured columns of concrete after water was pumped out of bases around them.

Salt Haying Days

Down paths far back in the memories of fewer and fewer folks lie details of such bucolic livelihoods as salt haying.

"It used to be, years ago when we went up there when my dad was haying, the mosquitoes were terrible," Milton said. "They used to have a smudge pot — you'd build a fire and put wet hay on top of it. The smoke would keep the mosquitoes away."

The meadows where they worked belonged to relatives. His father worked for Joseph W. Oliphant, who used to cut the hay. On each bale of hay was a number signifying its weight, and thus, the amount of money the bale was worth. Bales might weigh 250 pounds.

"They'd put it on a scow, and then they would tow it down the bay and load it in a freight car down there at Hilliards. There was a siding where they put a freight car in there. I used to ride down the bay on the scows of hay."

Those were the days when heavy horses worked alongside the men. The team pressed the hay after cutting it and raking it into a stack to dry.

"You couldn't use it wet; you had to have it dry when you pressed it."

Milton told more about the process. "This press, it was open at the top. The sides would come down on it also, but when they pressed the hay, it had the sides up and they would pitch the hay in the top.

"Before they put the hay in, they put three strands of wire underneath the hay where it would press. Then they put three strips of wood whatever the length the bale of hay would be, on each side of it, so that when you got ready to unload the hay to be pressed, they would take these wires and run it around and tighten up on it.

"They had horses to crush the hay. They would go right around in circles to bring the hay press together. The horse went around in a circle and the press kept going down, down, down."

Memories of life within a whiff of the bay include summertime parties on Milton's 26-foot boat. He used to take "all the kids around town" out for a ride. Other times, the 15 or so people aboard would party at the gunning shack.

"My sister would come and cook whatever we wanted. We'd get about half loaded. My wife, she never drank anything that I know of, but she always came along."

Martha Cranmer, the daughter of Martha Lawrence and Franklin B. Southgate, shared early-century memories of Manahawkin as well. Her family moved from Burlington County when an opening as station agent arose with the Manahawkin Railroad. Her father held the last station master post, from 1925 to 1936, when the railroad closed.

Martha remembered "anything you wanted" arriving by rail — maybe even a washing machine from Sears. One time, another brand-new washing machine arrived for the same household two days later — "nobody ever admitted they made a mistake."

Milton Cranmer was mayor of the town in 1955 and 1958, a member of the local school board, and has held offices with the Methodist church on Stafford Avenue.

— *Maria Scandale*

Charley Farley

"They spun yarns of the past that would make the hair curl on a brass monkey as they sat around the big potbellied stove and munched crackers from the nearby barrels."

Charley Farley, a house painter by trade, was also a grocer and snack shop operator in Manahawkin. Old-timers recall that he sold very large ice cream cones in his store where East Bay Avenue meets Parker Street. Friends found this manuscript that he wrote in his later years, before his death in 1965.

Certain events which took place in the little shore town of Manahawkin before the turn of the century whet the memory of a lifetime of years.

There were seven in our family, namely: father, Patrick Farley; our mother, Sara; one girl, Carrie; and five boys, Otis, John, Charles, Pete and Emerson.

Father was a veteran of the Civil War and a member of N.J. Volunteer 23rd Regiment. He lost his right arm in the struggle. I like to think of him as being able to chop wood, pitch hay or any other work as well as any two-armed man I ever saw.

We lived at the edge of the meadows near Barnegat Bay at the end of the tidewater of Manahawkin Creek, so our boat was a short distance from our house.

Our home was an old colonial type, built sometime in the 1700s. It was made of Jersey cedar, which was noted for durability. Most houses and boats of the region were made of it. The house was large, two stories, one with a big wide hallway that ran all the way through the middle and a wide stairway with a shiny hardwood banister down which we young ones slid. There were two chimneys, double wide with fireplaces both up and downstairs.

The old farm was an ideal place to raise a bunch of active kids. There were acres of forest and swamp lands, and stretches of meadows and fields, but it was not all play for us. We were obliged to do our share of chores about the place. We kept horses, cows, pigs and poultry and did much farming. I had to drive the team and plow at the age of 11. However, our parents were not unduly hard on us; we had time to have fun, also.

The wonderful bay was the place we liked best, for on it we could sail boats, catch fish of different kinds, and secure plenty of crabs, oysters and clams. The water was so pure in those days there was never any thought of pollution.

At an early age I learned to sail a boat and had a small garvey, one about eight feet long with a sprit sail and no centerboard. I could sail into the wind and far out into the bay. One day I saw a big dorsal fin of a shark cut through the water; then it disappeared, but soon surfaced toward the stern of my boat! It began to cut capers around me and under me until my little boat rocked like a cork on a rough sea. It frightened the daylights out of me, and I turned around and headed for the mainland as fast as I could go. After that, I never ventured alone far from shore until I grew older and had a larger boat.

That was not the only encounter with sharks. One day two of my brothers, Dad and I were sailing across the eel flats in his sharpie. The water was shallow, as there was only a half tide, and the eel-grass was dragging at the boat. It was a shallow draft boat, and with a good stiff beam wind we were slipping along at a good clip when off to the windward we saw a huge shark bearing down on us. Probably he was in pursuit of a fish, and had gotten out of the deep water onto the flats.

He was in a panic as he hunted deep water again, part of his body being out of the water. The shark was pushing a big wave of mud and water ahead of it in its mad rush, but it was making remarkable speed despite the shallow water, and headed straight for our boat! It evidently did not see us because of the murkiness of the water as it stirred it up.

Dad had the presence of mind to grab an oar and jab it into the head of the creature. It was enough to cause it to veer off to the stern, and miss hitting our boat, but only by inches. In making the quick turn with its powerful tail, it did plaster us and soil all the way to the peak with mud. We got a good view of him as he turned. He was longer than our boat, and the direction in which he was then going would soon take him to the deep water.

A great number of men of the town followed the sea in those days, either as sailors before the mast or as, in many cases, captains of ships. A number served in the United States Life Saving Service on the beach.

At that time there were such stations every few miles, manned by a trained crew through the winter months. They maintained a patrol night and day. A patrol from one station would meet at a half-way point with a patrol from the next station. There they exchanged checks. If a ship in distress was sighted, a flare was sent up by the patrol to notify the ship's crew that they had been seen. If the sea was calm enough, the lifeboat would be launched and they would row out to the ship. However, if the waves were too rough, a mortar was sent up to shoot a blue line over the ship, a lifeline being fastened to the ball and, if the crew over in the ship succeeded in getting the line, a larger one was pulled out and fastened to the mast as high up as possible. To this a breeches buoy on a pulley was attached, with a light hauling line on each end. One person at a time was strapped onto it and hauled ashore. At times it was a wet passage.

Many men followed the bay making a living by raising oysters and clamming and fishing for the market. Some, in duck and geese season, took spearmen out to points around the meadows, and maintained boats and decoys for that purpose. Others had large catboats, party boats or yachts, and took parties out for a sail on the bay. So the bay was a means of livelihood for many. Some fished offshore on the ocean side, two men to a skiff. That's what Rube Corlies was doing when he saw a sea serpent.

Some years back, I was operating a hydraulic dredge in Los Angeles Harbor, and a young Norwegian deck hand told me he had been fishing off Barnegat Light in the ocean, when a heavy fog with a rough sea set in. They could not find the inlet into the bay, but Capt. Raymond Palmer of the Life Guard came to their rescue. I told him that Palmer had been a schoolmate of mine.

The little engine and cars that ran from Manahawkin station over the bridge that spanned the bay to LBI we called the Yellow-Painted. People going to the beach transferred to the Yellow Jacket, so some of us boys would be on hand with wildflowers, whatever was blooming at the time, to sell to the passengers; wild magnolias were favorites. A

The "Yellow Jacket" in the meadows, with the Peahala Club in the background.

large patch grew in the swamp area near the "Y" where the train reversed itself. The water tank was there, too. When the little train pulled away from the station, we rode the steps as far as we dared. Sometimes by the time we jumped, the train would have kicked up such speed we would get a nasty spill down the bank of the track.

At times I was caught on the long bridge when the train came along. Then we had to get down on a timber cap and let the train roar over our heads. What a racket that made, along with an eerie feeling.

One time a man who wished to fish at the bay rode the train from town and the crew forgot to let him off. It ran a little way out on the bridge, then started to back up. Meanwhile, the man had gotten off to walk back. The only way he could save himself was to jump off the bridge. Made it in one piece, but lost his fish and tackle.

Snug at Home on Winter Nights

Mother was a very good cook and always set a splendid table of hearty food. She was a busy woman, looking after such a large family and usually an uncle staying with us, for whom to cook and wash and sew. What wonderful odors when she took those big, brown, crusted loaves of bread out of the oven. Then there were rows of delicious pies — pumpkin, huckleberry, apple, mincemeat and others. We always grew a large garden of various vegetables and raised enough potatoes to last the winters.

Three of us boys usually slept in one bed. Our bedroom was a large one on the second floor, with a window facing the bay. We slept on a big, fat, feather mattress with no springs, just slats to hold

it on the bed frame. When we had snuggled into its depths, we slept warm on the coldest nights. However, being slippery, the mattress sometimes got down between the slats, forcing them to jump out of position. Then we suddenly found ourselves in more or less of a predicament, with the foot of the mattress resting on the floor, and us piled up. We would stay that way for the rest of the night, not wishing to get up in the cold to straighten things up.

As the winter set in, the lighthouse across the bay inlet set its great light into motion, and its circling beam lighted up the ocean, bay and meadow with its orbit. As our house was within its radius, as it passed our window, it caused a friendly glow within the room.

When one of those terrible northeastern storms blew in from the sea, it hurled its mighty blast of fury against the weather-beaten sides of the old house as if it was trying to flatten it to the ground. So well was the frame constructed that never a tremble was felt. How we would snuggle even deeper into our bed, and think of sailor friends and relatives out on the wild sea, and how they must have welcomed the friendly light.

As a lad I remember a number of old ribs of wrecks sticking up out of the sand along the beach. One such was at Loveladies. After a big blow I would go there and pick up old foreign coins that were exposed by the wind blowing the sand from around them. Elderly men told of a circus ship being wrecked, and all the animals were drowned in the hold of the ship. When the passengers gathered on deck, huge waves washed them overboard, and all drowned.

Stafford Avenue east of the railroad. Tom Sprague's store, where the old-timers gathered to spin yarns, is at left, next to the Cavalry Cottage.

One time a Portuguese ship loaded with wines and brandies came ashore in a storm and broke up, spilling her cargo into the ocean. Her name was the *Armedis Pasqia*. Barrels and cases floated just under the water and were washed ashore for miles along the coast. Before the revenue officers got on the job, many barrels had been hauled to the mainland by folks from little towns nearby, and many were buried in the sand dunes and may still be there. Some people, it seems, occasionally knocked the head off a barrel and proceeded to get so drunk they forgot where they had buried them.

There were tales of old-time pirates plying their nefarious trade on Long Beach Island, also. It is said that during a storm they would put up false beacons on the beach and a ship, seeing the lights, would suppose they were in a harbor, and would be wrecked on the beach. The bodies of the hapless victims would be stripped of their valuables. Pirates even cut off the swollen fingers to get the diamond rings.

One quite elderly man in our town who had participated in these deeds lived near us and during a stormy night would pace the floor with remorse thinking about what he had done as a young man.

If vitamins have anything to do with good health, we must have been healthy. In the woods we were always eating what nature provided in the way of green things — berries and fruits. In the spring, tender leaves of wintergreen — also sweetbriar, sassafras and spice wood as well as tender shoots — a pleasing taste. If one dared to penetrate the mysterious dark depths of the Manahawkin swamp, the only growth of sweet birch could be acquired. I seldom had the courage. There were four or five huckleberry bushes, a patch of wild strawberries. I would eat all I could of this delicious fruit. There were two or three kinds of grapes; plentiful and luscious wild cherries grew along old rail fences. In the fall came the walnut and hickory harvest. Some plums grew on the beach, prized for wonderful jams and jellies. Wild rose hips grew in the marshes — tasty. Also wild persimmons — plentiful.

Between the first house on the road and the farm going to town, a distance of about two miles, there was a stretch of swampland with a thick growth of trees at the edge. The first house was old and in it lived a very old woman who was all alone, seldom seen, and it was said that she was a witch. Were we ever scared out of our wits when obliged to pass by that place! We always ran by, and used the far side of the road. One day I was alone, on my way to town, and was about to take off on a run past her place when, to my concern, I saw her at the gate. I was too confused to run or even move, and just stood there, petrified.

She just about finished me when she opened the gate and called, "Come here, young man." I was afraid to refuse, so I went to the gate and what a surprise I had. That good old lady had several chunks of honey in the comb and gave them to me! Never again was I afraid to pass her place.

That stretch of swamp had other terrors for me, though. On Stafford Avenue, Tom Sprague's store was a gathering place for some of the old-timers in the winter eves. They spun yarns of the past that would make the hair curl on a brass monkey, as they sat around the big potbellied stove and munched crackers from the nearby barrel. Among the narrators were retired sailors and veterans of the Civil War.

I was fascinated and sat in an obscure corner listening as they told the tales of pirates and shipwrecks. One man had been a prisoner of war in the South. He told of the terrible way they were treated and the appalling loss of life from starvation and neglect.

One dark night after staying longer than I should, I was on my way home when I came to the swamps. They seemed even more lonely and scary than usual. I was almost home, at a place where a small brook formed a pond. As I came to the pond, I heard a splash of an animal wading across it. At that time there were tales of wild animals being heard in the swamps. The local people called them catamounts. I was sure it was one of those. It was too late to run, but I saw what it was — the old black and white hound dog of a neighbor! No words could express my relief.

For spending money, we boys each morning gathered up the milk cows in town and took them to pasture on our farm; then we took them home in the evening. For that we received 25 cents a month.

Squire Hazelton, the father of Lee Hazelton, had a couple of cows which I drove. To us younger boys, Lee was a hero. I always said he could throw a baseball harder and farther than anyone in the world could. I could vouch for his hard-throwing arm. When I was old enough to play on the home team, I was the catcher and Lee sometimes did the pitching.

His dad had a yoke of oxen and at times hitched them to a cart and allowed us to ride. Besides driving cows, we at times got a job pulling or hoeing weeds in the corn fields. For that work, we received 50 cents for a 10-hour day.

A short distance from the house, near the creek landing on the edge of the meadow, the black soil showed that in the past there had been quite an Indian encampment there. The Delaware Indians had shucked their clams there, as a large pile of shells testified. There, too, they had strung beads and dried them in the sun for future use. Nearby was also a large grove of persimmon trees. When ripe, the wild fruit is a delicious one, and we worked right along with the opossums in climbing the trees to get them.

The limbs of the trees were brittle, and one day my older brother, Otis, was about 15 feet up when a limb broke. He came tumbling down in a good hard fall but escaped without injury.

I liked the persimmons best when in the winter one could climb to the top of a snowbank and pick the cured fruit.

Travels Afield Yield Lost Towns

I had often heard people speak of the "barrens," that they lay across the forested hills a few miles to the west of town, but I had never been to that area. One day my dad hitched up the team, and we drove there through the woods on an old road to the edge of that area. My first impression of the strange sight was of seeing a miniature forest stretching out before me as far as the eyes could reach. That really is what it was — a tract of land covered with small pine and oak trees.

One day my brother Pete and I decided to see something of the country south of us. So I made a canvas canoe and got together some camping equipment — all ready for the trip. When everything was loaded in the canoe and Pete and I got in, we had only four or five inches of freeboard. However, the weather was good and the water was calm with hardly any wind, so we had no trouble, and with two good paddles we made headway.

We entered the mouth of the Wading River where it flowed into the Mullica and, at the end of the tidewaters, came to a clean stream of fresh water. From then on, it was a case of hard paddling against a strong-flowing stream. The farther we advanced, the thicker the forest became until it formed a canopy over the stream. Then we rounded the bend and entered a clearing. Much to our astonishment, we saw close to the bank a large building in an empty canal. At the end of the building was a large water wheel sitting idle, as it had for many years. The building and the wheel were in good condition; in fact, the wheel looked like it would start turning if water was turned into the canal.

We entered the building and found it to be devoid of machinery, but on the floor was a huge roll of paper about six feet long and in good condition. We knew then that we were in an old, abandoned paper factory.

We walked from the mill to one side of it, and saw spread out before us quite a village, with neat rows of houses in good repair, paved sidewalks and iron lamp posts with lamps still in them. Something was wrong! Not a soul was within sight; no housewife going in and out of doors, no children playing in yards or streets, only a deadly silence. Finally, we realized that for the first time in our lives we were seeing a ghost town. Accidentally, we had run into Harrisville, and before us was proof of a vast amount of money having been spent for nothing, at some time.

The Harris brothers, wealthy merchants of nearby cities, purchased the property from the former owners who were running the sawmill — rather, what was called at that time a slitting mill. Lumber, instead of being sawed, was split and rived. The Harris brothers had started construction of the paper mill in 1815.

The project proved to be costly and a mistake for them. Their intention had been to make paper from meadow hay. Acres of it grew just below the factory, but the paper made from it proved to be of such an inferior quality that no sale could be found for it. Neither of us had a camera at the time of our visit, and we have been sorry ever since. Pictures taken at that date would have been worthwhile now.

We proceeded upstream from Harrisville a short distance and stopped at the old Martha Furnace. This was a lovely spot. There was a small lake and a clearing with large oak trees, and at the lower end of the lake stood the old furnace, still in good order.

We decided to make camp there and stayed a few days while looking the region over. We learned that in 1793, a man named Potter made the furnace by picking up small chunks of ore from the gravel bars of nearby streams. It is a strange kind of ore and is always growing or forming.

The ore was hauled to the furnace on wagons. When it was to be fired, a certain amount of charcoal was put in. Then the iron ore was added, also oyster shells. As the ore melted, it was drawn off and poured into the mold. It is said that the first cast-iron stoves were made at Martha's Furnace.

The local smelters and glass works of the area used a great deal of charcoal, so it was natural that much of the nearby forest trees were made into charcoal, and the jack pine of the region proved to be the best, because of pitch content, to make an extremely good quality of coal. It gave employment to a great number of men in the Pine Belt. Ned had done some teaming in the area after the Civil War, so he knew many persons who followed the trade. One time he took me to what proved to be among the last of the operations, to let me see how they made charcoal burn from the bottom up.

The wood was cut into two-foot lengths from smaller trees on an average of about six inches in diameter. A shallow round pit was dug 10 or 12 feet in diameter, and the wood brought to a peak, so it looked like an Indian teepee. At the base, a hole was left into which some dry kindling was put; then the entire outside was covered with turf from a nearby bog, and earth was piled on the outside. Small vents were left so the fire would get air; otherwise, it would be smothered. The men had to know their job in order to make a perfect burn. Day and night watching was necessary, and if the burn was too fast, with too much draft, the charcoal would be of an inferior quality, not worth much on the market, so a steady burn was required. Two men would team up and build a small log cabin near the workings so they could stay at the job.

Much charcoal was hauled into the Mullica River harbors and shipped out to other markets in different parts of the country. During the Revolutionary War, many cannons and cannonballs were cast at that furnace. Many a battle was fought on Jersey soil, and the Mullica River played a great part in the struggle.

Foundations Of Faith

When the population of a community grew, "free churches" sprang up as places of worship open to all denominations.

Historically, the Baptist and Methodist churches served as cornerstones in early Stafford Township, and this chapter focuses on their development within the community. By the mid-20th century, an influx of folks from other areas brought more diversity to the denominational base.

Pioneering preachers who trekked through the wilderness around the villages of early Stafford Township found little in the way of formal or organized religion.

The first evangelists who left records of trips to any part of the Jersey Shore belonged to the Society of Friends, commonly called Quakers. This society established a meeting at Tuckerton in 1704 and built a meeting house there in 1709.

Any other religious services in the early 18th century were conducted by missionaries or traveling ministers in private homes. "The Society for the Propagation of the Gospel in Foreign Parts," based in England, trained missionaries and sent them to what they saw as a "region of wild woods." Among the early ministers were Reverend John Forbes (1733-1738), Reverend John Miln (1738-1746), and finally Reverend Thomas Thompson, an Episcopalian who journeyed from old Monmouth.

"From Manasquan, for twenty miles farther on in the country, it is all one pine forest," Thompson wrote in his diary in 1745. "I traveled through this desert four times to a place called Barnagatt, and thence to Manahawkin, almost sixty miles from home, and preached at places as I went along, where no foot of a minister had ever come." Thompson found "neither religion nor manners," he declared. "In this traverse I had the first view of native Heathenism, just as thoroughly as I have ever since beheld. The inhabitants are thinly scattered in that region of wild woods. Some among them are decent people who had lived in better places, but those who were born and bred here have neither religion nor manners,

The aging Manahawkin Baptist Church, top, fronts an unpaved Main Street in 1900. By 1998, restorations and preservation are complete, at right. The first building on the site served both sides as a refuge during Revolutionary War battles. It was also an early meeting place for school classes. Now the church opens its doors as the Stafford Township Heritage Park Cultural Center after a community restoration project organized by the Stafford Township Historical Society.

and do not know so much as know the letter of a book."

On his return, Thompson sent Christopher Robert Reynolds, but because of his age and infirmity, Reynolds remained only a short time. Hostilities between England and the colonies had grown to such a degree that no other missionaries were sent over.

When the population of a community grew, "free churches" sprang up as places of worship open to all denominations. The first church built in Stafford Township was a "free church" constructed sometime prior to 1758 in the heart of Manahawkin on the Main Shore Road. As a reconstructed building, the site still exists on Route 9, surrounded by the graves of early settlers, shipwreck victims and Revolutionary War soldiers.

Baptist

The first organized religion in the town was a Society of Baptists formed on Aug. 25, 1770 with nine members. The Reverend Benjamin Miller led the church in affiliation with the Philadelphia Baptist Association. During the Revolutionary War, the church building served both sides as a place of refuge, and services had to be discontinued until the hostilities ceased. The church functioned as a makeshift hospital for militia members who were wounded in the "Skirmish at Manahawkin" outside its doors, Edwin Salter's *A History of Monmouth and Ocean Counties* tells us. In that battle, Captain Reuben Randolph's Manahawkin Militia clashed with John Bacon's band of "Pine Pirates." Several historians make mention of the bloodstains and bullet holes that were in great evidence in the church for many years later.

Because of the neglect suffered during this time by the discontinuance of services and the ravages of the war, the Baptist Society was not reorganized until 1801. The building, having fallen into disrepair, had to be rebuilt.

Another step in the Baptist church's formal establishment in the town took place in 1857 when the church was incorporated under the laws of the state of New Jersey as the Manahawkin Baptist Church

A Baptist parsonage, about 1900, on Route 9 near the church. Among its later uses was Presti's Italian Kitchen in the 1980s, and at the turn of the 21st century, Manahawkin's only bed and breakfast inn.

and Society. The trustees elected April 27, 1857 were Jarvis H. Brown, Amos B. Brown, John B. Crane Jr., Stacey Gennings and Joseph R. Oliphant.

Dedication of the new structure took place July 10, 1867, with the Reverend E. S. Browe as pastor. This second building is the one still standing, surrounded by the graves of early settlers, shipwreck victims, and Revolutionary War soldiers. Among its pastors were the Reverend C. A. Mott, who preached his final sermon in July 1878 before leaving to take a position in Vineland. The Reverend E. L. Stager became pastor in February 1880 but died on April 13, 1882 at the age of 35. There followed various ministers who usually stayed for one year. The first parsonage was built in 1882 near the church on Route 9.

One later milestone occurred in 1948, when a Bible school was started with eight students. The next summer heralded the advent of the first daily vacation bible school. During the time when the Reverend Earl Comfort was pastor in the 1960s, the congregation decided to build a new, larger sanctuary across Route 9 from the old building. The old church was leased to the Stafford Township Histori-

The earliest photograph (late 1800s) of the Methodist church on Stafford Avenue, top, which was dedicated in 1884. The tall steeple and round window are its outstanding features, as well as the two-color paint pattern. Scaffolding erected for repairs (inset) after the steeple was struck by lightning. The tall trees used as the prime supports of the scaffolding are said to have been cut by Ed Cook and crew from Cedar Run. The church in 1964, bottom.

cal Society. After periods of growth and outreach in the 1970s, the church purchased 36 acres on Hilliard Boulevard, where a brick sanctuary to seat 700 people was built through a bond program. The previous building, after a renovation, became the Stafford branch of the Ocean County Library. The church's Lighthouse Christian Academy opened in 1979. By 1999, an addition to the campus added a new library, four classrooms and a new office complex. By the year 2000, its enrollment in grades kindergarten through sixth reached 300.

Meanwhile, the historical society has reinvigorated the old building as the Stafford Township Heritage Park Cultural Center. With donations from the community and local contractors in the late 1990s, the historic landmark was refurbished for another century. It has hosted weddings, concerts, Lenape language classes, meetings and community church services.

Methodist

The Methodist church is another denomination that has celebrated a long history in Manahawkin and surrounding Stafford Township hamlets. The exact date of its organization in Manahawkin is unknown; the documentation available is a deed designating "a piece of land forty-one hundredths of an acre, located on what is now Beach Ave. north side, for the purpose of erecting a ME Church." Reuben Randolph, for the amount of $10, deeded the property on March 12, 1803. The church doors opened for the first time that same year. Trustees were Benjamin Seaman, Samuel Bennett, Edward Lamson, Benjamin Randolph, Henry Pearson, Thomas Randolph, Nathan Crane, Livi Camburn and William Randolph.

With the church probably crowded on Christmases and Sundays, members began looking in 1871 for a location for a larger building. By August 1872 their prayers were answered. The Stafford Land Company donated several lots on the north side of Stafford Avenue near the railroad depot. The frame structure dedicated in 1874 measured 40 by 60 feet. This church, according to the records available, was never really finished or kept in good repair. The congregation set up a committee in 1883 to study this problem and recommended rebuilding the church on the same site. This was begun on August 1,

1883 and dedicated by Bishop Harris on January 24, 1884. Today the same structure stands but has undergone many improvements and several additions.

The Methodist denomination made an organized effort in the late 19th century to see that a pastor continually served the area. One of the functions of the New Jersey M.E. Conference, when it met once a year, was to assign ministers to particular districts. It then became necessary for the community to provide housing for these men and their families. To meet this obligation in Manahawkin, the M.E. trustees secured a lot, deeded June 10, 1876, on Union Street from George and Anna Campbell, representatives of the Stafford Land Company. The new house built from the foundation up was finished by April 25, 1878, when the Reverend J. Rogers moved in. The congregation of both Manahawkin and Cedar Run churches helped furnish the home, even down to making large rugs for several rooms in the house. Josiah Sprague and Benjamin Carr were mentioned in reports on the construction. This house remained as the Methodist parsonage until the 1990s, when a new one was erected on the corner of Center Street and Beach Avenue on land donated by Milton Paul.

Meanwhile, church building efforts were taking place in the Cedar Run/Mayetta area. Nathaniel Bishop, when he built his sawmill on the Cedar Run stream, built a two-story structure on the Mayetta side in 1873. He had the stream dammed up during the fall and winter months, utilizing the water power to run the sawmill during the week. On Sunday, the hall in the upper part housed a Sunday school and services.

Residents of Mayetta and Cedar Run in the winter of 1872 had begun planning to build a church. The two villages banded together to call themselves "Unionville," but the name didn't stick. Townspeople decided on a design in December 1872 — a one-story gothic style with a belfry. By November 1874, the foundation stood in place. However, higher prices and dwindling funds combined to delay the project, and the sanctuary was still unfinished in 1876. An able workforce was available, though. Many men were out of work during the winter of 1877, so they decided to do the job themselves. From there it seems to have progressed steadily, if not speedily. The men raised a frame, covered it with clapboards,

The Methodist church on snow-covered Main Street in Cedar Run, top, at the turn of the century. The building was finished in 1880, utilizing local hands. Below, the building became the home of the Cedar Run Assembly of God in the early 1960s. The church organization also bought the adjacent Cedar Run-Mayetta school building to the south and preserved it as an activities center.

and brushed on two coats of paint by June 1878. With Edgar Cook organizing the construction, the steeple stood in all its glory by February 1880.

With all the work being donated during the winter months, the church rose without debt. It was fully completed, furnished and dedicated on December 15, 1880. The Reverend James Rogers of Manahawkin was the first pastor.

This church served both villages of Cedar Run and Mayetta. Parishioners walked there for services that were held twice every Sunday. Interior gas lighting came later, along with tin lining for the walls and ceilings.

In the summer of 1959, the Methodist congregations of Manahawkin and Cedar Run merged to form one church under the leadership of the Reverend Van Cleef. The combined church, for legal reasons, was incorporated on October 14, 1961.

At this time the congregation decided to add a Sunday school and nursery wing to the west side of the building. This addition, called "Fellowship Hall," was finished and dedicated on June 3, 1962.

The United Methodist Church in Warren Grove was built by Seth Corliss and one helper in 1874 as a simple frame building. The church still gathers folks for worship and special occasions. The congregation of about a dozen active members has upgraded the building's systems and in the year 2000 received money from the Charles B. Mathis Fund toward its plans to reconstruct the roof and repair the steeple.

Warren Grove historian Jack Cervetto remembered late summer Camp Meetings once a year, held in a pine grove and lit by kerosene lamps. The last one in Warren Grove was in 1928.

Denominational Diversity

As the mosaic of the community developed, other denominations grew.

The former Methodist church building in Cedar Run became the home of the Cedar Run Assembly of God in the early 1960s. The congregation grew from three families who had been meeting in Beach Haven, with the first pastor the Reverend Milton Thurlow. The church later bought the old Cedar Run-Mayetta school building, adjacent to the sanctuary. The building, which dates to the turn of the 20th century, became an activities center after renovations and the addition of plumbing. The sanctu-

The Warren Grove Methodist Church, founded in 1874, has been a longtime center of the surrounding area.

ary has undergone two renovations, first in 1973 and then in 1989, and the church built a parsonage in 1978. The Reverend James Occhipinti and his wife, Sylvia, have shared the distinction of being a husband and wife pastoral team who are both ordained ministers.

On July 1, 1965, the Lutheran Church in America sent the Reverend Rudolph Schneider to develop a congregation in the Manahawkin area. Seeds of the church had begun to grow as early as 1953, when mainland members of the Lutheran denomination on Long Beach Island began to hold Sunday School classes and monthly services in the vacated Methodist church in Cedar Run (later the Assembly of God). The services relocated to a store building farther north on Route 9 and then to the Oxycocus School in 1965. Ground-breaking for a new church building took place in November 1967, and the building was up and dedicated six months later. The congregation celebrated with a procession from the school to the current place of worship at 333 North Main Street, Route 9. The congregation quickly outgrew its initial facility and in 1980 expanded into an addition which more than doubled the size of the original building. A live outdoor nativity pageant has been an annual Christmas gift to the community.

St. Mary's Roman Catholic Church Parish Center in Manahawkin is an outgrowth of St. Mary's Church in Barnegat, whose first Mass dates back to March 1907, attended by 14 people. The Barnegat gathering soon became a mission church of the Church of St. Thomas Aquinas of Beach Haven. St. Mary's was officially incorporated as a parish in 1942. The first Mass at the new St. Mary's Parish Center on Route 9 in Manahawkin was said on July 3, 1976. Father Kenard Tuzeneu became pastor in 1992 and has overseen outreach programs such as Ken's Kitchen, offering hot meals for the homebound, needy and elderly. The year 1985 marked the dedication of St. Mary's Cemetery in Manahawkin. All Saints Regional Catholic School opened on the grounds of the parish center in September 1997 for kindergarten and first grade. A grade was added each year thereafter, and a new K-8 school was built at the corner of McKinley Avenue and Doc Cramer Boulevard. Plans also call for a large sanctuary next to the school.

The Ocean Reformed Church on Route 72 began on April 21, 1982. It was chartered with 100 members as a congregation of the Reformed Church in America, the oldest Protestant denomination with a continuous ministry in the United States. The Reverend Mark VanderMeer was the founding pastor. Worship services moved to a local school when the first official meeting place on Nautilus Drive was sold and torn down. The first services in the new building took place Easter Sunday, April 30, 1986, and the church became the Ocean Community Church in 1986 under the direction of the Reverend Dr. Philip Bakelaar. With the lifting of the building moratorium in Ocean Acres in the early 1990s came a housing boom and significant growth for the church. In 1998, two trailers were added to

A new Baptist church was built on the east side of Route 9, across from the old church, in 1968. With modifications, the building became the Stafford Branch of the Ocean County Library in 1989.

provide more space for Christian education while the church worked toward a building addition. Students from Princeton Theological Seminary periodically serve as assistants in youth work and women's ministry, as well as take part in the preaching.

The Christian and Missionary Alliance denomination in America dates to 1887. Dr. Albert Benjamin Simpson, a former Presbyterian pastor, refocused his work to begin an evangelistic ministry in New York City in 1881 and, later, an alliance for the promotion of missionary work. King of Kings Community Church in Manahawkin, belonging to the C&MA denomination, is growing into the 21st century in an 8,800-square-foot building that houses a worship center and a Christian-based recreation center. The church began with two families in 1991, and in October 1997, the church purchased the 4.75-acre property it formerly rented at 508 East Bay Avenue. Pastor Pat Sharkey's plans for the facility are that the church's main room serves as a worship center on Sundays, and during the week, hosts community activities such as youth basketball and volleyball leagues. In 1999, the church planted Lighthouse Alliance Church in Tuckerton. In the year 2000, King of Kings added Spanish language services, the only such weekly services in the area.

Thelma Cranmer

"A lot of people think, because they're old, they can't reach any goal anymore; that they can't do anything anymore. Just because you're old is no reason for you to lose it. But you have to use it."

If there is a secret to Thelma Cranmer's vitality, it might be that she rarely sits still. After she settles on the edge of a chair on the back porch with her flame-colored guitar, her knee starts keeping time. "What would you like to hear?" she invites. Finding her audience at a loss for impromptu requests, she launches into "Wabash Cannonball."

Like a locomotive, the voice gains momentum as it warms up, getting higher and sweeter, ending one song with a yodel, right on key.

Thelma shares this zeal with others who are less charged with life. She plays at nursing homes when she can get there. In an interview at age 80, she listed spare time activities as watching wrestling and playing pool. Ten years later, she was still exercising every day, she said, reaching and stretching to demonstrate.

Thelma was born in March 1909 to Benjamin and Eleanor Bradley Cranmer. Living her early years in Mayetta, she moved with her family to Manahawkin's Beach Avenue as a teenager. Her father was a Coast Guardsman in Barnegat Light; before that, a farmer and a bayman. Ben Cranmer's father, John, ran the general store in New Gretna.

Thelma's observations on life are going into a book, *The Joys and Sorrows of Growing Old.* Ever independent, she is trying to raise her own money to get the work published when it's finished. Checks from her columns still come in from the nationally distributed *Good Old Days* magazine.

"A lot of people think, because they're old, they can't reach any goal anymore; that they can't do anything anymore," she said, shaking her head at the thought. "Just because you're old is no reason for you to lose it. But you have to use it."

Her Irish grandmother from Philadelphia taught her a positive attitude — "take what life gives you," make the best of it.

Mayetta and Manahawkin Memories

From a compilation of Thelma Cranmer's writings over the last two decades.

I can see the old rambling farmhouse where I grew up, with a big woodshed and barns out in back. I can picture the fields, with the tall cornstalks waving gently in the summer breeze and Dad's vegetable garden stretching a couple of miles in the distance. I can smell the fresh earth. I see the same scene in the winter months, the snow-covered ground, nothing left in the fields but maybe a couple of corn stalks that were still standing, and I see the children sledding on the hills and hear their laughter. They are so carefree and happy.

Thelma Cranmer, at age 89, in 1998. Before moving to Florida, she shared her music with elderly residents in nursing homes.

Dad would bring home a small, silver-colored pail of beer that cost a nickel!

I can still smell the delicious aroma of baking bread as we kids entered the kitchen after school. Summer days, when we all sat on the back porch and watched Dad and Gramps weed the garden and then come in the yard and wash up at the pump outside. Then they would each get a drink using the dipper that hung over the pump.

I remember the marathon dances that went on for several days and nights. The big wagons that were filled with stacks of beer barrels pulled by large dray horses and how the driver would roll the barrels to the sidewalk and take them into the saloon. We kids had a penny to spend and would pick out the largest candy bar.

I remember the soap box radicals who voiced their dissatisfaction with our government by loud-voiced speeches on street corners or anywhere else they could find an audience. And they spoke it loud and clear in no uncertain terms.

The tin peddler came around once a month displaying his wares on the side of his wagon, and the pots and pans would rattle and make such a noise that as he entered our street, Gramps always said it was enough to wake the dead.

Our doctor was Dr. Hilliard, and it seemed that he had a pink pill for everything that ailed anyone. If we got sick, my mother just tied a white cloth to a tree or post outside, and he would be there before the day was over. No matter what the problem, the little pink pill was supposed to cure it. And it usually did!

Sometimes when the money was low, people would pay the doctor with eggs or vegetables, but he took care of them anyway.

We had no electric refrigerator and we depended on the ice man, Ernie Reeves. He was a kind and much-liked person, and patient, too. When he would go in to deliver ice on a hot summer day, we kids would jump into the wagon and steal chunks of ice. He knew but made believe that he never saw us.

In the spring, the gypsies came to town. We kids loved them, but Dad used to say you couldn't trust them. Gramps said, "Batten down the hatches. They're here again and heaven knows what scheme they have up their sleeves this time! Last time it was telling fortunes."

The gypsies camped by the cranberry bog next to our school, and we kids loved to watch them putting up tents and building cooking fires. I remember the man everyone called "Gypsy Dave." He seemed to be the big boss and had many tales to tell us kids when we dared to venture to their camp after school. The gypsies traveled south in the winter and came to New Jersey with the spring.

My sister and I did admire the costumes that the

ladies wore. They dressed in many different colors, mostly reds, yellows and a lot of purple. Their hair was jet black, and long, dangly earrings touched their shoulders. One time a gypsy woman told my fortune and she said I would be wealthy and live to a ripe old age in excellent health.

Back in 1917-18, my sister and I attended Cedar Run School, in the building that now is the activity center for the Assembly of God church on Route 9. We went every day, rain or shine, staying home only if we had a high fever.

The school was one room, and our teacher, Miss Bertha, was a dear soul but would not stand for any nonsense. We all had to behave and get our work done on time. Rules were strictly enforced: no swearing, no smoking and no fighting!

School was heated with a potbelly stove, and sometimes it was so cold that we had to keep on our coats most of the day.

No buses ran, so we walked the miles from Landing Road in Mayetta. My sister and I often had holes in the bottoms of our shoes, and we stuffed pasteboard in them, but it didn't help much. Our feet were usually soaked when we arrived home in the late afternoon.

We left home in the early morning, dinner pail in hand, and arrived shortly before the bell rang. Miss Bertha came out on the steps and rang a little bell that she kept on her desk. We all marched in and took our places in line, small kids in the front and bigger kids in the back. After we were seated she read from the Bible; then we bowed our heads in prayer, and after that came the flag salute. So began our day.

Those were the days to remember, when life was simple. We didn't need much to make us happy, and we had one thing in common — we were all poor.

If diet holds any key to longevity, Thelma's recipe is this: "I eat vegetables, fruit, yogurt. I eat a little bit of this and a little bit of that, but I don't overdo. I don't drink, I don't smoke. I quit at 37."

She wasn't one to get caught puffing away at age 15 in 1924. "No, they never caught me," she declared. "They caught some others; they used to smoke out in the outhouse. And once in a while they'd write something on the outhouse that they shouldn't, and my father would have a fit."

While on the topic of the only location for sanitary facilities back then, Thelma answered the question, wasn't it cold in the winter?

"It was cold, but we were used to it. And you always let somebody else go first. It warmed up the seat."

Talk about making the best of things!

Thelma recalled being 10 years old in 1919, watching a pot of water boil so she could take a bath.

"We used to have a big tub. We used to put it by the kitchen range. And everybody would take a turn taking a bath, everybody in the same water."

Even with conveniences as scarce as they were, Thelma Cranmer had life more rich, in many ways, than many around her. At least there was plenty of food to eat.

"We ate very well because we raised our own vegetables, and my mother canned them and we had enough to last us all winter.

"If you knew somebody that didn't have anything, you always invited them to dinner. Always."

Many years later, with her own daughter, she traveled all over the United States, spending four years in Alaska. Following her daughter's death, she has lived with her other daughter, Denise, and family in the Ocean Acres section of Stafford Township.

So, what are the joys and sorrows of growing old?

"The joy is the privilege of living so long. God has a reason for having us live so long. People say, 'It's because people love your writing, and because you go and play the guitar, and sing and make people happy.'

"Another thing Grandma always taught us: try every day of your life to do something nice for somebody. You don't have to do that much, just give them a kind word. There are so many lonely old people.

"The sorrows are, of course, with your health. What you have to have is a bit of a sense of humor to go through all this. And you need a lot of friends you can talk to. And we need family most of all.

"When you have something that you can't do anything about, you just have to leave it in the Lord's hands, but you have to have faith that he is going to help you the best way that is for you."

— *Maria Scandale*

Perhaps a Sunday or a holiday brought out the finest attire as a family posed on the porch of a stately Stafford home.

Hurley Conklin

"He was a master craftsman and a true bayman."

Noted local carver and Cedar Run native Hurley Conklin died in 1991 at age 77, but his decoys had already been prized by collectors for two decades. Among the last of the old-time Barnegat Bay decoy carvers, Hurley in his lifetime etched his mark on some 22,000 slabs of cedar, handfashioning the blocks into graceful and lifelike forms of waterfowl.

Carving had been Hurley's calling since he was 14. That year, local sawmill operator Sherwood Corlies gave the young boy some cedar blocks to carve. Corlies reportedly proclaimed of the results, "I'll have to put them in the closet because they look so real, the cats will eat their heads off!"

That was in 1928. Soon Hurley began filling mounting orders for sheldrake, black duck, brant, Canada goose, broadbill, bufflehead, sea gulls, shoveler, teal, pintail and canvasback decoys. He charged one dollar apiece for his work.

Conklin decoys have sat regally in collections of Senator Edward Kennedy and Andy Williams, among others. His carvings are well-known throughout the United States, Canada and Europe. What collectors call the "Hurley Conklin Classic" is a mantle bird from Conklin's decorative works, which he began carving in the 1960s.

"The most desirable decoys he carved were in the late '50s and early '60s," noted Jim Allen of Tuckerton, southeastern representative of the decoy auction firm Guyette & Schmidt, Inc. "The classic Hurley Conklins have a carved wing tip, an ice dip, which is a dug-out notch behind the head that allows the ice to peel off the decoys, and a streamlined body."

Only ten years after he died, Hurley Conklin goose decoys were fetching as much as $2,500 at auction. By the pair, his decoys were bringing $3,500 to $4,000, a figure that had doubled in a decade.

"If I had the money my decoys get now, I would be half a millionaire," Hurley told a reporter a few years before his death.

"If you have an opportunity to pick up a Hurley Conklin decoy, regardless of age, don't hesitate," wrote *Decoy Magazine*'s Dick Morton in 1989. "Just check the auction catalogs; the prices go up every day."

Conklin birds are termed "truly a blue-chip investment" by Jon Frank of Frank & Frank auctioneers. One reason Hurley Conklin decoys are coveted is because they are an art form that achieved a function.

"They're so aesthetically perfect," Frank elaborated. "They were nice and light, they were hollow, they would float well, they were weighted properly, and they had a great pattern for attracting wildfowl, which was extraordinarily important to people who were gunning.

"He was a master craftsman and a true bayman," added Frank. "He was one of the few people who was a true bayman who made decoys you could use as well as admire and put on the shelf. He used the traditional Barnegat Bay method of hollowed cedar construction, all hand-done and hand-painted

Hurley Conklin outside his workshop, 1955

with the traditional Barnegat Bay decoy paints. Hurley Conklin being a true bayman, by exposure to his natural habitat, had the artistic ability to copy and exhibit his talents in his wood carving and painting."

Hurley died in June 1991 with complications of heart failure and Parkinson's disease. The latter condition, according to his granddaughter, Regina Foster, was attributable to many hard seasons of clamming and working in the frigid bay.

But undoubtedly no one could have convinced a hardy, headstrong bayman to live his life in any other manner.

"He was one of the old-timers," his granddaughter declared.

"What's unique about how my grandfather used to clam," she added, "is that men usually use a clamming basket to hold onto. He used to hold onto his boat — a 17-foot garvey. He used that as his clamming basket."

Hurley left the area to serve in the Army's armored division during World War II under General George S. Patton in North Africa, and settled in Manahawkin when he returned. He had earlier worked for less than a year for the Civilian Conservation Corps in Idaho because he yearned to come back home.

Spending outdoor hours eeling, cranberrying and fishing, he was also a duck hunter and a guide for the Marshelder Gunning Club.

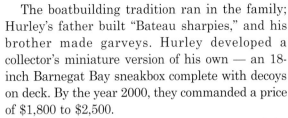

The boatbuilding tradition ran in the family; Hurley's father built "Bateau sharpies," and his brother made garveys. Hurley developed a collector's miniature version of his own — an 18-inch Barnegat Bay sneakbox complete with decoys on deck. By the year 2000, they commanded a price of $1,800 to $2,500.

The master's techniques live on in some of the best carvers of the next generation. Award-winning carver Bill Oler of Beach Haven and his father, Walt, used to visit Hurley three times a week, beginning almost exactly ten years before the day Hurley died..

"I studied under him for approximately 10 years. After breakfast, we'd sit with Hurley in the shop and watch him carve. He'd criticize what I had carved; he'd tell me what I did right or wrong. If it wasn't up to his specifications, he'd let me know about it.".

Professional carver Jamie Hand of Cape May County also counts Hurley as one of his mentors. "He taught me most of what I know. He took me under his wing, so to speak. A lot of carvers don't want to trade secrets, if you will. But Hurley Conklin would say, 'Change this a little bit; carve this a little differently.'"

Now Hand, one of the young men who listened, takes pride in passing Hurley Conklin's knowledge to others. "Anybody who asks me the methods I use, I'm free with the information, just like he was with me."

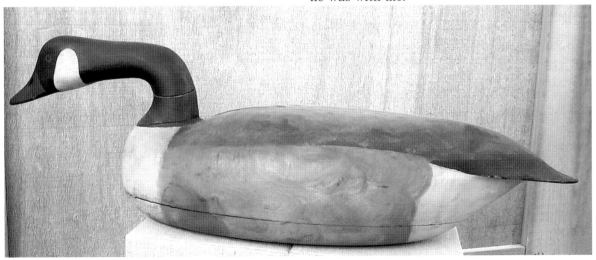

A 1960's-era Hurley Conklin brant, top. Above, a classic Canada goose.

Gone But Not Forgotten

At one time on the corner of Route 9 and Old Broadway stood a huge buttonwood tree. The local men hung deer from its many branches as they gathered at the Esso station there to swap hunting stories.

Gone are not only the many personalities that shaped the past of Stafford Township, but many of the structures in which they plied their trade.

One of the oldest was the Manahawkin Tavern, the meeting place of the Manahawkin Militia during the Revolutionary War. It commanded the northeast corner of Beach Avenue and the Main Shore Road, the old name for Route 9. A house-store combination took its place in 1900, built by Elmer Cranmer. He and his wife, Jennie Cranmer, lived in the house for the 50 years that she was a teacher and principal of the elementary school down the street on Beach Avenue. The house changed hands many times thereafter. At one time the Baptist parsonage, it later housed businesses as varied as a hardware store to a tattoo parlor. At the turn of the 21st century, it is an ice cream parlor in a style reminiscent of an earlier century.

Across Route 9 from the house were three places of business, as well as an icehouse, a private home, and two lakeside cottages. One of the businesses was a building known as Cranmer Hall. Cranmer Hall was used for many purposes, some of them a public meeting place, Johnson's Luncheonette and offices. It was built in 1888 by C. H. Cranmer on the east side of Route 9, and later moved across the road.

When Cranmer built this structure, he built it around the town's second elementary school, which had been abandoned and sold in 1887 when the Beach Avenue school opened. The building and surrounding properties were sold in the late 1980s and it was torn down in 1991, along with the two cottages by the lake.

A small gas station replaced the first site of Cranmer Hall. Rufus Cranmer was the first to run it, and later Leo Lamson operated a repair shop there before it, too, disappeared to become a parking lot.

The National Hotel, circa 1900, before its expansion to the rear. The lamp on the corner burned with kerosene.

Another meeting hall, just to the south of the first site of Cranmer Hall, came onto the Manahawkin scene in 1900. Richard Stager originally built it as a movie house, and early silent movies played to accompaniment by piano. A stage at the western end of the building could be closed off by a large curtain. When movies weren't showing, the hall held political rallies, debates and school ceremonies.

Since those early days, the building has been used as a store; local residents will remember finding clothing and toys there. The Elks also used the building as a meeting place and headquarters. It finally burned down.

Back behind this store and the Cranmer Store stood an icehouse at the edge of the lake. The building dated to the late 1800s. Ice was cut from the

The National Hotel, the Hall store, and the Triangle Garage, seen from the intersection of Main Street, Bay Avenue and South Broadway, about 1920.

A view of semi-rural Main Street, top, looking north. The Latch Farm on Main Street 9 (above and left), about 1900. The entrance to Deer Lake Park is now situated there.

The former Cranmer Hall, a meeting hall built in 1888, was a private residence in this 1945 view. The structure was originally located east of Main Street. As Johnson's Luncheonette, below, in 1964, the building stood at lakeside.

surface of the lake with large, two-man saws. Packed in sawdust for insulation, the blocks lasted all year in the icehouse. In the summer, peddlers took the ice door-to-door to those who owned iceboxes, as well as to the hotels on Long Beach Island. When electricity replaced iceboxes with refrigerators, the building became an ice manufacturing plant until 1950, when owner Elmer Aker sold it. Aker's uncle, also named Elmer, had started the plant in 1926.

The Sealtest milk company bought the building to store milk and dairy products, which were delivered fresh to the doorsteps of the neighborhood. Progress caught up, and because of a lack of business, the dairy company left. The old icehouse became a furniture storehouse until it was set on fire and quickly burned to the ground in October 1974. The cause was officially labeled arson; some thought it a professional job.

In front of the icehouse on Route 9 and to the south of the movie house was the Cranmer Store. This landmark site had a long history. A store was built in the 1770s by William Aumach, who wanted

to set up a business for his two sons, Elijah and John. The general store dealt in hardware, charcoal, coal and other necessities. Henry and Horton Gulick later bought it. The string of subsequent merchants included Randolph and Abbott, Allen & Son, Joshua Lamson, Charles Sloan, Sprague & Oliphant, Al Brown, I. M. Inman, Lewis Peckworth and the Peckworth Brothers.

The icehouse by the lake (above), became a dairy (below) with the advent of refrigeration, then a furniture warehouse before it burned in 1974.

In 1880, it was Charles H. Cranmer's turn. It was well known that if Cranmer didn't have an item in stock, he would order it for you. A barn in the back by the lake held a horse and wagon at the ready for deliveries. The owner passed the business operation to his clerk, Woodie Shinn, while he turned his interests to real estate. Later, Charles "Charlie" Farley operated a food store there under the name Quaker Foods. A Firestone dealership followed, run by Frank Marini, until he moved his business to Bay Avenue.

After Cranmer sold the building, it became, in turn, a poodle parlor, meat market, ice cream shop, grocery, auto parts store, boutique, and finally a hobby shop before it was sold again, boarded up, and then condemned and torn down in August 1985.

Moving south from the Cranmer store on the west side of Route 9, the next building was razed in 1998 to expand Manahawkin Lake Park. At the time the park project began, it was the home of Althea Fredrickson, built in the late 1800s by William S. Sprague.

Continuing south to the only remaining private house on this side of Route 9 North, the building very close to the road is known as the Carr house. It also was built in the late 1800s and stands as a demonstration of the architecture of that period.

Just to the south of this house was the original bathing beach. The area in front of the old wooden dam was deep enough for diving into the lake. A pavilion stood out over the lake, connected to the sand by a boardwalk. Mothers could sit in the shade in the pavilion while they watched their children play in the water.

At one time on the corner of Route 9 and Old Broadway stood a huge buttonwood tree. The local men made it a center of attention when hunting season came. They hung deer from its many branches, as they gathered at the Esso station there to swap their stories. Russell Horner opened this station in May 1932. During hunting season or not, this was the busiest intersection in town, and Russ knew everyone in Manahawkin. His Esso was the first full-service station here.

After Horner built another station to the west in about 1966, Haig Choolagian managed the sta-

tion for Esso until 1978. By that time, too many changes had taken place and Exxon decided to close the station. The tanks were capped, the station boarded up, and the pumps removed. In 1989, a bulldozer razed the property. A real estate developer had purchased the ground for an office building, which has commanded the corner since 1990.

On the other side of Route 9, at the junction with Stafford Avenue, Carroll's restaurant parking lot sits on the site of the old Manahawkin Hotel. The gathering place, later known as the National Hotel, gradually grew from a three-story house to a four-story hotel with dining rooms where there had been porches. It was extended outward on two sides to enlarge the rooms. The building burned in a major fire.

Bell Telephone built its first exchange and over-

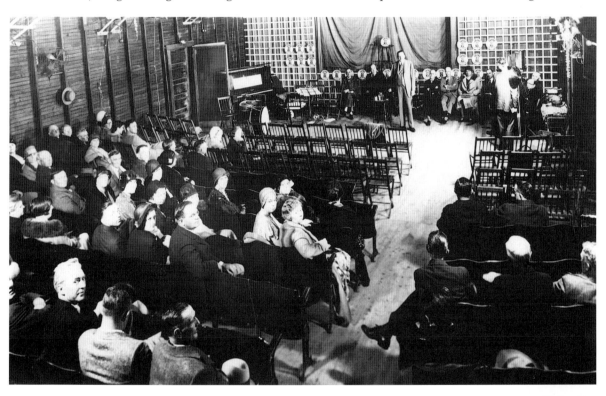

A political rally in Stager's Music Hall, top, probably in the 1930s. Built as Manahawkin's first movie house about 1910, the hall took on a different focus as Phoebe's Clothing in the 1960s, right. The building was torn down in the 1980s. In the year 2000, children played at the site on the playground in Manahawkin Lake Park.

seers building just behind the old hotel. A nearby tower served to send and receive signals. Operators inside worked the switchboards by hand, using cables to connect the circuits to different destinations. Operators stamped tickets on clocks to time the beginning and end of each call. The building and tower were torn down when an automated system replaced the old. A new building was built directly east of the former one.

Moving south from Stafford Avenue along the east side of Route 9, the building that holds the Diamond Mine and other businesses was built in the 1880s by a Mr. Hall. He bought the property from Ed Brown and built a store with rooms above. The parking lot of this building, along Bay Avenue, at one time held the Triangle Garage. A Dodge and Plymouth dealership was the next occupant; later Joe Bennett purchased it and operated Bennett Chevrolet there until he moved the business to Route 72. Joe Bennett sold the business in 1998 and retired.

The first automobile dealer in Stafford Township was Matt Cranmer, who located a Chevrolet agency in Mayetta. He built his showroom from the old Cedar Run elementary school. After he passed away, Lou Macaluso purchased the property and ran a used parts and hubcap business. He kept horses and a track at the back of the grounds. The property was also one of the first Harley Davidson dealerships in the state, if not the first, local Harley enthusiasts say. In 2001 the property was sold to become a storage facility for contractors, and the school building was demolished.

Also in Cedar Run, W. S. Cranmer, who was very active politically in Ocean County, ran several businesses from one building on Route 9. The huge building served as a rooming house, a store and an

Built around 1870, C. H. Cranmer's General Store dispensed groceries and sundries at the turn of the century, above, and in 1964 was showing signs of neglect, below. The building, located on the lake side of Route 9, was one of the last 19th-century commercial structures of old Manahawkin. It was condemned and torn down in 1985. Historians say a store had occupied the site since the 1770s.

insurance office. There was even a gas pump out front at the curb. The activity there was quite a contrast to the abandoned, boarded up facade of later years. Suddenly one Halloween night, the building

caught fire and was destroyed.

Route 72, when it was first built, was to be a limited-access highway. That began to change in the 1970s with the building of the drive-in and an airport. Neither still exists today. As beach-bound traffic turned Route 72 from a byway to a highway, it became a magnet for businesses. The 1980s and 1990s saw both Shop Rite and Kmart move from their former Bay Avenue enclave near the meadows to more expansive sites on Route 72. Wal-Mart built on the property that was once the airport, along with Radio Shack and Karin's Kurtains. In 1998, a Hoyts movie theater opened up in the same mall.

Russell Horner operated the Esso station at the corner of Route 9 and Old Broadway from its opening in 1932 for more than 30 years. The Manahawkin Drive-In was a local attraction on Route 72; now a Home Depot stands in its location.

The 1898 Class of Miss Carrie Crane at the Manahawkin School

In this vintage photo, the class was identified in 1949 as: (first row, seated, from left) Lulu Horner, Naomi Bunnel, May Predmore, Helen Crane, Annie Horner, Mabel Cranmer, Lily Walden, Essie Johnson, Jo Clifford. Second row: Earl Hall, not identified, Joe Horner, Harry Corliss, Russel Horner, Ben. Paul, Jennings Gaskill, Hugh Walden, Ernest Paul, Peter Farley, Gertie Bolton, Bessie Soper. Third row: Bertha Johnson, Eva Patterson, Nellie Elberson, Joe Oliphant, Irve Johnson, Harry Giberson, Ed Perrine, Firm Cranmer, Walter Bolton, Walter Cranmer, Carrie Reeder, Maggie Stevens. Fourth row: Harry Dalman, Steve Palmer, Pierson Bennett, Charles Farley, Gus Predmore, Abe Dalman, Joe Wilkins, Rufus Cranmer, Roy Jackaway, Henry Johnson, Lloyd Johnson. Top row: Howard Dalman, Ernest Reeves, Della Paul, Carrie Crane, Grace Clifford, Ira Reeder, Clem Stevens, George Cranmer, Leon Cranmer.

The Three R's

Many of these schools were open for only six months or less. This was due to many factors, not the least of them the financial problem of raising taxes in each community.

For many rural areas of New Jersey, formal education and the rudiments of "readin', writin' and 'rithmetic" came quite late compared to other states. In Colonial times children remained uneducated if parents did not instruct them in the home.

As more European settlers came to this area, they opened private schools, called "dame schools," operated by women who had some formal schooling. According to some residents, a private school was located in Manahawkin on Beach Avenue, built from tax money after the Revolutionary War. Parents had to furnish classroom supplies and pay tuition to cover the cost of the teacher's salary and the building's heat.

Naturally, not all families could afford to send their children to school. This hardship eased for many residents when Stafford Township passed a bill in 1820 that tax monies would be used to pay the tuition for children whose parents could not afford it.

Finally, in 1828, the state Legislature passed a bill authorizing townships to raise money by taxation to build and repair schoolhouses. Ocean County established district schools. In 1838, a new law required townships to create a committee of three to handle school funds and management. The Old Stafford Township School Committee in 1840 operated schools at Manahawkin, Mellville (now Brookville), Waretown, Barnegat, Poplar Neck (now Cedar Run), Westa Cunk (now West Creek) and Cedar Bridge. The Cedar Bridge School fell to a forest fire in 1878.

A law abolishing tuition passed the Legislature in 1871, designed to give all children the opportunity to learn. The law gave rise to a number of one- and two-room schoolhouses in the township, which were supported by both state and local taxes.

Many of these schools were open for only six months or less. This was due to many factors, not the least of them the financial problem of raising taxes in each community. Hunting sea-

The old Cedar Run School, top, and its students in 1895. The horse and carriage stalls at right are for church-goers next door. The school closed in 1907, but the Route 9 structure in Mayetta later did interesting duty as a Harley Davidson motorcycle shop, left, a bicycle shop and an automobile showroom. It was still in use in 1991, right, as an auto parts salvage business. When the property changed hands again in 2001, the new owner cleared away the old cars and hubcaps that had become a landmark in themselves.

son and the cranberry harvest also claimed part of the year, since whole families participated. Also, in the days before vaccines were available, schools closed when outbreaks of communicable diseases such as measles, influenza, chicken pox and infantile paralysis raged through the community.

Cedar Run School closed in 1907, and students from Mayetta and Cedar Run began riding the bus to Manahawkin School on Beach Avenue. The school in what was then Cedar Grove, now Warren Grove, did not close until 1931. The Manahawkin School had been enlarged prior to that to accommodate all the pupils in the township. Since about 1932, many small schools have been abandoned in favor of a larger consolidated district, with pupils bused in from the outlying rural areas.

The year 1887 saw a "new" two-story schoolhouse on Beach Avenue that was used until January 1951,

The last Cedar Run schoolhouse, built in front of the older school in about 1904, closed its doors in the 1960s, and was later purchased and preserved by the Cedar Run Assembly of God.

when the Township Elementary School, now called the Oxycocus School, was built on Route 9. The Beach Avenue School was abandoned by the Board of Education and sold to Whalon's Furniture store to use as a warehouse. It was neglected and burned down on October 18, 1974. The local first aid squad built a garage and meeting room on the site.

The Oxycocus School grew with the enrollment between 1958 and 1970. The Intermediate School on McKinley Avenue, a $20 million, 16-classroom building for 464 pupils in grades four, five and six, was built in 1975.

More population growth led to another school on McKinley Avenue, which opened to students on September 5, 1990. With this larger intermediate school in place, the older building became the McKinley Avenue Elementary School.

Growth in the Ocean Acres section of the township required a fourth building; this opened in time for the first day of school in September 1999. The $10 million

The Warren Grove schoolhouse was built soon after a fire in 1878 destroyed a school shared by both Warren Grove and Cedar Bridge communities.

The Manahawkin School on Beach Avenue, circa 1910, top, and below in 1964. The school bell rang from 1887 to 1951.

school sits on a 13-acre site at Nautilus Drive and Buccaneer Lane.

Until 1957, the eighth-graders from Manahawkin Grammar School rode the bus to either Barnegat or Tuckerton high schools — the board of education decided which one on a yearly basis. Once a choice was made, the board kept that choice for several years. The year 1957 marked an educational milestone when Southern Regional High School opened on a 45-acre tract at the intersection of Route 9 and Cedar Bridge Road. The $1.5 million school would serve all of the Southern Ocean County area and southward through New Gretna.

It was quite a transition for the students and community to establish an identity for their new school. The choice of school colors came to a vote. Barnegat had claimed red and black; Tuckerton was already blue and gold. Under the consolidation, black and gold became

Whether they liked it or not, students at the Beach Avenue school in 1910 opened wide for the Rural Dental Ambulance. The clinic on spoked wheels probably provided the only dental attention some children received.

Southern Regional High School's banner colors. There were other adjustments to be made — Barnegat and Tuckerton were rivals on and off the fields. The coaches and teachers insisted that discipline and communication were the order of the day.

Southern Regional opened its doors to 825 students, under Superintendent Dr. Sampson Smith. The original nine-member board of education was appointed by the county superintendent. Smith resigned his position on Dec. 16, 1957 after the board of education rejected, 5 to 4, a resolution which called for replacing his progres-

A bus that Stafford Township children rode to school in 1920. The vehicle looks sturdy, but safety features have come a long way.

sive "general education" program with a more traditional curriculum.

The original budget was $637,075 for 1957-58. By 1962-63, the district was spending $1,184,007. The enrollments for this period grew each year: 1958, 930; 1960, 1,072; 1961, 1,200.

On November 7, 1958, the school board hired Harry Q. Packer as the new superintendent. In June 1960, Packer refused to give contracts to seven new teachers. It caused such a controversy that many other teachers resigned, and substitutes had to be called to fill the gaps. The controversy spilled out into the community. By the fall of 1963, Packer had been replaced by Robert W. Allen. Allen remained through the 1975 school year. John Hadden arrived the next September, but resigned his position on June 30, 1977. Hadden had twice received votes of no confidence from the teachers. William

Wright took over the superintendent position on October 1, 1977. Robert Schiller followed him in 1981. Dr. Robert Daria arrived in September 1985 and took over as superintendent.

The middle school had opened in September 1970 to house grades seven and eight. In 1993, because of overcrowding in the high school, the board of education placed a referendum for a $28 million high school building, but the public voted 3-to-1 against the venture. The board then sought the use of more modules or "trailers" to relieve the overcrowding. The school buildings' population seams had been bursting since at least 1989 and 1990, when mobile units were first rolled onto school grounds.

The school district acquired approximately 200 acres of buildable ground, as well as wetlands, in 1989 and 1990. A new administration building on

The exact year is uncertain, but the camaraderie is evident among these Manahawkin schoolchildren. At left, rear, in the derby hat is Stafford Superintendent of Schools J. R. Steelman.

Teacher Mae Cranmer's class

Front row: Julia Jarossy, Evelyn Hadsell-Wozar, Anna Poland Parker, Mary McKinley, Katherine Giberson, Anna Boreedy, Ethel Sprague-Cranmer, Marie Stiles. Back row: Bannell Liefred, Filmore Shinn, George Shingloff, Emil Parker, Mae Cranmer, Roy Rostein, Harry Ridgeway, Amos Michel, Earl Abbott, Josephine Anzesi, Bob Cranmer.

Cedar Bridge Road opened in 1993.

Meanwhile, a new school facility was still needed, but disputes over the scope and cost continued. Daria resigned amid disagreements with the policies of the board of education in April 1995. Interim superintendent Arthur Criss, a former district administrator, temporarily replaced Daria. In July 1995 the board of education hired high school principal Kenneth Arndt to take over the position the following September.

A new building for the 11th and 12th grades was proposed at a cost of approximately $22 million. The school board went back out for a $4.7 million referendum in 1996 for a science addition and renovations to the existing building. Ground-breaking for this new structure took place in September 1996, with the project completed by September 1998.

The school year 1997 brought expansions to the outdoor recreational complex. Two practice football fields; six soccer, field hockey and lacrosse fields; and two baseball and two softball fields were added.

Arndt retired January 1, 2000, and James Kerfoot assumed the superintendent duties.

Two nonpublic elementary schools operate in Stafford Township — Lighthouse Christian Academy on the Manahawkin Baptist Church grounds, and All Saints Regional Catholic School on the grounds of St. Mary's Parish Center. Lighthouse Christian Academy opened in 1979 and instructs grades K-6. All Saints Regional Catholic School opened in 1997 for kindergarten and first grade, and has expanded to a K-8 school on a site at the corner of McKinley Avenue and Doc Cramer Boulevard.

Pearl Cervetto

When her husband and her father built their house, they wired it for electricity because they heard that the utility lines were finally coming to Warren Grove.

Few know Warren Grove as Pearl Cervetto does. Pearl has lived in the rural Stafford Township settlement for all the years of her life but one. Her late husband, Jack, was Stafford's mayor four times during their 60-year marriage. "He loved Stafford," Pearl proudly reflects. His 1964 chronicle, *A Brief History of Stafford Township from 1664-1964,* remains one of the few complete compilations of the township's lore.

But Pearl is a rich source of her own memories, of a later Warren Grove, a small hamlet in the Pine Barrens that has been overlooked by passing motorists for a long time as they travel Route 539 to the shore.

"Just as many people lived here then as live here now," she said. "About 200, maybe a few more now, 'cause they built a few more homes."

The house where she was born is still standing. It's the blue one across from the firehouse, but when she was a little girl there was no firehouse. There were forest fires — those memories stand out vividly.

"I remember them going all around us. Well, they didn't have all the equipment to fight the fires like they have now. What could you do? Thank God, they didn't get that close."

Pearl's maiden name was Holloway. Her father, William Holloway, married a Corliss. On Pearl's mother's side the family can be traced back to the Reeves, the Warrens who settled the grove, and even further back to the Penns — as in William Penn.

Pearl's father and his siblings were orphaned very young in isolated Warren Grove.

"There must have been at least six kids and they were left there to raise themselves," said Pearl. "I think maybe the aunt — my grandmother's sister — went there to try to help them out, but she had her own family. It was very hard.

"Their parents died of TB. My father said if they got hurt or lost in the woods, nobody ever came to help them. He wasn't the oldest. There were three about the same age — him, Alva and Marianne Holloway — but they had to raise themselves and then the state took the property. They had no money to pay the taxes. They lost a lot of property."

But her father was a man who could do anything to survive. He was primarily a carpenter, but he also mossed and pine-balled and hunted and farmed. He married, started his family and built the blue house she was born in.

"We had a garden, chickens, and we raised turkeys. He did a lot of mossing, baling moss. My husband did that, too. They picked it out of the swamp." The sphagnum moss, which can hold twice its weight in water, was used by tree nurseries to keep roots moist. It has since been replaced by other materials, but is still used to a lesser degree by the floral industry.

"The moss grows all around the trees in the swamp," Pearl said. "We own the swamp. I wish we didn't."

The next steps after collecting the moss were drying and baling. "I still have three balers in the outbuilding. You put the moss in one end, turn the crank and the bale comes out the other. I used to help turn the moss to dry it, but I never baled it. To dry it, you would lay it out in the sun on the ground and just keep turning it over. Mossing was a big industry around here."

Little Schoolhouse in the Grove

Pearl attended a one-room schoolhouse on Sim Place Road. The building is a hunting club now.

"We had eight grades in one room, so we got in on everybody's questions and answers. I was the oldest one when I graduated from there, the same year they closed the school. Then they bused the children to Manahawkin."

Pearl isn't sure how the advantages of her quaint schooling weigh against the disadvantages. "I don't know if I was lucky or not. I think I missed out on a lot of things," she decided. "I only went to high school for two years. My mother was sick and she needed me, so that's what I did."

Pearl remembers two teachers. "Mildred Lees from Pleasantville boarded up here. She had one or two students in each grade, about 20 children altogether.

Pearl Holloway Cervetto on her Warren Grove property.

"Rebecca Wilkens was the last teacher and she was the one that kept falling asleep. I would go up and ask her to give me a lesson and she would be asleep. Well, she was a middle-aged lady and she had a boyfriend.

"She told me once, she was so tired she had put her clothes in the refrigerator and took a chicken upstairs to her bedroom by mistake. Wasn't that funny?"

In the summer the children splashed in the swimming hole at Sim Place. "We called it Coffee Beach because it was cedar water. It looked dirty but it wasn't."

The big event in town was the camp meetings held at the Methodist church. Pearl's grandfather Corliss donated the land for the church and helped build it in 1874. The camp meetings took place in the field next to the church. The meetings would make money to pay the minister for the year.

Pearl remembers, "They all came by horse and buggy, or horse and wagon. I still have some of the lanterns they used to hang up in the trees for light. The gathering thing was a real thing back then, a real social event. I remember the horses and wagons tied to the trees, and good food. People came from all over, from Barnegat and farther away. Later they came with cars."

When Pearl was young, it was unusual for a car to come to town.

"Not many people would travel Route 539 when it was a dirt road. You couldn't even get through to Tuckerton. The road was so sandy, the first hill you'd get stuck. That was 60 years ago. Then they finally put the road through and that was good. We could finally do our shopping in Tuckerton."

There was no doctor in town. "Dr. Carmona was about the only one ever came up here when you got sick, and that was when the roads were finished.

"We didn't have mail service; someone went from here to pick up the mail in Barnegat. Then finally they decided to have a post office here but the name wasn't Warren Grove; then it was Cedar Grove, and they had to change the name because there was another town in New Jersey called Cedar Grove. They changed it to Warren Grove. The Warrens were the people that settled the area; they were relatives of my mother's. I don't really know what year."

From Iron Ore to Electricity

"Cedar Grove is old. People first came for the iron ore. They used to mine it here and they took it on wagons to Stafford Forge. And they did a lot of charcoaling here."

Charcoaling was the process of burning pine and oak to make charcoal that fired the forges.

"I can still see spots out here in the woods where they charcoaled," Pearl said. "Nothing ever grew back; it just stayed sand.

"I do remember about the time I got married there was a couple of men still charcoaling, but that was more down towards Bamber."

Pearl's future husband was seven years old when he came to Warren Grove with his parents during World War I. His father worked in a wool factory making uniforms. His mother brought the children to Warren Grove, and young Jack loved it here, but after five years, his family moved back to Garfield.

"He went to school here and whatever grades they gave him ... he had to do it all over again when he got back to the city," said Pearl. When he came of age, he moved back to Warren Grove.

Pearl knew Jack because all of the boys played ball next door to her house. "I was a kid, I was eight years old, and they would always holler for water. I was the water girl. But then we didn't go together for a long time because I was too young.

"Then he got a car and he asked me out and that was it. When we were married, he was 30, so I must have been 22. He was Catholic and I was Methodist, so nobody would marry us. We tried lots of different places. We just kept driving. We stayed all night in one place, so we went up to the courthouse, so the judge married us. In the same room where we were getting married, a couple was getting divorced and the things they were saying to each other! And the things they were calling each other! I thought, what am I getting into? But we were married 60 years."

When her husband and her father built their house, they wired it for electricity because they heard that the utility lines were finally coming to Warren Grove.

"The government put it in for the radio tower. We didn't have telephone service until 1939. They had one in Sim Place — that's three miles over in the cranberry company there. They don't allow anyone back there now. My husband used to have keys to the gate so we could get in there all the time and get cranberries if we wanted to.

"We didn't have electricity until three years after we moved to this house," Pearl said, thinking back. "We had all the wires, we were wired for it and we were going to have our own generator, but then they put this in along with the telephone.

"I was scared to death of that telephone," Pearl declared. "I had never touched one in my life. And my cousin, she worked up in the office at Clayton's Log Cabin, and she said, 'I'm going to call you!' She knew I was getting the phone connected the next day. I was scared to death when it rang! "There was seven on the line — it was a party line — but I didn't make many calls a week. I didn't want to.

"The old days were hard," Pearl said. "You had to really be prepared. You had to write everything down when you went shopping, because if you forgot anything, you couldn't run back to the store.

"We had kerosene lamps and you had to be careful around the kids. Kids would come over to play. When I got married, all I had was a little two-burner kerosene stove and I had it set on a dough box. A dough box is … they used to make their dough in a box and then they'd turn the lid over and they'd roll it out."

In those days, a wood stove heated the kitchen. "We gave a potbellied stove to the Old Stone Store in Stafford for the historical society."

Pearl was a housewife who stayed home and raised her son. She used to drive a school bus — "Well, it was a station wagon" — for about five years to Manahawkin and the high school.

She also helped her husband with pine cone collecting and mossing. There are two concrete buildings in the yard. One Pearl still calls the moss house; the other is the pine cone shop. "I used to help with the pine cones and turning the moss. He would gather the pine cones, and he had men to help him do that.

Jack Cervetto, right, with Palitine Gun Club President Ellsworth Harris in 1975, discussing the Pine Barrens and how they were gradually being spoiled. The Pinelands Comprehensive Management Plan wouldn't come for another five years.

"He bought a dump body truck. He was the only one around with a dump body truck and he was in great demand. Every job there was around, they needed it; otherwise, they had to shovel by hand. So he bought this new truck down in Vineland, and I didn't like it at first because it was a lot of money. But anyway, he made good with it.

"He would take it out in the woods with two, three men with him that lived around here, elderly men that didn't have anything to do … they'd take a bushel basket and go out and get the pine cones and then they'd dump them right in the body of the truck. They picked the cones when they were closed.

"He'd come back and they'd dump them off the truck and I'd go out and put them on the trays and put them in the pine cone house, where there were heaters to pop them open. You had to watch careful that they didn't catch fire. They'd burn fast with the seed and the pitch.

"I'd stay there all day picking out the pine cones that would open up and putting them in bags, counting them. Then they'd take them to New York or Jersey City." They were wholesaled to the floral industry for Christmas decorations.

"Then we had the cranberry bogs … we mostly made cranberry sauce."

For entertainment, the Cervettos could go to the Albert brothers' homestead to listen to some real country music, the kind made with spoons, wash tub and fiddle. Jack was also a Mason and belonged to the Tuckerton lodge, so they visited Tuckerton quite often.

After Jack Cervetto died in 1995, Pearl's sister lived with her on the homestead until she passed away. Pearl closed up the house and went to Florida for a year with her granddaughter, Terry Bayer, and her husband. "But it was too hot in Florida," said Pearl, "so they came up here with me instead."

Terry reminded her that Jack Cervetto had kept a list of every person who lived in Warren Grove and when they died and what they died of. "I don't know how far back it goes. We just found it. He was really a historian; he really kept track of this area," Terry said.

"Grandpop also donated the land for the Warren Grove Fire Department," she prompted Pearl.

The building at the entrance to the Cervetto property is known as "the slave shack," but it is not known who owned the slaves who reportedly lived there.

"Yes, the first meeting when they incorporated was held right in my dining room," Pearl replied. "Grandma's family, the Holloways, owned all the land around here. So all the buildings here came from her family — the firehouse, the church, even the graveyard."

The Reevestown Cemetery, built on land donated by Pearl's grandparents, is on nearby Route 532. "There are Indians buried there," Terry said. "Not Cato and Lash, the last Indians in Stafford; they are in Manahawkin in the cemetery on Stafford Avenue. But there are 13 Indian graves."

Only residents of Warren Grove can be buried there, and the stones mark the resting places of many relatives.

"Jack was built like an ox," said Pearl. "He was 87 when he died and a good worker right up to the end."

Pearl owns 600 acres of swamp. Jack Cervetto bought the land from Abe Gerber years ago and intended to build cranberry bogs. He never finished his dream, but his grandchild might. Terry and her husband are looking to do something traditional with the property, rent it out to a grower or lease it to hunters.

"Now, don't give anybody the impression that I'm a wealthy woman because I own all this land," Pearl instructed. "I'm really tax poor ... you can't do anything with it except maybe turn it back to cranberry production."

The entrance to the Cervetto property is a dirt road past the church, into an oak and pine forest. A little building on the right is known locally as "the slave shack."

"We don't know who had the slaves or what they used them for," Terry said. "It's always been called the slave shack. Later, men who worked the sawmill would stay there. It's an historic building. Grandpop put a roof on it to preserve it, but it's deteriorating, and I think someone should preserve it like they have the railroad station and the Old Stone Store. I don't know how many slave buildings are left around Manahawkin, but it's an original building."

Just past the shack, a collapsed tin roof and some interesting but unrecognizable metal rubble mark where a lumber mill once stood. "There was a sleigh in one of these buildings," Pearl said, "but then it was in there when the building caved in."

On a sand road along the bog dam, there are blueberries still fruiting. The sun bakes down. The cedars are bright against the blue sky and some swamp maples have already turned a crimson red ... the first hint of autumn.

The bog dam is a huge reservoir of the Wading River watershed, Terry tells visitors. "You have to pay an awful lot of taxes for 600 acres and no income coming off it."

"This is one of the last plots that isn't owned by the government," Pearl sighed.

Sweet-smelling water lilies float on the pond; beyond are the cedar swamps.

"My husband loved the trees," Pearl reflected. "That's why I'm burdened with this, really. He loved it. He wouldn't sell it."

— *Pat Johnson*

Daughters of Ma Bell

The coins dropped as the operator counted two dings for a dime, one ding for a nickel, a bong for a quarter; then she dialed the number and stamped a ticket on a clock. Time was now running on the conversation.

Not so very long ago, before deregulation and downsizing became household words, the telephone company was affectionately called Ma Bell by all who worked for her. Ma Bell was a lifetime employer. She took care of your hospital bills; she had savings plans, pension plans; she allowed for paid vacations and kept track of seniority. For many women in the Stafford area, you couldn't get a better job.

In Manahawkin, Ma Bell was the New Jersey Bell Telephone office on Stafford Avenue, also known within the company as the Barnegat toll office — Barnegat because the Manahawkin office was a consolidation of all the small offices from Barnegat to Tuckerton, including Long Beach Island.

The office was a plain building with one door that operators entered after punching in the secret code on a key pad. Inside were two long rooms with switchboards from one end to the other. A sea of blinking lights flashed patterns as the switchboards signaled every call. The intonations of operators announcing themselves filled the room.

"Operator," a customer would request from a phone booth, "connect me to this number."

"Surely," the operator would reply, just as she had been taught to say, while quickly looking up the charge in her handy flip rate book.

The coins dropped as the operator counted two dings for a dime, one ding for a nickel, a bong for a quarter; then she dialed the number and stamped a ticket on a clock. Time was now running on the conversation.

"Your three minutes are up now; please signal when through," the operator would announce politely. Politeness was mandatory.

A light next to the slot went out when the customer hung up. Immediately, the operator stamped the ticket, hit the coin drop button and collected the "toll."

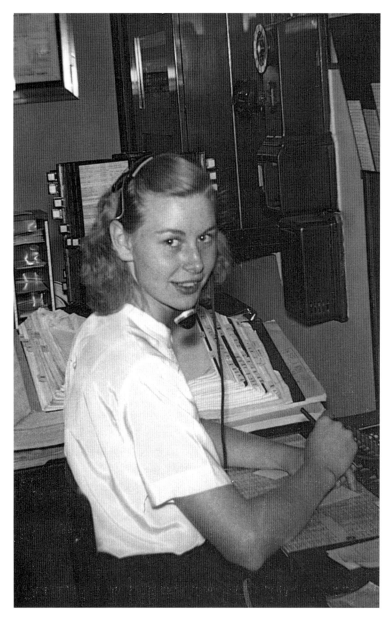

Minnie Richards started at New Jersey Bell Telephone in the 1950s.

calls, she could hear the peals of thunder and the rain hitting the glass and the laughter of a bunch of vacationers crammed into the booth.

The work of an operator could be monotonous. Each was acutely aware of time passing in three-minute increments. Sometimes while staring straight ahead at the board, an operator would daydream till she was tapped on the shoulder by a supervisor.

Although the women worked shoulder-to-shoulder, it was against the rules to talk. Still, some learned to speak quietly while casting sidelong glances at the supervisor's back.

Then there were the drunken callers who fumbled with money, or the perverts who knew there was a female voice at the end of the line for the price of a dime.

But for those women who gave the telephone company a lifetime of work, the friendships and the benefits were good. Six former Manahawkin telephone operators shared those switchboard memories one day when they reunited at Hannold's restaurant.

Dial E for Efficient

Ginny Ferns remembered when she worked with just two other women in an office above a storefront on Beach Haven's "Brick Row." She was transferred to the Beach Arlington (Ship Bottom) office, and then to the Manahawkin office when it was built in 1946. She worked there 25 years; altogether she worked 42 years.

"I worked with Betty Willets in Beach Haven. I started work early because I came from a family with 12 children, and we had to get to work," Ginny told her listeners. Both her son and son-in-law joined the company.

"Almost all of our children worked there at one time or another," added Winnie Hopf.

Winnie worked for Ma Bell for 42 years, eight months and six days. "But who's counting?" she joked.

The operator performed other duties, connecting long-distance, person-to-person calls or the credit card calls that were new in the early 1970s.

Her heart would pound when she heard the occasional "Operator, get me the police!" but most of the calls she attended were timed coin box tolls.

When it rained, people on Long Beach Island would run off the beach and line up to make calls at the closest phone booth. This was the operator's busiest time in the summer. As she answered the

Minnie Richards also clocked in at the Manahawkin office for 42 years. There were seven operator positions when she started; that grew to 125 before downsizing began in the 1970s.

"When I first started in 1947, the mainland couldn't call the beach. Everything had to go through an operator; you couldn't dial long distance," Minnie recalled.

"We had an emergency list for everything — fire company, ambulance, Coast Guard. The first thing people would do if there was an emergency was to call the operator. We didn't have 911 in those days. If you wanted information, you got us operators — we did everything."

Catherine "Kate" Cranmer had been on the job for almost 31 years. "I went to work to make money."

"We all did that," Winnie agreed. "And we picked a good one, too. The checks were always on time."

Next to her was the group's former boss, former chief operator Clare Maher. Clare was chief at Stafford for 25 years and worked with the company for a total of 33 years.

Clare remembered that bracelets were given out for perfect attendance. "We were also recognized with service luncheons. If you had 20 years or 25, they would give us a service luncheon and we could pick the guests — up to 25 people — and we could pick the location. It's so different today; the young people, the yuppies, don't plan to stay with a company for too long. But when we were working, that was a real objective, to get 25 years somewhere."

Clare's telephone career began when she ended another career prospect that was less than rewarding. "I put an application into the telephone office up in Boonton and also put it in the hosiery plant," she said. "I was called to come in as a desk clerk at the hosiery plant; I think I worked there three days. I never realized how awful it was to work in a factory. The office that my boss had was assigning work to all the workers and they got piece work; they got paid according to how many stockings got knitted. And if they thought they weren't getting enough work ... I never heard such swearing in all my life and never since then — from these women! By my third day my mother said the telephone company had called and they wanted me to come into work the next week. I never left a place so fast as that one."

Ethel Rosenholm was recruited by the first chief operator at the Manahawkin office, Bessie Ellis.

"I didn't even want to go work for the telephone company," Ethel said. "I worked in the post office, and every day Bessie would come in and get the mail and say, 'Why don't you come work with us? We have indoor plumbing,' which I didn't have. The post office had an outhouse. If the place had caught on fire, there wasn't a tea cup of water to throw on it.

"I had to handle all those mail bags and no place to wash my hands, no bathroom and $320 a year salary. So Bessie said, 'We pay better.' Anyway, my mother thought it was a good idea, too, so I went and filled out an application.

"When they hired me in '44, they weren't hiring married women, so they hired me for the duration of the war," Ethel continued. "I was called a temporary employee, and when I retired they gave me that application with that on it, 'hired for the duration of the war.' So 38 years later the war ended, I guess."

Bessie Ellis also trained Kate. "I was so scared of Miss Ellis. I couldn't hear the bells for the pay phone. Miss Ellis would ring them and ring them and say, 'Now can't you hear that?' But I was too nervous."

"She lived right across the street, so she could keep an eye on us coming and going," Minnie said. "When Ellis left for the evening, she would tell us where to sit and be sure to sit with a position between us so that we couldn't talk. She used to call the operator and time how long it would take before someone answered. We all answered the 597 (Manahawkin) numbers first."

"We had a dress code that changed over the years," added Kate. "It was very strict with Miss Ellis; you wore stockings and you didn't chew gum.

"In defense of Miss Ellis," Kate added, "I'd like to say a couple of good things: She was very service oriented; she believed in punctuality. And when it was time for you to go, I never remember having to wait to be relieved. There were lots of things good about her — she was just strict."

"If you worked well you got along much better with her," Ethel said. "If she taught you something, it was correct; there was no half-way about it. In the old days when the office was in Barnegat, she went door to door selling telephones, literally. She was service oriented."

Lil Brescia joined the table. She had worked only six years off and on, she said, because then she went to college.

"It was a good place to work for kids," Clare noted. "It was a good place to make money for your tuition."

"That's true — Ma Bell put a lot of kids through college," Winnie agreed.

"I had a scholarship, but I still needed money for college," said Lil.

"Another thing," added Clare, "we learned how to save money because the telephone company had all of these plans. You could have $2 taken out of your check every week and have it put in a savings account, save it, or you could buy U.S. savings bonds or AT&T stock, all out of the payroll, and we learned early how to put a little bit aside. Right now we just got our November dividend checks and that check is my Christmas money."

"I pay my taxes with mine," Ethel told the group.

"I get such a kick out of it when MCI and Sprint call with all those plans," Clare said with a laugh. "After all that Bell Telephone has done for me, they've got no chance."

The Connection Must Go Through

The telephone office never closed, though sometimes it held just one woman keeping the lines of communication open.

"We had to work all night. One week a month, all night," Winnie remembered.

"Another thing about working nights is that a lot of times you would be the only girl the whole night," put in Minnie.

"If you had to go to the bathroom, you had to run up the stairs real fast," added Ethel.

"I liked the overnight shift," Clare decided. "I enjoyed the 10-to-7; then you had the whole day off."

Lil liked it, too. She often clammed during the day to make extra money and then worked the night shift.

"Remember, in the old days, if you called in sick they would send a nurse out to make sure you were really sick," reminded Minnie. "They had a home visitor."

"I had a gall bladder attack one time and I couldn't work," Winnie said. "So, I called up and said I couldn't come to work and Ellis said 'Well, you have to.' I couldn't even hold my head up. I went."

"There were lots of old chief operators that were tyrants," Clare observed. "Maybe they had to be to keep the employees coming in on time."

The one and only thing that could halt a connection was a competing telephone company.

There were plenty of independent telephone companies before deregulation, noted Clare. "There was Northwestern and several others. If an office was mad at us and we had calls going into that office, they just wouldn't answer us."

But even a natural disaster was no excuse. Not storms nor fire nor dark of night nor holidays could stop New Jersey Bell.

"More than once we had a horrible forest fire and they closed the Parkway; we still had to come to work," Clare remembered.

"It would have taken a national crisis to get us out of there," declared Winnie.

"Whenever there were any natural disasters, the more people who would come in, the better," Clare said.

"We were the lifeline, really," agreed Minnie.

"When you think of it, we didn't know how important we were," Winnie said.

"I remember going to work in a blinding snowstorm," Kate began her story. "My husband drove me all the way from Warren Grove, and then I found I'd forgotten my glasses. He had to go all the way back again to get them for me because I couldn't work without them."

"I think the saddest thing was you had to work Christmas or New Year's Eve," said Clare. "Unless you had the seniority, you had to work it. So many a Christmas I was very unhappy."

"I used to come home from college and work Christmases and whatever," added Lil. "It was money."

"I always worked Christmas Eve so that someone else could have off — someone who had kids," affirmed Kate.

"The last 10 years that I was working," Minnie remembered, "Joan or Marge Dryer would put the Christmas schedule up and then you could call one of the occasionals to come work for you —"

"And, boy, there would be a race to that telephone," Winnie finished.

"The last Christmas I worked was in the plant department, where they did the repairs," Ethel said. "And there was a girl there who was scheduled and she had two little children and I was scheduled off. I said, 'I'll work for you so you can be home with your kids.' And so I was there alone and the door buzzer rang and there she was with my Christmas dinner for me. And she had everything — pumpkin pie, everything. Everybody called me up and wished me a Merry Christmas. I had the best Christmas, I think, in years; I had a ball."

The Manahawkin operators banded together in a bowling team. They attended each other's baby showers, which were sometimes held in the office lunchroom.

"We shared the bad times and rejoiced when there were good times," Kate summed up.

"The number of baby showers and food — Kate always made a turkey for Thanksgiving," added Clare.

"We had parties to end parties," declared Ethel.

"We were like a family," as Ginny saw it.

"When my mother was bedridden for a good many years and she lived by herself, I said, 'Mom, if anything happens, all you have to do is call the operator and tell her you're Minnie's mom and right away they'll know who you are and they'll get me,' " Minnie said. "Now you dial for an operator and you don't know who you're going to get, where."

"I don't even know how to call from a coin box anymore. I hate when I break down on the road and have to read the directions first. At one time all you had to do was drop a dime in the coin box and call the operator. Look what technology has done for us."

Clare complained that when she called an 800 number recently she couldn't get through.

"Sometime soon we'll have to dial 10 digits for a local call," predicted Ethel. "That's coming because of all the demand on the companies."

When technology phased out their jobs, operators had to make other arrangements to stay in employment with the company, Minnie said.

"They realized the office was going to close sometime in the '70s — and, of course, we all laughed and said that will never happen — anyway, it happened. So from '71 to when the office closed in '77, whenever a job became available they would let us know. In '73 a job became available for me, so I left operating for a job with the company in Atlantic City.

"A few people had to retire; a lot of them went to different places like Atlantic City, Toms River, Freehold — one girl went to Cherry Hill.

"I finished the last 15 years of my career in the telephone company in Atlantic City," Minnie said. "I wasn't alone; lots of other people had to commute.

"It doesn't seem like 42 years. Most of it was very pleasant. Even when I went to Atlantic City, I hated it at first, but then I met so many nice people down there — I miss it."

— *Pat Johnson*

The Bell Telephone central office on Stafford Avenue in the 1960s; eventually it was torn down.

Lucille Bates-Wickward

"People come here thinking they've found a place in the middle of nowhere, but it's really not."

Lucille Bates-Wickward can stand the oven's heat, but after all these years, she wouldn't mind getting out of the kitchen. The owner of Lucille's Country Cooking would travel, see how some other people live, then come home to spend time with her grandkids.

Keeping the warmth in the Warren Grove landmark since 1975 has meant that at 4 a.m., the pies went into the oven, and it wasn't until 8 o'clock at night that the last heavy cooking pan came out. Every day but Christmas.

She has "delegated" more of the chores lately, but she's still been the main ingredient to the place's charm — Lucille on the other side of the counter mixing from table to table as comfortably as mashed potatoes meet butter.

If anybody else bought the place, they would by requirement genuinely like people — talking with them, standing over the stove for them, treating them "the way you'd like to be treated."

Some customers have been "regulars" so much that if mom knew she'd be an hour late from work, she'd tell the kids to go to Lucille's after school. Lucille would sit them down with a box of crayons. If a neighbor ran out of celery, she'd call Lucille and ask if she could send her kid over for two stalks.

From the kitchen, Lucille has been able to tell by the order slip who was sitting at the counter waiting for it, and how they'd like it done.

But customers have found Lucille's Country Cooking to be full of surprises, more than the plain panel exterior advertised. You'd expect deer hunters because the spot is an official weigh section. But you never could know who might walk through the door.

When he spent time in Atlantic City, Merv Griffin sent somebody in every Friday to pick up two pies, blueberry and apple.

Joe Piscopo found Lucille a couple of years back. She wasn't sure of the face at first — "because I never stayed up that late."

Lucille Bates-Wickward dishes out some good humor at her Warren Grove restaurant counter.

The comedian wanted seriously healthy food, turkey on wheat bread with a side of nutritious juice. Ever joking, Lucille craned her face over to his and compared the match to him and his girlfriend. "Now, who does he look happier with?"

To newcomers, Lucille's popped up like an apparition from the cranberry bogs. There weren't any other restaurants around it in Warren Grove; heck, there never were many other buildings.

But then, Warren Grove, population 300 in 1999, is an exceptional place in its own right. What other spot on the map sprawls across four townships and two counties? Where else do zoning rules say you need 17 acres to build a house?

With all that space between them, no wonder locals come in ready to talk. The listener gets a taste of what's really going on: the deer will be fat this year — the woods are full of acorns.

Dinner, soup to dessert, has been found for the same price as a single sandwich on the Island. On the menu, variety has been the order of every day — meat loaf, clam chowder, omelets so big you'd swear, as one customer did, that an ostrich laid the eggs.

"It's the only place in town you can get Belgian waffles," declared a road department worker on his way out. Then he paused, realizing the size of the town he was talking about. Oh, well.

"The atmosphere, that's what we come here for," pronounced the man happy with his omelet, Bruce Groendyke. He wore a hat proclaiming his affiliation, "Manure Movers of America, Local 239." Organic gardening is his hobby in Hightstown. He and his mother, Lois, were heading home from Brigantine via Route 539.

"People come here thinking they've found a place in the middle of nowhere, but it's really not," Lucille said. She did allow that "a lot of people tell me it's halfway to where they're going."

A customer once stepped in and announced that he had been passing by for 20 years and finally decided to stop.

"Why today?" Lucille shot back, re-enacting the exchange with a jaunty tilt of the head. "I just want to know what made you stop today?"

There are times in Lucille's when nobody's talking, if everybody wants it that way. Coffee cups clink on saucers and pages of newspapers rustle until somebody new walks through the door.

Lucille wasn't sure at first, after her husband died, if she could handle running a restaurant by herself. It had all started when he had mused, "You know what? We could have a hot dog stand."

They started selling breakfast and lunch; he died three years later. Friends encouraged her to reopen,

Growing Up in 'Hawkin in the '40s and '50s

The Manahawkin race track circled the gravel pit off today's Doc Cramer Boulevard. Here in about 1950, the middle car was driven by Manahawkin's Huck Fredrickson and sponsored by the Harold Tess Sr. Garage in Mayetta. One day, Huck turned over seven times and got gasoline in his eyes, but emerged all right otherwise.

Lucille Bates-Wickward shares her recollections.

Manahawkin was a perfect place to live, growing up in the '40s and '50s. I have many fond memories of events and people. Life was like a Norman Rockwell painting of rural America.

In the summer, most everyone in town went to the local lake and pavilion. We often packed our lunches and picnicked there. As kids we spent hours playing around the waterfall at the spillway, sliding down the boards that were all slippery from the moss. In the winter, the lake stayed frozen for many weeks — great for skating. We had a nightly bonfire.

The local roller rink, located where the flea market is today, provided a year-round activity. Every teenager in a 20-mile radius knew where this place was located.

There was a dirt track for car racing. My parents had two hot dog stands there. I'm sure my brother, Tim Michel, got his fever for stock car racing at these Sunday races. I went on to have a hot dog stand, and later to own Lucille's Country Cooking in Warren Grove — thanks, Mom and Dad.

As young people, we all looked for a job. Of course, that was back before video games and computers. We found jobs picking berries in the local blueberry fields, babysitting, clamming, delivering papers, running errands, pumping gas, waitressing, or working as New Jersey Bell Telephone operators on Stafford Avenue. Many local girls found a great future at the Bell office.

My mother and father did not have a formal education. They were good, honest, hard-working people. My ancestors go back to the early settlers in Barnegat and Egg Harbor — Chadwick, Ridgway, Michel, Taylor.

My father had a trash route on Long Beach Island, before there was a public works department. In the summer, my mother had to drive his second truck to keep up with the work created by the increase in residents. This was in the 1940s, and women truck drivers were rarely seen.

We raised pigs. All neighbors on Oxycocus Road knew us well. When the pigs broke down a fence, we all had to get out of bed in the middle of the night, "rounding" them back into the pen. My daughter, Diane Lohr, raises pigs in Warren Grove today.

We also raised chickens. I used to pick out the feed sacks with prints so my mother could make me a dress. My mother is no longer alive, but I'd still like to tell her thank you again.

Kay Stienerson started the first Girl Scout troop in Stafford. I was a member of that troop.

Al Goldberger was the eighth-grade teacher and principal of the school at the same time. The football field at Southern Regional High School is named in his memory.

Bert Paul drove the school bus; Sadie Paul taught school. Minnie Courtney was the school nurse. Elsie Sprague filled the air of the old school on Beach Avenue with her most famous peanut butter cookies and baked macaroni and cheese. If you went to the Beach Avenue School, you well remember what this lady could produce in a five-by-five kitchen.

The traveling salesman sold Porter Salve — you could do just about everything with it. The "Rag Man" came around in an old truck calling out, "Any old rags for sale?" I don't know if they bought the rags from people who came out of their houses, or what. But it sent me running for home, because I thought he was really looking for kids.

In the corn fields, we used to play hide-and-seek until the farmer caught us.

Another memory — the deer hanging from the tree in the center of town at Russ Horner's gas station. Each deer season, the town was a sea of orange. At Christmastime, Dick and Gladys Fraser had a train set that was assembled with all the little scenes around it, and they shared it with the other kids in town.

Even before Route 72, summer traffic was heavy, since everyone used the two-lane Bay Avenue. The wooden drawbridge backed up traffic for hours.

With the nearest hospital in Atlantic City, we had seven-day-a-week, 24-hour-a-day duty from "Dr. Bob" Irvin, the only town doctor.

School activities were very well attended, especially if Barnegat and Tuckerton High — rival teams — were playing. Volunteers for first aid, fire company and PTA were plentiful.

On a more rowdy note, the National Hotel was known by the locals as the "Frontier Playhouse," because every Saturday night someone went through the front picture window.

We had four diners and two little restaurants in town. Louise Hannold served an open-face barbecue pork that was out of this world. There were no Chinese restaurants, but Yep-Yow had a florist shop on Bay Avenue. Some of us would go in to browse because we hadn't seen an Oriental person before. There were no malls, but we had Phoebe's and Smartie June's. Of course the selections were few, so we all dressed quite alike. There was no bus service, but Rose Cranmer drove many of us to events outside of Manahawkin. No credit cards were in our wallets, but Bill Soper extended credit to many locals in the winter. Everyone paid him in the spring. Thinking back now, so many people were nice to us, and I'd like to thank them, but they're no longer around.

I believe Stafford is developing well under good people. My father, Amos Michel, served on the local council for four years — I'm proud that he helped make a difference also.

Manahawkin is still a great place, but Warren Grove is the hidden secret. I can't imagine living anywhere else.

and over the years her four kids helped. They all still live in Warren Grove.

"I always knew where they were," Lucille said. "They've all grown up to be OK. They learned to talk to people of all walks of life."

Lucille stopped chatting to rap with a salt shaker on the counter, signaling the young waitress who was getting something from the kitchen. A man had settled onto a counter stool a minute or two earlier. "I'm not in a hurry," the customer assured her.

"I can't stand to see somebody sit there that long," Lucille said, turning back around. "I want to at least get them coffee."

The waitress appeared through the swinging door. "Hi, honey. I didn't know if you knew he was here," Lucille explained. A clank and a swish, and

the aroma of fresh coffee invited the man to stay awhile.

If a new owner were ever to stand behind the counter, he or she would be carefully chosen. Some inquirers have thought they'd like to run a restaurant, but Lucille wasn't sure enough. Even when retirement comes, Lucille wouldn't let go of her own apron strings entirely. She would still keep on catering for private affairs.

"Something we're doing is right," she allowed. Her compensation over the years she described as "enough."

"I'm not a wealthy woman. But a person could make a good living here. If they want to treat people good, they'll make out fine."

— *Maria Scandale*

The Old Stone Store

Local historians say the building that became the general store by the lake was built in the mid-1700s by Reuben Randolph.

The date 1838 carved into the southeast corner-stone marks the year when the exterior was reinforced in stone by Benjamin Oliphant, who had bought the mill complex and a large tract of land there. The stones they used have been traced to the "iron stones" found in and around Warren Grove.

An account book of the Oliphant family store for the year 1803 shows one typical entry: a gallon of apple whiskey, 10 pounds of pork, 24 pounds of rye flour and two gallons of molasses.

The next owner of record was Michael Sprague, who operated the store until 1888, using the enterprise's central location as a meeting place for

Old Stone Store and grist mill, above, in 1905. The mill was destroyed by fire in the 1930s. The abandoned store, below, a few months before a 1964 blaze left the landmark a blackened shell.

the township committee during his membership. The store was also pressed into service as a recruiting station at the time of the Civil War.

In 1888, another Benjamin Oliphant took over. The first Benjamin Oliphant had died in 1873.

Customers came and went until about 1901, say local residents. The building later became a residence.

Around the end of World War II, locals noticed the building was starting to deteriorate. From disrepair, the

Flames breaking through the roof are a challenge for firemen during the April 23, 1964 battle, top left. After the fire, the store is left gutted and charred, above right. Through persistent efforts of preservationists, and stone-by-stone reconstruction, the Old Stone Store stands as it did in the good old days, below.

structure declined to abandonment, then vandalism. It burned in 1964.

Plans and hopes for restoration date to about that time, when the township committee, echoing hopes of the community that the landmark would not be lost, sought funds to buy and restore the building at a reasonable cost.

It was finally taken down and all the stones were marked and moved to an Ocean County maintenance garage.

"Jack Cervetto and I worked 12 to 13 years off and on to try to save the old building," recalled Ed Hazelton. "Finally we went to the board of freeholders and asked them if they would incorporate it into the A. Paul King Park, which they did.

"In due time, the freeholders had contractors come in and work on it and move the stone back. We put the 1838 cornerstone back where it originally was." The township and the community pitched in.

"It's the same stone that's in the original building," said Hazelton. "The only difference is, with the original building the stones were laid flat. We lost a lot of the stone when we moved it, when the walls crumbled down, so in order to have enough stone to do the job to its original condition, we put the stone on edge."

The reconstructed Old Stone Store on Old Broadway, dedicated in 1979, stands as a reminder of Manahawkin's early commercial activity. The Stafford Township Historical Society maintains the building with the goal of outfitting it as a museum that will someday be open year 'round.

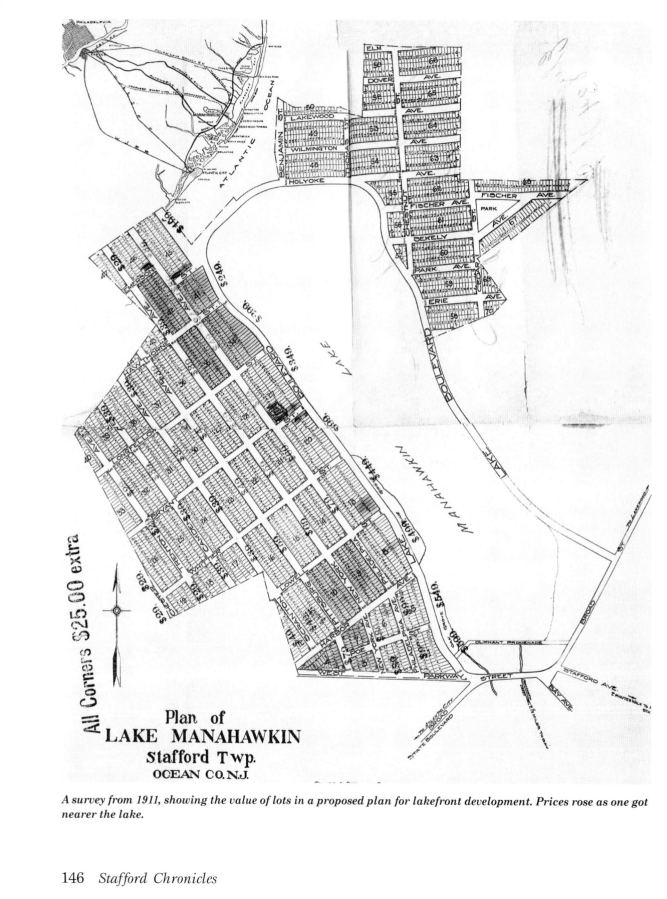

A survey from 1911, showing the value of lots in a proposed plan for lakefront development. Prices rose as one got nearer the lake.

Manahawkin Lake

*Childhood memories
grew, romances
blossomed and the
more seasoned
generations reflected
on the times
of their lives.*

Gazing across a timbered-out cedar swamp in the 1740s, Reuben F. Randolph saw that with a little construction, the swamp adjoining the village could deepen into a functional lake. Strong natural banks stood along the north and east sides, so the only requirement was to build a dam with a spillway along the south end. Manahawkin Lake would become the focal point of the town, for both economic and recreational pursuits.

With lumber a growing industry in the outlying areas, Manahawkin would thrive on its own sawmill, Randolph thought. So, during the spillway construction, the men excavated a deep sluiceway at its base to install a "power wheel." The creek that rushed out of the lake, powering the sawmill and draining into Barnegat Bay, became known as Mill Creek.

Other mills sprang up, scattered along the streams feeding into the lake as well as those below it. At one point, as many as 11 mills operated various industries at the same time. The lumber industry prospered, with ships carrying its cedar, pine, and oak to ports along the Eastern Seaboard. Later, a new railroad transported the lumber. Residents trusted the lake for clean, potable water, at the same time that it invited them to dive in for a cooling swim.

Before the age of refrigeration, the frozen lake was the area's commercial source of ice. In 1891, Firman Cranmer built an icehouse for the Oliphant brothers and rebuilt their farmhouse on the hill just south of the lake. In 1813, Benjamin Oliphant bought all of Reuben Randolph's enterprises and erected a large gristmill and a sawmill along the south side of the lake near where the Old Stone Store stands today. Once the mill wheels began turning, Oliphant had a ship built to carry white cedar lumber and grain to southern ports. As a businessman on the local scene as well, he opened a store and sold general merchandise. Benjamin's two sons assisted and later became partners.

Manahawkin Lake has held a key position at the head of town since the 1700s.

The enterprise was known as the "Firm of Benjamin Oliphant, Samuel M. and Joseph R."

In order for patrons to walk among the various mills and the store, the landowners built a walkway that stretched along a marsh, past the lake and over the dam. This walkway became known as "Oliphant's Promenade."

In later years, the side of the lake bordering Route 9 was still a social gathering spot. It drew the residents to its shores in all seasons. In the summer, all ages gathered lakeside to swim, launch their boats, and fish. In the winter, the pastimes switched to ice skating and ice boating. A pavilion next to the bathing area sheltered parents trying to keep one eye on their youngsters while hearing the news of the neighbors. Not far from the swimming beach was an ice cream and soda shop, which

dripping, barefooted children probably reached laughing and running. The National Hotel was just across the street. Childhood memories grew, romances blossomed and the more seasoned generations reflected on the times of their lives.

In 1976 Manahawkin Lake entered a new phase when Ocean County purchased the land. County funds built a bathing beach along the southwest shore, equipped with a small recreation and picnic area. The county also built a new concrete spillway to replace the old wooden structure.

By the late 1970s and early 1980s, the lake's ecological balance was suffering. Over the years, development upstream had allowed more stormwater runoff to reach the lake, carrying silt and pollution with it. The lake became shallower, which in turn further harmed its water quality. The lake's bath-

The pavilion on the lake, a spot to sit and talk or keep an eye on the children.

to an abandoned gravel pit, where it sat until it was utilized as fill material on projects throughout the township.

The dredging restored the lake for swimming. Stafford Township Councilman and Environmental Commission Chairman John Spodofora maintained records of ongoing water quality tests of the lake. In the first 10 years since the lake was re-opened for swimming, tests have indicated that it met the state's safe swimming standards 99 percent of the time. The councilman has a letter from the EPA designating the lake restoration project as the most successful in the United States. He was presented the Theodore Roosevelt Conservation Award by President George Bush in 1990.

The township applied for $1.2 million in state funding to buy land along the lake in 1995, and bought the property in 1996. A Green Acres grant provided $317,125; the rest came through a low-interest, 20-year Green Acres loan. Another $1 million loan covered Phase I and II of development of a seven-acre park. As 1999 dawned, so did the first phase of landscaping and construction around the eastern shore of the lake.

The township council hopes the new Manahawkin Lake Park will again become a center of family activities. When the blueprints are fully realized, the park will come alive with a playground, bike paths, and a basketball court. A boat ramp and a fishing pier are planned waterside, along with a bathing beach. A band shell at lake-level, with seating built into the existing hillside, will complete the picture. The plans included a replica of the original pavilion on the same spot that the earlier pavilion occupied, and paths would lead strollers along the lake as they did in the days of "Oliphant's Promenade."

ing beach was closed between 1985 and 1995. The Stafford Township Environmental Commission and county officials conducted a comprehensive study to see what could be done.

The project became a community effort. Volunteers took on the tasks of conducting aerial surveys of the lake from private planes. Photographers helped shoot the infrared survey film needed to chart the lake, and Southern Regional High School science students and ecology club members worked alongside the Stafford Elementary School Trash Busters and Pitch Pine Kids. The students conducted environmental studies that were needed before the restoration could proceed. Volunteers pitched in, collecting water samples and asking the federal Environmental Protection Agency to grant money to restore the lake.

The $412,000 EPA grant came through in August 1990, with the county matching that amount. After many delays, in February 1994, a dredge began working to deepen the lower part of the lake and redirect the water's flow toward the bathing beach. The dredge also scraped the lake bed to create an infusion of pure groundwater and to allow some of the old artesian wells to flow back into the lake. The average depth of the lake before dredging was 16 inches, and after the project was completed, 8.5 feet.

Pipes carried the dredged silt under Route 72

The Lake in Its Perpetual Time and Place

"This place is like no other," Stafford Township Council President John Spodofora professed of the lake that he and others have strived to bring back to its former focus in downtown Manahawkin. "As long ago as I can remember, growing up in the '50s and '60s, Manahawkin Lake has always been the centerpiece of our town. The gazebo was there, an ice cream parlor and the diner. It was where everyone went. This was the social gathering spot for Stafford Township."

The lake was a place for all seasons and all ages, and that may be why, when he spearheaded the restoration effort, so many others joined in.

The boyhood native recalled moments of his own youth. "All summer long, all the kids would be there, swimming at the beach. In the evenings, we'd sit in the gazebo, meeting friends and socializing into the wee hours. On days when it was too chilly to swim, we'd fish. After every fall game at the high school, we'd end up at the diner by the lake. Even in the winter, the lake was the place to be. We would ice skate for hours with friends and family.

"Many of our fondest memories of being in the downtown area revolved around our lives at the lake. It was our second home. We built rafts to explore the lake and to find the best fishing spots. I even learned how to scuba dive in Lake Manahawkin before I joined the Navy as an underwater demolition team diver. It was quite an experience."

As if memories about the lake weren't enough, legends abound.

"We had a great time making up stories about the Manahawkin 'muck monsters,'" John smiled. "For a time, we outdid each other with tall tales of giant snapping turtles. They got bigger with each telling." His smile faded. "But we were scared, really scared, by the old-timers' stories of a mysterious Model-T Ford at the bottom of the lake, complete with a person still inside!"

He shook his head and smiled again, remembering. "In later years, everyone was looking forward to whether the car or skeleton or both would actually show up as we dredged the lake." Neither did.

The real history of the lake and its surrounding area is not as dramatic, but interwoven forever with the town's growth. "The reason for Manahawkin's very existence centers on a huge cedar swamp that sat right on this spot," John reminded. "The trees were phenomenal here, straight and tall, making them valuable for shipbuilding. Jersey white cedar was the most desirable wood for making vessels, and we had it in abundance."

The lake continued to offer a livelihood, even in more recent years. "When I was a kid, we used to trap muskrats up at the headwaters of the lake. Some men made this their primary source of income for many years. This lake was many things to many people."

And it will be in the future, he hoped. "We have a vision to restore the grandeur of this historic spot," the councilman said as he spread his arms wide. "As our town continues to grow, we hope to provide people with a place to go. A place where they can interact with each other, to socialize and relax, even to dream, just like in the old days. Maybe we can bring back some of the old-time atmosphere and environment that was so important to our formative years as we were growing up."

The development of Manahawkin Lake Park has had as many twists and turns as the old Lenape Indian trails found nearby. The town first tried convincing the county to purchase the site outright, but ended up buying it instead. Why? "Simple," said Spodofora. "To keep the spot from becoming another Wawa convenience store." As the council president saw it, the whole downtown area could be restored to meet the future. "We're already seeing Route 72 blossom into Kmarts, Wal-Marts and Home Depots," he said. "Now it's great to see Old Bay Avenue and Route 9 becoming home to antique shops, bed and breakfasts, restaurants and professional offices."

The pedestrian bridge over the spillway at Mill Creek, links the township park with A. Paul King County Park on the opposite side of the lake. A $170,000 grant enabled its construction.

"We plan to also use this park as a way to make people more aware of our history and heritage," the councilman said. "The historical society has been very much involved in the development of the park. They envision a series of plaques along the path that point out various key moments in Stafford's history. Maybe one day we'll have little monuments that commemorate the people and events that shaped our heritage."

— *Jim De Francesco*

Two unidentified women support themselves during an ice skating outing on the lake, opposite page. From the spillway, above, looking beyond the boaters at the lake, the land stretches nearly undeveloped.

Stafford Lake, Manahawkin, N. J.

The year is unrecorded, but the scene of boys bicycling at lakeside is timeless. And from a vantage point atop the spillway, circa 1930, the sight and sound of rushing water sent a refreshing feeling.

Louise Hannold

"They still come in from years ago. They come in to see if I'm still here."

Louise Hannold is Stafford's reigning business queen with a spatula for a scepter. Born in 1918, she has owned and worked at Hannold's Restaurant at 621 East Bay Avenue since 1945. She doesn't regret her more than half-century spent serving homestyle food and specialties, and has no intention of retiring soon.

It was a long trip to a place she's never left.

Louise followed her sister to Manahawkin from her childhood home in Newark when she was 11 years old. She remembers Stafford as a quiet country town. "There were lots of dirt roads, no sidewalks. They still had the old swimming hole in Manahawkin Lake and the pavilion. It was real nice."

Her sister had married into the Mascola family, who owned and operated Jimmie's Restaurant and Tavern on Route 9 until selling it to the Carroll family in 1957. "When I came down in 1929, I came down to help my sister with her baby, and after a couple of months I was washing dishes in the restaurant," Louise said. "She broke me in to be a waitress."

When the Mascolos built the Manahawkin Barbecue at the lake, Louise also helped her sister there. "I was almost 12 when she pushed me out to waitress. Then she started to teach me how to cook. We all learned a little bit when we were home because I came from a family of 13. That's a big family. We all had to learn to fend for ourselves. So she pushed me out to cook for her customers, first at Jimmie's Restaurant and Tavern, and then at the Barbecue.

"We knew everybody in town and everybody's name," Louise said. "Now I know people, but I can't remember too many names."

Louise went back home to finish school in Newark, but quit school to go to work when she was 16. "I didn't like to go to school at all."

In 1941, her whole family moved to Manahawkin.

Louise Hannold in the place she loves best.

It's probably no surprise that Louise met her future husband, Edward, while she was waitressing. "He used to come in and order milkshakes. I was about 17 when I met him. I was 21 when I married him."

In 1944, when Edward got out of the service, the couple bought the Barbecue. They operated the drive-through establishment by the lake for one year, and then moved to the spot on East Bay Avenue where Hannold's is now.

"We moved because people that owned the property wanted about $1,000 a month rent for the ground. So we just up and moved. We took the building apart, put it on a big truck and moved it."

Louise recalls that the first year they ran the Barbecue, they kept it open 24 hours a day. "People used to come to my place after the bars closed around 3 in the morning and they got kind of rowdy," she said, "so we started closing at 2, just before the bars closed. There was another diner down the road, so they went there. And then about 6 a.m. we would open up again."

At first, the serving space was limited to a counter. "Originally I would cook out front and serve right over the counter. Then after about five years, we built the dining room. We could seat 49 people, and 15 at the counter."

The counter and the roof over it are all that remain of the original structure. But as time goes on, even the rest of Hannold's has gained the vintage feel of hometown, a blending of '50s, '60s, '70s and neighborliness.

"We were busy then," Louise reflected on the earlier years. "This was before they built the new causeway, and there weren't that many restaurants around. Now there must be about 300 or more. There's lots of competition."

As the new dining room at Hannold's got busier, Edward left the job he had working in the gardens at the F. P. Small estate in Harvey Cedars. "He quit there and worked with me and I taught him how to cook," Louise said.

"Then we used to open up at 5 in the morning

Most of the businesses along Main Street that provided the backdrop for the bathing beach are gone. In their day, though, the grocery stores and refreshment stands were close at hand for kids after a swim.

for the fishermen and work until 12 midnight sometimes. But we were young then; we didn't mind. We still catch a few fishermen in the morning. They still come in from years ago. They come in to see if I'm still here.

"We served barbecue, hot dogs and hamburgers. Then people used to say, 'Gee whiz, we'd like to have something else once in a while.' So we started to serve dinners, and once we put the dining room up, we used to serve a hundred dinners a night from 4 o'clock until 8. And if you said we close at 8, people would come in at five to 8 and we'd have to stay until 10.

"We served dinners right up to the week my husband died in 1974," Louise said. "And then I tried to do it for a while, but it was too much. It would have been OK if you could close at 8 and get out of here by 9, but 12 midnight and being by myself ... I said no way."

So, in recent years, she has closed the restaurant at 2 p.m., after coming in at 7 a.m. to get things going by 8 a.m.

There was nothing much but Hannold's at that end of East Bay Avenue in the late '40s and early '50s. "The bowling alley was built in 1959. There was nothing on the highway, just a little house next door. The road was just a dirt road.

"There wasn't even that much traffic. The only heavy traffic was on a Sunday. Other than that,

nothing. The only time it was bumper to bumper was when the old drawbridge was up."

Dancing in the Dining Room

While the new causeway was being built, the workers used to eat at Hannold's. There were other amusements to draw people to Manahawkin at night. Besides the bowling alley, there was the drive-in movie theater and the old skating rink.

"Years ago we used to have a juke box in here, and I used to let the young people dance. We never had a problem."

Louise is still young at heart and quick on the grill. When someone asks, she attributes her youthful looks to her own cooking and hard work. "Restaurant work is hard work, but I like it and I get to socialize with people. I really like it.

"I'm the only one in the family that's not retired. I enjoy what I'm doing. I'm happy. I make enough to pay my bills and spend money on what I want ... and not worry about where the next dollar is coming from. People say, 'Why don't you retire?' but I like doing what I'm doing. Why should I retire?"

Louise likes cooking up "crazy specials," and contest judges seem to appreciate the creativity. Over the counter is a trophy from the Chatsworth Cranberry Festival for her cranapple cheese omelet. The contest rules required that cranberries be used, and left the rest up to the cook. Her answer was an omelet featuring cranberries with cheese, bacon and apples.

One special on the menu has never been served — the sardine club sandwich.

"Many years ago, Maine Sardines ran a contest, and I made up a sardine club sandwich and I won. I came in third, and I won a trip to Chicago and about 10 cases of sardines." The sandwich on her menu is in homage to the winning recipe.

"I create a lot of sandwiches. I get an urge to do something different. I had half a dozen mushrooms and asked myself, 'Now what should I do with them?' I took the stems off and dipped them in eggs and fried them up like you would eggplant, and I ran a special portobello sandwich with other mushrooms and fried onions and parmigiana. Nobody ever heard of it, but they tried it and they liked it.

"That's one of my crazy sandwiches. Another crazy sandwich is grilled cheese and egg ... or grilled cheese and eggplant. It's not on the menu, but if I have the eggplant, I'll make it."

Louise's recipe for BBQ beef is the original from 1944. It's her own recipe and she never gives it out. "Even if I did, they couldn't make it anyway. I make five gallons at a time. Most people sell the beef all chopped up in the sauce. I serve it sliced. It's pretty popular."

The owner still peels her own potatoes and makes her own french fries. "I don't like the frozen stuff."

Ever since she started working in the restaurant when she was 11, she has worked continually except for welcome breaks each autumn.

"When my husband was alive, we used to close from Labor Day until after Christmas and travel. Things were very cheap then. You could go away and stay at a motel for $20 a day. We used to travel across country. He used to have a license to fly a Piper Cub, and he used to fly all over. We drove cross-country five times. I didn't like flying too much in a small plane, but I went anyway.

"Now I'm open year 'round. I might take a week or 10 days off for a break in the winter."

In her spare hours outside the restaurant, Louise has been an energetic organizer of the annual Stafford Township Founder's Day parade and pageants. The trophies she has won for the parade floats rim the walls in the dining room. The flatbed she decorates each year is kept in her garage.

She has run annual beauty pageants for the Veterans of Foreign Wars, Barnegat Light Post 3729: the VFW Sweetheart Pageant for ages 14 to 18, and the Poppy Queen Pageant for ages 4 to 7. She runs a separate pageant for Southern Ocean County Hospital, and also raises money for Deborah Hospital. In 1988, the VFW voted her "Citizen of the Year."

Retirement? Someday

In 1974, the Hannolds were getting ready to exchange the pots and pans for retired life. "We had a buyer for the place, but then when Edward passed away, I thought I'd better keep it.

"Maybe it would have been better if I had gone out to work," Louise mused. "I'd be getting a pension now, like most of the women I know ... a telephone operator or something like that. But I'm happy. I have a lot of fun.

"In the morning it's a riot around here because I have people coming in and I have a lot of seniors, some widows and bachelors, and before you know it, they start talking and they get to know each other. Sometimes when they start talking about years ago, they find out that they graduated together. That's happened a lot in here.

"Regular customers look forward to seeing each other and us. If we're not busy, after they finish eating we'll sit there for a whole hour and talk. Today, four ladies sat there for an hour and a half. We were busy in and out, but not that I needed another table. So they sat there."

Hannold's is closed on Sundays, though she used to be open seven days a week. "They are still trying to get me to open up on Sundays. 'We'll bring a whole bunch of people,' they say. I say, 'Nah ...'

"Some Sundays I pretend I have nothing to do with the place at all."

But for the other six days a week, she greets her regulars waiting outside her door at five minutes to 8. And she's ready to make anyone who stops in a regular.

On the front of the restaurant is a sign her husband put up:

There is no place like this place anywhere near this place so this must be the place.

It has been for Louise Hannold.

— *Pat Johnson*

Dan and Barbara Soper

"Yes, I am a native.
And I'm glad
it shows."

As Stafford Township began to grow, new customers to Soper Cabinets stopped in from north Jersey towns and the western metropolis, ready to build part of their lives here.

"I bet you're a native," they surmised as they watched the cabinetmaker, Dan Soper.

"Yes, I am a native," he proudly replied. "And I'm glad it shows."

Dan and his wife, Barbara, are as "native" as it comes. Dan Soper inherited the same surname as the first full-time residents of Surf City. Sopers native to England had first settled in Huntington, Long Island before migrating southward to Long Beach Island. By the early to mid-1700s, the first Sopers reached Soper's Landing, between Barnegat and Waretown. In the early 1800s, some settled in Manahawkin and took up trade as baymen and oystermen, according to records researched by Dan and Barbara's daughter, Rhonda Traut.

The couple were chosen as grand marshals of 1998 Stafford Township Founder's Day Parade because, as one planning committee member put it, "their family has been here forever." Another reason was because, in a quiet way, they're one of those families who make a community go 'round.

Daniel and Barbara spent their lives in Manahawkin raising five children on the family homestead along Jennings Road and volunteering their time for many activities their kids have been involved in, including Cub Scouts, Girl Scouts, Little League, and the soccer teams. When Barbara first joined the PTA, the school library was a tiny 10-by-10-foot room, with the mothers taking turns acting as librarian.

Dan has been a volunteer with the Stafford Township Fire Co. since 1955 and has served as president and assistant chief. He also spent many hours as a member of the township school board. Barbara's work with the fire company auxiliary since the late

Dan and Barbara Soper were chosen as grand marshals of the 1998 Stafford Township Founder's Day Parade.

Barbara was once told by an agricultural extension agent that "there aren't any hickory trees in Ocean County."

Dan carved a niche for himself in the business community by knowing a skill that no one else had perfected.

Soper Cabinets was founded in 1962, but its roots are older. "I had started in the woodworking business in Forked River in 1951, working with Chester Treloar Millwork. One thing led to another." From custom millwork like entrance door frames, the job extended to "anything anybody wanted out of wood."

Later, working for a Forked River lumber yard, Bock Supply, Dan had a chance to branch out. "The owner didn't know anything at all about the cabinet business. He said, 'How about you taking over the cabinet business?' I said OK," he recounted, the tone of the OK sounding a lot more like *You bet!*

Sitting in their comfortable living room, Barbara pitched in. Actually, woodworking has been a "lifetime" pursuit for her husband. "He got awards when he was in high school. He spent all his time in the woodworking shop. So it's more or less a natural talent for him."

"I have a wood lathe out in the shop that I bought when I was 16 years old," Dan said.

"How'd you get the money for it at that age?" one might ask.

"Worked," he would answer.

Enterprising young men in Dan Soper's day — he was born in 1933 — often worked their way up the ladder from whatever rung they could reach.

Still a kid, he delivered the Philadelphia *Evening Bulletin*, and emptied the ashes out of a neighboring woman's furnace. "That's how I got the money for the lathe."

1950s includes years as president and treasurer.

Dan Soper's father, Henry Mills Soper, saw to it that his children each had a neighboring plot of Manahawkin land on which to base their lives.

The nearly one-acre lot where Dan and Barbara live is a tranquil place on the old portion of Jennings Road. Today, it connects southward to Route 72; then, it was a dead end into a "two-rut sand road that went down to Mill Creek."

"There are more than 100 hickory trees on the lot," Barbara and Dan have counted. A granddaddy tree in the front yard must have liked Manahawkin.

His first official "job" was at the Lakeside Diner, located as the name suggests, on Manahawkin Lake. Washing dishes, six days a week, 10 hours a day, paid $25 a week.

"So when they offered 75 cents an hour at Treloar's, that was quite an increase!" he laughed.

Much later, when he bought Chester Treloar's building, around 1964, "that was quite a step, I'll tell you," he said. Of course, by that time, he was already married to the former Barbara Ann Martin of Beach Haven Crest, and the couple had three children.

Installing the cabinets that went into many a home from Toms River to New Gretna and Long Beach Island, the craftsman worked mostly with birch, and "a tremendous amount of knotty pine." Wood always added warmth, but the trends were, at times, not to be explained. "There were a lot of brick orange countertops, and people would use avocado appliances with that," Dan recalled, shaking his head.

In 1969, after he sold his shop in Forked River, he talked to Bill Flynn, owner of Home Lumber. Dan was able to set up his own cabinet shop as part of that Manahawkin establishment.

When Flynn died, Dan went back into business for himself and leased a shop at Dee Lumber on East Bay Avenue. History repeated itself. "The president said, 'I don't know a thing about kitchen cabinets ...'"

In October 1982, Dan built his own shop on Indian Road, where Soper Cabinets stands today. His older son, Fred, operates the business, with younger son Tim and grandson Fred.

"It's still keeping the family busy."

A woodworker he has been, but a decoy-maker Dan does not profess to be. He was told he is related to noted decoy carver Sam Soper as a "second cousin once removed." His mantel holds a Sam Soper brant found for him by collector John Hillman. "I don't want to misrepresent myself and call myself a decoy carver," Dan said as he picked up a small bufflehead he had carved in a preening position. But it is an exquisite piece, nonetheless. "I did three in my life."

Fire Company a Part of Life

"If I was talking to you years ago and the siren rang," Dan said, "you'd be here by yourself." Barbara laughed in agreement.

Such was the business of a volunteer firefighter.

Ubiquitous fire calls interrupted anything and everything.

"They were lucky they were dressed part of the time," Barbara laughed, describing members trying to stretch gear on over bathing suits, on the run. There was no state law then that said you had to be fully dressed before riding.

The old drawings in children's books of firemen hanging on the back of a careening fire engine are another evaporated image. "That's against the law today."

As Stafford Township inflated through growth spurts in the last generation, community spirit suffered growing pains. The fire company's fund-raiser called "door tagging" — "that was the name for going house-to-house raising money" — didn't always get a caring reception in the new parts of town. "They'd say, 'We're only renting here.' I guess they didn't realize that house could catch fire, too."

Some fires in town were quite memorable, like the night in 1974 that the old grade school burned. "That was a bad fire; very dangerous. It collapsed one wall. It came down and hit a guide line pole and shook the wire on the poles on the street where the apparatus was," Dan remembered.

No one was injured, but Manahawkin lost a landmark.

For active fire company members, volunteering was a seven-day, 24-hour job, the Sopers said. Besides drills and keeping up to date on equipment, there were mutual aid calls to towns such as Tuckerton. "The old movie house, the church where we were married — the doggone things all burned in the middle of the night, and it was cold!"

For a forest fire, a man might be out for two days. So were the women at vigil that long — worrying, and making sandwiches and coffee for the crew. It wasn't uncommon to break for breakfast at the closest firehouse after spending the night near the blaze scene at, say, Warren Grove, "sleeping on the fire truck," Dan said.

Recovery from a stroke can leave a person in the position to treasure what's good around him.

Barbara has never been too far away. Her family and his family, and the other older ones in Manahawkin, have been entwined for generations. On their wall is a picture of the Manahawkin School graduation, 1909. Barbara pointed out two boys in the first row. "His dad and my grandmother's

A view from the Methodist church steeple, looking northwest, in 1964.

brother, Herschel Horner, went to school together. I think that's neat."

Barbara's family has deep roots in Manahawkin, too. Her great-grandfather, Harry "Dad" Horner, born in the mid-1800s, was a well-known basketmaker who lived in the house on Route 9 where the Cornucopia gift shop is. He used to hang his baskets of local white oak up in the trees, where Route 9 travelers couldn't miss them.

On Barbara's mother's side, she traced the Johnson line back five generations in Manahawkin. Harry Horner's wife, Evaline Johnson (1874-1947), was the daughter of David, who served with the N.J. Volunteers 9th Regiment in the mid-1800s.

Through the efforts of the Sopers' daughter, Rhonda, the Sopers also learned their lineage far beyond Daniel's parents, Henry Soper and Freida Homeyer. Henry was a child of Philip Soper (1864-1927) and Sallie Letts, who also lived their whole lives in Manahawkin. Philip's father was Isaac, born in 1814 in the Barnegat-Waretown area, who first married Rebecca Haywood and then Elizabeth Hazelton.

Dan returned to woodworking after illness forced a year's layoff. "The first thing I did after my stroke was a baptismal font for the Methodist church," he described. "It was octagonal in shape. For the water, I used one of the old collection plates from 1922.

"It was fun doing," he said, but it got done only through his wife's help. "We worked on that for five months."

Reflecting on his life while walking slowly outside to the yard, he said, "I've slowed down since. But I have plans."

Not surprisingly, they involve woodworking, and family.

"I want to build a nanny's rocker. It's a combined rocking chair and cradle. It would be for a small child, with a doll.

"Originally, before Rhonda had her baby, I told her, I said, 'This is going to be for our next either granddaughter or great-granddaughter.' Well, at that point, she almost knew she was having a boy!"

— *Maria Scandale*

Barbara Eismann

*"People really
believed in
healthful sea air.
In fact, I remember
when they started
taking soil from the
mainland to build
on the beach. People
were concerned it
would contaminate
the air."*

Growing up and living in Manahawkin has been very sweet for Barbara Eismann, who with her husband, Larry, has owned Lucille's Own-Make Candy Shop since 1954.

Barbara's family has been in the area at least since her grandfather Howard Conklin's time.

"My grandfather was born in Cedar Run. They used to pay him $5 a game to pitch for the baseball games, he was so good. He'd play for either Manahawkin or Cedar Run; it didn't matter to him which one as long as he got paid.

"He also used to ride a bicycle three hours from Cedar Run to Northfield to court my grandmother Ida.

"We used to call her our 'hot tea grandmom.' I don't know why. Maybe she liked to drink hot tea," Barbara began telling her family memories. "But she was a little woman and she ruled the family with an iron fist. She was my mother's mother. She had a son that was 45 still living with her; and if he left dishes in the sink or he sassed her, she took the broom to him."

Howard Conklin used to run the railroad bridge, a job that yielded many stories in itself.

"How he happened to work there — my mother, Mary, was sickly and Dr. Hilliard told my grandfather to take her over to the beach for the salt air and sunshine. So my grandfather got the job as drawbridge tender for the Pennsylvania Railroad. His job was to lower and raise the drawbridge for the trains. He turned the crank by hand.

"One time the train was over on the Island and it had to get back and the bay was rough, so my grandfather got in his rowboat and he started rowing out but he wasn't getting very far. It was too hard to row, so he tied the boat up, dove in the bay, and swam to the drawbridge."

When Barbara's mother was a young girl, the causeway was "one long bridge," as Barbara described.

The candy business has shown sweet success to Barbara Eismann.

"On the north side of the first Causeway bridge, you'll notice there are some pilings sticking out that kind of slope up. Well, those were put there to break the ice up when there was one long bridge and they had trouble with the ice running into it. You'll notice when the bay does freeze over, the ice does go up those."

In her own younger days, the span to the island was actually several bridges, but they were still made of wood. "Sometimes when it was real quiet you could hear the bridges rattling with all the cars going over them."

Brother in a Box

Howard and Ida Conklin were also caretakers for a gun club on Cedar Bonnet Island that has since been torn down.

"That first street, where the Dutchman's is now, that's where Grandmom's hunting club was. And there was nothing there then — just one other house. A little girl lived there and my mom used to go play. They would make boats, get hold of cardboard boxes and put tar in the seams, and she would launch them in a salt marsh puddle. Being a typical child, she was going to give her brother a ride. My grandmom was in the house cleaning and she happened to look out, and Mother had put her little brother in the box. She had the box tied to a string and when she yanked it, her little brother fell into the bay. Grandmom had to run down and save him."

Barbara recalled many wonderful stories about her mother's childhood in a Manahawkin of earlier times.

"Mother would also make mud pies with wild duck eggs and bake them in the sun.

"With the salt air and the sun, my mother became strong — she wasn't sick anymore. People really believed in healthful sea air. In fact, I remember when they started taking soil from the mainland to build on the beach. People were concerned it would contaminate the air.

"When my mother had to go to school, she had two ways of going. One was she went to school by train at 6 o'clock in the morning, and took the 6 o'clock train home at night. They had a lady over in Manahawkin to take care of her, but being a kid, she roamed Manahawkin and she knew all the old people and she learned all about flowers and how to do this or that. The other way to go to school was my grandfather would take her on his motorcycle. And they said if they hit a bump, her father would just grab hold of her dress and pull her back down on the seat."

Barbara's mother's married name was Garrison. Barbara was born in her grandmother Garrison's house on Bay Avenue at the end of Jennings Road in 1934. The house stood until 1999, when the townshp tore it down to build the new town hall.

"Up until I was married, I only lived in two houses — my grandmother's house, and when I was 4, we moved away from there to where I lived on Stafford Avenue. I lived across from the Methodist church. It's now the parking lot of the fire company.

"So I grew up in Manahawkin proper, on Stafford Avenue and Union Street, and with that group of kids ... there were 10 or 12 of us and we would play hide and seek in people's yards. A group of us would run all over town and you didn't have to worry about getting hurt or anything like that. You could sleep with your doors open. It was nice."

The Garrison house was next to a field they called the commons. The lot stretched between the railroad and the church, and it became a popular baseball field.

"Sure, I knew Doc Cramer," Barbara noted, of the major league baseball player who was a Manahawkin hometown boy. "His daughter Joan and I went to school together."

A Dog Named Muggins

"There was always hunting around here," Barbara said. "Can you imagine anyone walking down Beach Avenue today with a shotgun over their shoulder like they used to?

"This dog I'm going to tell you about was named Muggins. The mother of the dog was a thoroughbred hound dog that belonged to my grandfather. The father of the dog was mixed Airedale and police dog. Muggins had one ear that stood up and one that lay down. My brother bought him off my grandfather for two nickels. But my grandfather was the type who would slip you a dime or a nickel to go get ice cream, so my brother got his money back three times over.

"My dad trained him to be a hunting dog. I can remember my mother hollering at my father. He would take a hot dog and run it across the kitchen floor and this dog would just sniff it out, following the trail.

"Anyway, my father worked for Kings' and they had thoroughbred hound dogs, and they made fun of Muggins. But Daddy always came back with his quota of rabbits with Muggins, and they didn't with their purebred hounds. Mugs was good.

"Muggins also stole rugs. He had a rug behind the stove and it got smelly; my grandmother threw it out. Well, a little while later, he brings home this rug and we didn't know who it belonged to. We didn't find out till years later, when a neighbor was talking about how she had thrown a rug over her railing and came back for it and it was gone. And she described it and Grandmom went 'uh-oh.'"

Barbara's father worked at Howard E. King's Garage. "He sold Fords and Mercurys, next to where the Diamond Mine is today. That building used to be the American Grocery Store. Also on that corner was Bill Soper's Meat Market and the drug store. You were allowed to park in front of them and you didn't have to worry about getting run over when you crossed the street.

"During World War II, the ladies had a canteen in King's showroom for the servicemen who were traveling. They had coffee and doughnuts. They had it once or twice a week, so that the boys would have some place to wait after they got off the bus. My mother was involved and naturally she took me with her. I remember they had a sign with all the names of the boys in town that were in the service on it.

"Also, during the war, our church (Methodist) had a speaker in the belfry. At 12 o'clock, someone would go there and start playing hymns, just for 10 to 15 minutes, and one of our local men would sing over the speaker. It was nice; on your way home, it was peaceful and you knew the community was safe.

"At that time, the Baptist church was closed and the Lutheran church wasn't built. It was just the Methodist church."

"There was a little building on Stafford Avenue that belonged to the Hazeltons and that was the apothecary shop — Dr. Lane's Pharmacy. They later took it down to Smithville.

"Cranmer had a lumber yard and his wife, Jennie Cranmer, was our eighth-grade teacher. She taught my grandfather in kindergarten and she taught my aunts and uncles and my mother. My brother's class was the last class she taught, but she was the principal when I was in the lower grades.

"The kindergarten was in one room, first and second in another, and third and fourth another. There was three rooms downstairs and two rooms upstairs. The big room upstairs was fifth and sixth, and the seventh and eighth was in the principal's room in the back. It was two flights of stairs and you got your exercise running up and down the steps.

"I can remember at lunchtime walking home from school. First you would stop at the post office and then go home for lunch. And you knew everybody in school and their parents, and sometimes their grandparents. And if you did something wrong, your parents knew about it before you got home.

"When we graduated from eighth grade, we used to have our class picture taken in the Methodist

This 1930s or '40s-era postcard was labeled "The busy corner." Barbara's father sold Fords and Mercurys at Howard E. King's garage, visable behind the Sinclair gas bays.

church. My husband is standing right behind me in our picture."

A Match Made in Candy Heaven

"I married into the candy making. I married an outsider. My husband, Larry, moved down here in the second grade and we've been friends ever since.

"He was the new boy in town — he had been going to school in Philadelphia and he wore stockings and knickers and suspenders and a tie. I bet we broke many a pair of his suspenders. Well, he dressed different than we did — we wore flannel shirts and dungarees. But his mother wouldn't buy new clothes for him until the next year.

"Being a new person was difficult because then we Stafford natives were the majority. It's different now; now we're the minority.

Lucille's Own-Make Candies was named for Barbara's mother-in-law. Before the Eismanns moved to Manahawkin, they had a luncheonette in the Tacony section of Philadelphia.

"They had a soda fountain and candy, and her mother would make the pies and cook for them," said Barbara. "And then the war came along. During the Second World War, the federal government froze prices, and Dad Eismann wasn't charging enough to make the business work. Also, Larry's health wasn't so good. Their doctor told them to get

him out of the city, so they got the old house on Bay Avenue. Dad Eismann had different jobs around, and then he opened up the store."

The original shop was a penny candy store that also sold ice cream. "They moved the store several times, and then she got into making candy," Barbara said. The shop was at 449 East Bay Avenue, a good location because it was in the path of everyone who was going over to Long Beach Island.

When Lucille's opened in 1947, Larry started working there after school, Barbara said. "They made chocolate and fudge. They started out with just a small cream beater. The creme filling is a liquid when you first start out. A cream beater is a piece of machinery shaped like a big cake pan and a motor with three blades on it, and as that went around in a circle, the creme would become a solid. Then they would have to roll the cremes by hand. If you were real good, you could roll two cremes at once.

"Mom Eismann coated every piece of chocolate that came out of there by hand. She had a puddle of chocolate and how you know it's the right temperature is if it's cool to your lip; if it's hot to your lip, you're going to have gray chocolate because it doesn't dry right. The center also has to be the right temperature. You can't coat a cold center with warm chocolate — it's going to go gray. So she would do all this by hand and string them. She was very fast."

When Barbara got married, she joined in the work, but not as candy-maker, at first. "I was never fast. I was never taught to make the candy, only to sell it and later to do the office work."

They also had a store in Beach Haven behind Kapler's Pharmacy. The shop in Brant Beach was established in 1965. "When we started wholesaling and business grew, we moved over here to Route 72.

"We made taffy at one time, but then it got to the point that Larry was over here on weekends and all hours and — hey, you have to have a life, too."

Remember Yellow Jackets?

"Like everything else, candy goes in and out of fashion," Barbara's experience told her. "When we first opened, we used to make hard candies called Yellow Jackets. You'd pull it out of the paper and you had a little silver hammer that you'd hit it with and crack off a piece. It was hard, chewy candy like a taffy.

"We used to make haystacks — that's a molasses coconut. You'd roll it so it would look like a haystack. Seafoam was a candy that would just melt in your mouth. We'd make two or three different flavors of that. Divinity — a vanilla with nuts in it.

We used to sell a lot of plaited mint, a mint that they would braid in bars.

"Now we sell mostly fudge and salt water taffy. We make all our fudge and we have always cut it up in little squares. Since 1947, been cutting it up in little squares. People sometimes ask us why we don't have it in chunks, but we think this way you get more flavors in each box.

Yes, candy has been good to the Eismanns, Barbara said. "I'd do better if I didn't eat as much candy, but I love it. I like the fudge when it's warm ... and the caramel when it's warm. Well, the trouble is — I like it all."

It's hard to imagine a more enjoyable job, but Barbara had another vocation in mind when she was young.

"I always wanted to be a beautician, and I went to New York to beautician school. I never practiced hairdressing because my husband didn't want me to work! And I didn't work for the first year we were married, but after that, I worked all the time.

"My husband always said it was an awful thing he did to his best friend: he married her and put her to work!"

— *Pat Johnson*

Mud City and Mallard Island

"We'd have friends and family visit often. They enjoyed walking alongside the bay, going out on the dock at sunset and then gorging themselves on the clams and fish that we had caught fresh that day."

One area of Stafford Township that remained relatively unaffected by growth and development as the town celebrated its 250th anniversary is an isolated strip of land bordering the bay along Old Bay Avenue. Today, some longtime residents of the marshlands known as Mud City and Mallard Island look back fondly on quiet days gone by spent working and playing on these picturesque lowlands where the township meets the bay.

Sigmund "Ziggy" Kalicki first came to this edge of the bay in 1937 and recalls the majestic views and quiet surroundings that initially drew him. "There were only a few houses, then, north of Old Bay Avenue," he recalled. "We used to walk up these 'mosquito ditches,' as we called them, and get a whole basket of crabs in less than an hour. But things changed as more people came in."

He remembers the old wooden bridge spanning the waters to Long Beach Island and the backed-up traffic on weekends every time the center drawbridge would open to allow a boat to pass underneath. "The natives wouldn't like it at all. Sometimes the cars would be tied up all the way back to Route 9 and beyond. What a mess!"

Ziggy explained the boundaries of Mud City and where Mallard Island begins, defining what has become years of confusion over the matter. "Where Margo's Boats is now was a ditch where the old railroad tracks were just north of the original bridge. The trains went right by the span, and that's the area known as Mud City. It really runs from where Tonneson's and the creek was right to the edge of the bay — only several hundred feet or so. The rest here is Mallard Island," he said.

Recognizing the potential of a spot so close to the main artery leading thousands of tourists and visitors through Manahawkin to the Island every summer, Ziggy Kalicki decided to build the area's first Stewart's Root Beer franchise on the spot where the Mud City Crab House Seafood Grille and Market stands today

Sigmund "Ziggy" Kalicki has called Mud City home since 1937 and has been known as its "unofficial mayor."

at East Bay Avenue and Marsha Drive.

"Before the 1962 storm, we got the permit, but the storm delayed our construction. When we opened, though, it was a great operation, with car hops, trays that hung from your window and curb service, just like in the movies."

Motorists who were caught in the traffic jams to and from the beach would be served right at their cars on the road as the Kalicki crew fanned out, taking and delivering orders.

"We had a very successful business there for over 18 years," the owner recalled with a smile. "Since I sold it to the Spaghetti Pot in 1984, there have been several food operations there."

But it was the charm of Mallard Island that evokes the fondest memories for Kalicki and others who have called this marshland and its single, winding road home for decades.

"The fishing and crabbing were always great here. We'd have friends and family visit often. They enjoyed walking alongside the bay, going out on the dock at sunset and then gorging themselves on the clams and fish that we had caught fresh that day. Those were the days!"

Causeway Shack's Gunning Club Days

Known now as the unofficial "mayor of Mud City," Ziggy Kalicki also gave insight into the origins of the famous "fisherman's shack" that now sits south of the Causeway and has been the subject of countless paintings and photographs over the years.

"It wasn't always there where it sits now, crumbling away," he said. "We had it over here on the other side of the road for most of its life. It was a gunning shack for the duck hunters. They had a club over here on the north side of Route 72 where they would gather to go out hunting in their sneakboxes and in the duck blinds along the bay shore.

"My brother, Chester, and I knew Hank Thomas and his friend, Huey Singleton, who worked at DuPont in Parlin and who would come down often to hunt. That shack you see today was originally their gunning club headquarters just about every weekend.

"The really interesting thing, though, was that their wives used it more than they did." Ziggy grinned. "While they were waiting for their husbands to return from the hunt, they would spend hours sitting around a long, hand-hewn table to play cards. It was just penny ante poker, but they took the games quite seriously — sometimes raising their voices and having good-natured arguments over who really won a hand or what cards were played."

When the shack got overcrowded, Huey Singleton decided to move the structure to a better location, and the Kalicki brothers said that wouldn't be a problem at all. "My father was a house mover for many years and we knew how to do it," Ziggy said. "Nobody else around here knew about such things, but we did."

Singleton had gone from being a renter of the cabin to becoming its owner, courtesy of his associates at DuPont, according to Ziggy. " 'We have to move it because of the new Route 72 highway that's

Bonnet Gunning Association

East of the Mud City train stop (Hilliards) was the last stop before reaching Long Beach Island. It was called Martins on the railroad schedule.

The building on Cedar Bonnet Island that became the Bonnet Gunning Association was built after 1887 by Humphrey Martin and run by him and his wife, Malinda. When the train left there, it crossed over the drawbridge and continued to Long Beach Island. The old-timers before the 1920s knew the sportsmen's club as Martin's, while the younger generation were growing up around the Bonnet Club, as it was known after its purchase by the Bonnet Gunning Association. Fishermen and gunners who frequented the Bonnet Club were advised of the best spots by keeper Phineas Cranmer, and fed by his wife, Rebecca. Their son, Alden, also lived there year 'round. Local men recall that the Bonnet Club was "one of the real gunning clubs" of the area, attracting wealthy fellows from the city.

The gunning association was under renovation as The Duck Inn marina in 1964, above. Its rooms still housed summer renters at the turn of the 21st century.

Railway travelers could stop at Martin's or continue on to Long Beach Island.

The City of Mud

Ever wonder how Mud City got its name? Ed Hazelton knows the story. The setting is Avenue A, about 1924.

"Next to our house, Harry Randall and John Horner bought a lot and they had Luke Courtney build them a little bungalow. Luke Courtney had my Uncle Henry Hazelton, who was a carpenter, help him.

"Those old fellows took a post hole digger at times and went down in the mud as far as they could, then put the piling in, and jumped up and down, using their weight. They used a cant hook to turn it around, and jumped up and down, and pounded with a tuck — that was a heavy pipe with a handle. And by the time they got done walking around on the meadows between all these pilings, plus the tide coming up, it got awful muddy.

"They would lay their tools up on top of a piling or a joist, and the vibration would make it fall off in the muddy meadows. You'd pick it up and it'd be all wet and muddy. So this happened two or three times to Uncle Henry, and the last time it happened, Uncle Henry says, 'The damn mud!' He says, 'C.H.' — that was my grandfather, C.H. Cranmer — 'C.H. ought to name this the City of Mud.'

"And from that came Mud City.

"Somebody else tells a different story, but I know — I was a kid and I saw it." — *Maria Scandale* coming in,' he told us, and we made plans to get it across the road to a piece of land he bought," Ziggy remembered. The gunning club building was jacked up and rolled gently to its present location in the early 1960s, where it hosted more hunters and their card-playing spouses.

When Huey Singleton died, his wife, Stella, continued the tradition and would often visit with the Albert brothers (founders of Albert Hall) on their small farm in Waretown.

"She would still come down here to visit her old haunts on Mud City and Mallard Island, though. They all kept up their interest in duck hunting and, of course, playing those card games," Ziggy said.

When the federal government began declaring much of the area as designated wetlands back in the '80s, the gunning shack and much of Mud City and Mallard Island were seemingly limited from further development, preserving the marshland in its present state for generations to come.

"Back in the 1930s, there were only four buildings that comprised Mud City, and one was the old hotel that also served as the train stop beside the bridge," Ziggy explained. "It's the building that Margo's Boats has now. My other brother, John, developed it and called it after his wife's name, which was Margo."

The original structure was known as Thomas Cranmer's Bay Side Inn, built about 1917 and the scene of many pleasant stays overlooking Mud City and the bay beyond.

The other three houses were owned by "very good friends," according to Ziggy, but were occupied only during the summer months.

"The only full-time residents were the clam diggers who made their living from the bay." That living was disrupted by the two big storms that hit the island — the 1944 hurricane and the Great March Storm of 1962, which covered Mud City and Mallard Island with several feet of choppy salt water, Ziggy remembers vividly.

"By far the worst was the 1962 storm when the water got all backed up in the bay for several days. I remember wading through waist-deep water and slipping into a drainage ditch, which soaked me to the skin."

At high tide, he "borrowed" a rowboat from a shed belonging to one of the local clam diggers to float out to see his property on Penguin Road. "The water was so high, it swept tons of eelgrass up to the roof and even blocked the doorway. It took days to clean up."

Today, the longtime residents seem to take solace in their relative isolation, far from the "maddening crowds," as they put it. Rapid development in other parts of the township hasn't yet touched their tranquil preserve on Mallard Island and the remnants of Mud City.

"When Beach Haven West was first built, we wondered if we would be inundated, too," Ziggy said. "Thank God that was not to be. This is where we live, and we like it just fine, just the way it is."

— *Jim De Francesco*

Calvin Conklin sold oysters and clams, both to the wholesale market and to people who stopped by the restaurant at the east end of Bay Avenue. Customers could also rent a rowboat and get a taste of the bayman's life for themselves. The establishment was located at the Hilliards train stop.

Burrel Adams

"When my brother and I were growing up, my mother used to tie a rope around our waist and let us fish out the window."

Burrel Adams was just two years old in 1923 when his father moved the family from New Gretna to a house in the middle of Barnegat Bay. His father took the job of bridge-tender on the old swing bridge that connected Cedar Bonnet Island to Long Beach Island, and then manned the newer drawbridge, built in 1928, until the concrete causeway was finished 31 years later.

Most of the bridge-tender's house hung out over the water. It was pictured on postcards of the times. It wasn't a very big house for the family of four, Burrel said, but it had a big porch on the front and the view was expansive. All the windows looked out across the bay.

"When my brother and I were growing up, my mother used to tie a rope around our waist and let us fish out the window," recalled Burrel, who now resides on a wooded lot in Tuckerton.

"My dad used to shoot ducks off the back porch. There were plenty of ducks and geese in the winter time. He had a sneakbox and a ladder going down to the boat so he could go out and get them."

The nearest dry land was Cedar Bonnet Island, which at that time had only half a dozen houses on it.

The bridge to Long Beach Island was called the Long Bridge because it stretched in one continuous wooden span from Mud City, then named Hilliards, on the mainland to Bonnet Island and Cedar Bonnet Island, where the drawbridge completed the link to Long Beach Island.

The Long Bridge was built of pine planks. "You could hear the cars from the time they hit one end to another. They would rumble all across."

The planks, coated with creosote, were very flammable. A cigarette thrown from a car was enough to start a small fire. Part of Burrel's father's job was to jump in his Model T and rush down to extinguish fires started when a motorist threw a butt out the window.

The original bridge was a swing bridge, operating like a turnstile. The tender opened or closed a section of bridge by dropping a big Y-shaped key into a slot, then slipping poles into both arms of the Y and walking in a circle. This motion turned gears in the bridge, opening it to allow boats to pass through the channel. If Burrel's father was away, his mother would have passengers get out of their cars to help her.

A converted tractor motor powered the drawbridge that replaced the swing bridge.

At that time the Tuckerton Railroad still ran on a railroad bed built on the north side of the bridge. Made of cinders and heavy timbers, it was real solid, Adams said. It was elevated to the height of the bridge. When he was a boy the Barnegat City line and passenger cars had been discontinued, having been replaced by buses and automobiles. But a freight train to the fisheries and lumber yards of Ship Bottom and Beach Haven passed across the rails twice a day. An approaching train had to stop and wait for the railroad bridge to close, because it was kept open until the train arrived.

"So, the train got into Mud City and you could see the smoke stack puffing away, black smoke and cinders, as she stopped at Hilliard's Station, where Margo's marina is now.

"Our mother had her wash out on the line, and when the wind was blowing from the railroad, we used to have to stand and watch for the train. When we saw her coming, my mother would run out and take the sheets down."

Some of the train bed is still there under the weeds and trees at the end of the causeway on the western side of Ship Bottom, Burrel said.

His family's unique address posed a dilemma as to which school Burrel would attend.

"When I started school they had a problem, because the center of the drawbridge and channel was the boundary line between Stafford Township and Ship Bottom," he said. "Technically we were living in Ship Bottom, and I was supposed to go to school in Beach Haven. At that time I was seven years old, but as it turned out, the state already decided to build a new bridge and they knew they were going to move us, and move the house to Bonnet Is-

Photojournalist Burrel Adams captured the 1930s and beyond with his Speed Graphic camera.

land. So we got permission that as long as I walked down to the end of the bridge in Stafford Township, I could go to school."

When the state finished the new drawbridge, they moved down to a house on Cedar Bonnet Island around 1927. "I remember the date because when Lindbergh flew the Atlantic, we were in that house."

Burrel had a few playmates in the Fackler family, the only other family that lived on Cedar Bonnet Island. Adams' playmates were twins Billy and Betty and their older brother, Jack. They lived for a while in the old Bay Side Club, where their father was caretaker, and then moved into a house where The Dutchman's Brauhaus is now.

"Their father, Charlie Fackler, got a small building, a houseboat or something, and set up a small store for bait and so forth, and then he got a liquor license and started Charlie's Bar and Restaurant. And it was quite a famous place around here."

The patrons were mainly from the beach, locals from Ship Bottom, Surf City and Harvey Cedars. Across the street, the Van Kestern started a bar and restaurant called Van's.

At that time, Burrel and the Facklers all went to school in Manahawkin by hitching a ride on the school bus that was taking the Island girls and boys to Barnegat High School. The Manahawkin Elementary School on Beach Avenue had five rooms. The first and second grades were on the first floor and were taught by Miss Irene Hazelton, who later married Paul Cranmer. Her sister, Edna, had the third and fourth grade.

"Miss Edna lived a couple blocks over from the school," said Burrel. "Her mother would make up her lunch every day, and she would send one of the boys down to pick up her basket."

Also on the first floor, Miss Mae Cranmer taught the fifth grade. On the second floor, the sixth and seventh grades were taught by Maude Black. The eighth grade was under the tutelage of the principal, Jennie Cranmer. The class size got smaller as the years went up; eighth grade had the fewest students because many left school to go to work.

"We learned worldwide geography. You had to learn all the continents; you had to know your globe," said Burrel. "The globe was a big thing; we loved to play with that. You learned the distance between places and all sorts of things. Then we had the big pull-down map of the world and the United States. We had to know all the states and their capitals.

"You learned a lot by rote besides your book. You had to give oral reports — you got called on and you better have something to say when you stood up. Then we had to learn the state of New Jersey, too; all the counties and local history. When we graduated from grade school, we were given a copy of the state constitution.

"We had a helping teacher, too, named Sarah Hernberg. She was also the state representative who would pop in unexpectedly during the day and would rate the teacher. And when she came in, we had to know all the things about the county. Many times, the New Jersey superintendent of schools, Charles Morris, would come with her and they would talk about the Revolutionary War.

"Then we had J. Henry Bartlett. He was an old Quaker from Tuckerton, and he would come and talk to us about the Indians and different things from the locality. One of his favorite things was to ask some child, 'What is your last name?' And they would tell him and he would say, 'All right, your grandfather was such and such, your great-grandfather was such and such, and your family goes back to this or that.' We thought it was a pain in the neck. I never liked history back then. I didn't like history until I was in the service and came back home again, and then I got interested and tried to catch up on everything.

"Most of the things they gave us on the Indians I still recollect. We had to learn the basic language of the Turtle Clan, one of the clans of the Lenni Lenape that came to Manahawkin. The Turtle Clan, the Wolf and the Turkey Clan used to come to this area. The Turtle Clan came to Manahawkin to the bay to get their clams and fish. They had a limited vocabulary. We learned their alphabet and the language. If you read *The Tides of Time*, a section on Stafford Township Indians was written by us schoolchildren.

"Now at that time, Quaker Oats came in a big, round cardboard box and we took a piece of rubber and stretched it over the top to make a drum, and we learned an Indian song. It was like a chant, and then we went 'yo!'"

Across from the school on Beach Avenue was a big field where the boys played baseball.

Since Manahawkin's baseball celebrity, Roger "Doc" Cramer, lived next to the field, he would often supply the balls, bats and gloves for a game. When Doc was playing a game on Long Beach Island, a baseball scout spotted Cramer and Doc signed with the Philadelphia Athletics in 1928. Every year after that the town kids were taken to Shibe Park (later Connie Mack Stadium) in Philadelphia for Doc Cramer Day.

"Jimmy Mascola had the bowling alley" (six lanes in what is now Carroll's restaurant), "and he also had the business of handling all the bottled soda, like Nehi, a popular drink, and, of course, Coke. He had this big panel delivery truck for the soda, and every year on Doc Cranmer Day he'd fill it up with hay and we'd pile into it and he'd drive it to Shibe Park in Philadelphia, the Athletics' home field. We got to see the game, we had free popcorn, peanuts and hot dogs, and we got to go down to the dugout and meet the players.

"We were about 12, 13 — teenagers, because they didn't take any younger kids. One year we went in and Babe Ruth was playing, but he didn't hit any home runs. We wanted to see Doc hit a home run. He played center field. We all cheered when he came out."

For fun activities, besides the bowling alley and Stager's Music Hall where silent pictures, medicine shows and slide shows were the regular entertainment, there were swimming and skating on the lake and a firemen's carnival each year.

"Everybody came from all around to the firemen's carnival at the lake," Burrel said. "It was during the Depression and there were wheels of chance and bingo with prizes like a five-pound box of sugar, a pound of chocolates or a waffle iron."

For shopping, Manahawkin had stores like Phoebe's, which kept up on the latest styles for women. A dry goods store, Niesa's, was in a big, old building behind the railroad station on Stafford Avenue. The owner stocked thread and bolts of cloth.

Burrel's family would also go to Tuckerton on a Saturday to shop and visit with relatives. He and his brother were dropped off at the matinee at the Community Theater on Main Street. In later years, Burrel's future wife, Alva Cullison, was an usherette.

Capturing Island Society on Film

"I got into photography because I made a pest of myself," Burrel remarked. "When I was in the seventh grade, I met up with Monk Lynn. I think his real name was Howard or Harold. He was the original Lynn (of Lynn Photo). I met up with him because he used to hang out in Charlie's Bar on the Island.

"He had this camera and he was always taking pictures, and it fascinated the heck out of me ... and he had a studio over in Surf City. I went over there and I bought a camera for something like 79 cents. It was called a Univex, Bakelite with a glass lens. I took the film over to his place to have it done and I saw these pictures that he had around the place. He was a great photographer. He had an eye for it.

"So I got interested. I kept pestering him about how he did it. So one time when I asked him how he developed pictures, he said, 'Now look, are you really interested?' And I said yes, so he said, 'I'll tell you what, you ask your father if after school you can come over and I will teach you about photography. But I will not pay you. Because if I pay you, you'll be here for the money, but if you are really interested, you'll do what I say and stick with it.'

"So I asked my dad and he said, 'Well, OK, if you want to work without money. I'll tell you one thing: I'll know where you're at every night.'

"So that's what happened. Monk used the correct approach. For weeks after I went over, all I did was clean up all the messes in the darkroom, clean the trays — all the dirty work. But in return for that, I got to stay in the darkroom and watch him make the prints and the enlargements.

"The more I watched, the more I loved it. And I bought my first flash camera, a box camera put out by Agfa. Then I started to take pictures of people. I used to go with him and carry the equipment. He did all the high school pictures in Tuckerton.

"So I had this camera and I would go all over the beach shooting pictures. I had a terrific group of negatives that were all lost when I went into the service."

The young photo buff started taking pictures professionally when he met Jack Lamping, the public relations director for the Long Beach Board of Trade. Lamping asked Burrel if he was interested in taking pictures for the board and later convinced "Ham" George Willits Parker, publisher of the *Tuckerton Beacon* and *Beach Haven Times*, to hire Burrel as a free-lance photographer.

"Ham said, 'Sure, and as a matter of fact we have a Speed Graphic camera here that nobody uses,' and he brought it out. Well, this was like somebody bringing a Cadillac out. My gosh, a Speed Graphic!" The Graphic was the typical camera that you see newspaper photographers holding in old movies, Burrel explained.

In the late '30s, the dollar a print that he got paid was a respectable wage, especially for a job he enjoyed. So young Burrel gladly went out on his own as a photojournalist. With Jack Lamping at Board of Trade functions, he met celebrities and officials.

"Then there was a society page that appeared weekly in one of the Philadelphia papers; it was either *The Inquirer* or *The Bulletin*. The Board of Trade would try and get as many pictures in of

Drawbridge and causeway across Barnegat Bay.

prominent people vacationing on the Island as we could. So we would go over to the yacht club in Beach Haven or up to the Engleside at the tennis courts and we'd photograph these people. I especially remember Big Bill Tilden, the tennis champion.

"After I graduated from Tuckerton High School in 1940, I decided to set up business for myself and I scraped up enough money to start it from my paper route on Cedar Bonnet Island. I sold *The Ledger, The Camden Courier, The Bulletin* and *The Record.* I also sold magazines.

"Along with the paper route, every week when I collected, I learned what people had been doing during the week because my mother was the social column writer for the *Tuckerton Beacon* for Cedar Bonnet Island. She didn't really care that much about it, so I would get the information and I did the write-ups for five cents an inch. The content of the columns were things that seem silly now, but it was a big honor then to say, 'I went to Atlantic City and had dinner at a certain restaurant' or 'I went to Atlantic City and went to Blatts' store,' which was a big store. So I would get these things and rewrite them, and out of one inch I could get an inch and a half or two inches. So I wrote a lot and people liked it. I did that for years and Mom would get the check.

"In line with that, when I went overseas in the service in England, Ham Parker, who was still the head of *The Beacon,* sent every enlisted man a free subscription to *The Beacon.*

"In the barracks, a lot of guys would get their hometown papers and we'd exchange them even though we didn't know the people involved — because it was still something from home. So I would get *The Beacon* and pass it around and these guys used to laugh. Marion Leek was a lady who was always in the social columns. She was always doing something and they'd say, 'Hey, Adams, what's Mrs. Leek doing? Did she go to Atlantic City again?' They got the biggest kick out of it, 'cause nobody else's paper had anything like it."

Before he entered the service, Burrel took all the money he had saved and bought another camera. At that time, you had to have an ID card if you had a boat, used a boat or rowed in a boat. You had to have a yellow card with your picture on it and your thumb print, three copies of it. So every member of the fishery had to have one. And the fisheries in Barnegat Light, Beach Haven Crest and Ship Bottom employed hundreds of Scandinavian fishermen. Also, anybody who lived down here and had a sneakbox or a garvey, anyone who went out in the water had to have one.

"Monk Lynn called me up and said he couldn't be bothered with making these things ... he charged $2 to make the set of them, and they had to be ready so they could take them to Atlantic City to the Coast Guard to be signed by the commandant of the Coast Guard.

"It was actually a hardship for some people, but you had to get it done.

"When Monk said, 'Why don't you take these pictures?' I said, 'Fine.' So I started taking these portraits and I took hundreds of them. I still have many negatives of these portraits I shot for $2 apiece."

When Burrel entered the service, he went to the Army Air Corps photo school.

"I was supposed to be an observer; that meant I was to fly with a camera. But things changed on that. We were the 13th bomber group to come into England. At that time, they were killing photographers really fast because of the section of plane where you had to sit in, a thing in the floor in the radio room you had to crawl into, called 'the coffin.'

"You had to lift the lid and sit down in it. It was just ahead of the ball turret where the gunner sat. It was a big, long thing. It had holes in it in various locations and when you sat down in it, it was miserable cold because of the air blowing through. The German fighters would try to get the gunner in the ball turret and, missing him, they would hit the radio room. They were killing photographers faster than (we) could supply them.

"So about that time they came out with an automatic camera, a beautiful job. There was a toggle switch that was tripped by the third bomb that was dropped, and the camera would go *click, click, click* as the bombs were dropped. So photographers were no longer flying.

"At first we griped about it until the first mission came back and we had to clean out a section of the radio room. The radio man was killed. A 20-millimeter shell had come right up through the camera section and blew up in his face. We had to go and take the automatic camera out. I didn't like it; it made me sick, but it had to be done. The guy behind me when he saw it said, 'Thank God we don't have to fly.'

"So I worked in the photo lab, did public relations. I could carry a camera anywhere in England because I had a badge. I got to take pictures of bombed-out areas where civilians weren't allowed. I also got to photograph stars that came to the USO.

"The Glenn Miller Orchestra was stationed right in town, and they used to jam and jive at the USO Club in the evening. They were sent to London and assigned to the U.S. Army Air Force band, and every night they would come in the USO Club. They were a great bunch."

But it wasn't all glamour.

"Every plane that came back in, we had to photograph all the bomb damage, every bit. And because I was the smallest person in the group, skinny and short, I got stuck taking pictures in places nobody else could get into. I had to crawl around inside where the gas tanks were. They'd put you inside and you had to take a picture."

When the war was over, Burrel came home to Stafford to find that when his family had moved from one house on Cedar Bonnet Island to another, they hadn't taken the boxes of negatives he had stored in the attic. Many of the pictures of the beach were irreplaceable because the area didn't look the same.

"When I came back from overseas, my parents naturally thought I would settle down on the Island. But when I saw what was happening, I said 'no way.' I could see what was coming. They were building houses everywhere. They were talking about eliminating this and that, and they cut down the forest. There was no more forest left in Surf City or Harvey Cedars where there used to be a big forest.

"There had been a bad storm in '44 that had wiped out a good bit of it, and they were hauling in sand and gravel to build houses on it.

"Barnegat Light, where the lighthouse is, used to be a big forest, too, with beautiful holly trees — the prettiest and the biggest I've ever seen — and cedar trees. Up near the beach, where the lighthouse stands, were these old, gnarled cedar trees that had been sandblasted. When we were kids we used to go and play in the forest around there.

"What had changed the most was all of those people moving in and building houses."

So Burrel, with his wife, moved to Oxford, Pennsylvania, for five years but eventually returned to the area, settling in Tuckerton.

Whenever they can, weather permitting, Burrel and Alva get in their car and drive to Stafford, cross the "new" causeway and continue to Barnegat Lighthouse State Park, where they walk the nature trail and enjoy a small sensation of the Island's past.

— *Pat Johnson*

Perry Inman

"We were never rich; we were never poor. We never went to bed hungry. We lived off of clams, seafood of all kinds, and had one wonderful life."

When talking with Perry Inman, sit back and listen — to tales, all true, of whaling ancestry, of sea monsters, of peril on the ice. Of witnesses to rum-running, of a brother born in a gunning shack.

Listen to the lively lilt in the anecdotes of the native shoreman who hopes to tell them till he's 100.

Perry Inman traces his lineage back to the second family to settle in Great Swamp, the town now known as Surf City. Aaron Inman, born November 29, 1709, came from Rhode Island and bought land from an earlier settler by the name of Soper.

The first Inmans were successful whalers. Rising above the oceanside enterprise of cauldron and furnace, where blubber bubbled and boiled, was the lofty Inman whaling lookout mast. Inmans of old spent days in the "crow's nest," scanning the horizon, "sweeping the sea, searching for the great moving bulk of a whale," as Perry and Jane Inman's daughter, Cindy, imagines.

Spotting a whale, the whaleboat crew sprang into action, launching their boat for the chase. If they were lucky, they towed the beast to the beach, where it could be cut into haulable pieces.

Whales sometimes became helplessly stranded in the shallows. When this occurred, local men often shared the wealth. It happened once in 1803 at Absecon Island. As the locals celebrated their good fortune, a man named Inman appeared and claimed a portion of the profits. Although the men protested, Inman won his share in a court of law by proving that the harpoon which had actually caused death was his own.

It was a different leviathan that Perry's father, John Robbins Inman, encountered five generations and 200 years removed from Aaron.

"You've heard the story, without a doubt, about the sea serpent," Perry began. "Well, my dad and Uncle Rube were the ones out in the boat."

Perry's father and Rube Corlies had set their net the night before to catch bait. In an 18-foot sea skiff, they launched from Surf City one summer morning that began like any other.

"They would collect their bait in the morning and they would row until they got clear of the breakers; then they'd put up their sail, and they'd sail off three miles to what they call the sea bass grounds," said Perry.

"This morning when they went to lift their net with the bait in it, this sea serpent came up out of the net with its mouth full of mossbunkers, and, Uncle Rube said, eyes that big."

Perry and Jane Inman in 1998.

His own eyes wide, even though recounting the story for the hundredth time, Perry made a circle with his hands the size of a dinner plate.

"It was a snakelike creature the way it looked, with the dangling tentacles like a squid would have.

"Rube said Dad picked up the sprit on the sailboat to push it against the sea monster. According to Uncle Rube — and I think I probably heard Daddy say that, too — he said, 'John, don't put that sprit' — that's a long gadget they used to use on the sail — 'don't touch that beast with that thing; just drop that net and let's get the H out of here.' And that's what they did.

"As they dropped the net, the sea serpent headed towards open water. They say when he made his run to get away from them, he took a lot of net with him, that he stirred the bottom up. They were in water that had to be seven or eight feet deep. He took half of their net with him when he left; he must have torn the net just all to pieces.

"Now, there were two or three other boats, with two men in each boat. They could see that there was some kind of commotion, but they never got a real good look at the sea monster — until they saw it going to sea. Then they saw it on the top of the water. They said that days before this happened, there was one report of a shipwreck, a wooden ship, and lots of people think that could have been the sea monster floating around."

Perry's birth on November 8, 1914 was less spectacular, one would have to say, than that of his brother, firstborn John Elwood Inman.

Parents John and Amanda Corlies Inman were the keepers of the old Bonnet Club on the south side of Lazy Point, which, as Perry explained, is a long stretch of land that can be seen from the Causeway bridge sticking out from around Fourth Street in Surf City. Years ago, it was nothing but marshland. As keepers, the Inmans lived there.

"My oldest brother was born in the old Bonnet Club," said Perry. "When Daddy knew my mother was about ready to give birth, he left one evening in a 12-foot sneakbox. He either sailed or rowed, I don't know which, over to Mud City, and he had to walk from there up to Manahawkin, and get old Dr. Hilliard. He hitched up his horse and buggy, rode down to Bayside again — that's what they call Mud City now — and they went across.

"Mother had a midwife with her, of course: Sherwood Corlis' wife. Sherwood was my mother's brother. Aunt Olive was the midwife. Dr. Hilliard stayed two nights and three days before Jack was born, and guess what the bill was? Five dollars."

There were eight children in all, by the time the last one came in 1921. After John, there arrived Willard (1905), Joseph (1907), Amos Marvin (1909), Rachel Martha (1911), Oliver Perry (1914), Bertha Myrtle (1916) and Eva (1921).

Perry and the former Janie Birdsall moved to Manahawkin in 1948.

But growing up in Surf City brought memories of its own: camping on High Island to clam with dad and brothers, and staying for a week; picking cranberries and huckleberries when the only road that went to the bay was an old gravel path; neighbors taking turns to help butcher one another's pigs.

"We were never rich; we were never poor. We never went to bed hungry. We lived off of clams, seafood of all kinds, and had one wonderful life."

It's been long enough now that Perry doesn't have to change or leave out the names when he tells his stories, he has decided.

"One winter night, it was a calm evening, a knock came at the door and we let them in and it was my first cousin Alice Jones, who married Frank Jones, who was ex-Coast Guard. She was with her friend Angie Lukens, whose father did everything in town (Surf City) back in the mid-'20s — water superintendent, borough superintendent, anything that was necessary to be done except lighting the lights on the street corners — my brothers did that — and they would put just the amount of oil in there so they would go out at a certain time of the morning.

"Back to the liquor story. They walked up to the ocean this one night and they heard noises and they saw a pile or two at the end of the street. They peeked over the dunes and they could see what was going on. They were landing liquor right on the beach. The bigger boat was off behind the bar, and they would run ashore in a smaller boat.

"So Alice and the others rushed up to Uncle John's, as she called my dad, and said, 'Call the Coast Guard, they're landing liquor on the beach at the end of Ninth Street. We just saw the whole thing.'"

Ninth Street was in the district of the Ship Bottom Coast Guard Station, but Perry's dad called the Harvey Cedars station, too, figuring Ship Bottom might need help.

"Well, as it ended up to be, they suspected that some of the Ship Bottom Coast Guard might have known what was taking place, because they didn't get there until way after," Perry recounted. "By the way, my brother was in the Harvey Cedars Coast Guard Station at the time. They had orders before they went there — 'Don't shoot to kill; shoot in the air just to scare them away,' you know. There was one new Coast Guard there. Evidently he hadn't heard of the instructions, so they managed to catch one man that night.

"They asked him, 'Why the hell didn't you run with the rest of the guys?' He said, 'Those bullets were coming so damn close to my head that I decided I'd better fall down.'"

The crew came back to Perry's family's house to use the phone.

"Ed Arlen was number one man with the Harvey Cedars Coast Guard Station. When he came in to use the phone at our house, he said to my dad, 'Did you get any of that liquor yet?' My dad says, 'No, I haven't seen a drop of it.' So, our telephone happened to be in what we called our summer living room, which we never used in the wintertime. Ed had to go in there to use the telephone. He said, 'John, I thought you told me you didn't have any of that liquor.' He said, 'Well, I fell head over heels right over two or three cases in the middle of the floor.'

"Dad said, 'Those damn boys of mine must have brought them in there.'

"I don't know to this day what ever happened to that liquor.

"When it came time to prosecute this one man who was stupid enough to fall down, why, they couldn't find enough liquor to present as evidence in the case. Not only state troopers but everybody else had helped themselves to the liquor."

With that remembrance, Perry laughed again.

Perry Inman belonged to the first aid squad in the 1950s when there were only seven members.

"I'm telling things that I couldn't have told years ago."

'Stay the Heck Off of Salt Ice'

"A story that should be told to everybody," Perry said, concerns staying off saltwater ice. "Any ice is dangerous, but salt ice is triple dangerous."

Perry never skipped a Saturday hunting with his sister Eva's husband, Ken Houssell, who was keeper of the Sandy Island Gunning Club. But there was one Saturday he almost missed, and wished he had missed.

The bay was frozen over. They never came close to hunting for anything but solid ground.

His brother-in-law asked if he would help walk a 10-foot aluminum boat carrying some kerosene across the ice to the island. The clubhouse was running out of fuel for the fire.

"Here we go off with two five-gallon cans of kerosene sitting in the stern of his boat and him pushing on one and me on another one. Everything is going fine, and we got almost dead-center of the channel, where I know there is 18 feet of water, and what happens but *kerplunk*, down goes everything.

They had the good fortune to stay close to the boat when they fell in. "I don't know what happened but the good Lord did it," Perry attributed. "I climbed that boat, got in the bow of the boat, half full of water, Ken holding onto the stern."

Salt ice does not run deep, Perry explained. Though the top surface of that ice appeared perfect, there was a strong tide running beneath it.

"He said, 'What are we going to do now?' I said, 'We better say a prayer.'

"I said, 'Well, here's what we're gonna do; it's the only thing we can do. You're gonna be the outboard motor, Ken. Turn around and put your butt up on the back of that boat and kick like that.'

"We didn't even have an oar," Perry remembered. "Stupid!

"I said, 'I'll sit on the bow of the boat and I'll break the ice, until we come to that hard ice on the edge of the channel.' "

Once there, they would find only three feet of water below the ice.

The plan worked, and they walked the rest of the way to the clubhouse, where the fire was still lit.

When walking on other parts of the bay, men of that time knew to carry a long cedar pole; some were as long as 12 or 13 feet. If a person fell through the ice, the pole, carried parallel to the ground, would lodge on the ice around the hole.

As Perry explained, "If you break through and you have one, you can get back out on top of the ice again that way, just covering the hole up that you break."

As teenagers, he and Rudy Reiser had sense enough to carry a pole when they walked out to watch his dad and brothers spearing eels through holes in the ice at Main Point Sunk. The place was so named because the water off Main Point was deep. Perry's dad was not glad to see the boys join them.

"My dad and my brother gave us holy heck."

Perry recalled a time when the pole that Paul Cramer carried saved him. Paul was the brother of Doc Cramer, the baseball player.

The moral of the stories: "Stay the heck off of salt ice!"

If walking on the frozen bay was dangerous, driving on it was another thing altogether, as Perry told.

"Rudy Reiser and young Dick Zachariae, both of them were very good friends of mine. Dick would do anything on a dare, and I don't know whether anybody dared them to do this, but this was one day I had common sense and told them they were nuts if they did it," Perry's recollection began.

They had their car way past the bay end of South Second Street in Surf City.

"He had a '28 four-door Chrysler, which was a heavy car. They drove down off of the end of that street, and they came out at the bathing beach on 10th Street, driving along on the ice.

"They didn't go through and they went across some very deep water at one point, I know. When I had told them how crazy they were, they said, 'Well, we're going to leave the doors of the car open.' I said, 'That is a good idea, but you're nuts.'"

Making the Move to Manahawkin

The fishing industry provided some work for young men. When trucks replaced the railroad, Perry took the opportunity to drive the day's catch to New York markets.

"Rudy Reiser and I used to drive trucks into Fulton Fish Market for Charlie Butler from Barnegat Light. Rudy didn't even have a license at that time, but we'd drive the truck in anyhow whether we had a license or not," Perry recalled.

At this point in the story, Perry's wife reminded him that she drove around Manahawkin for three years after the two were married in 1945 "and never had a license."

A lot of things were different then; one of them was the makeup of the community.

"Everybody from Manahawkin knew each other," Jane said. "I came from Barnegat and he came from Surf City, and we built here and it wasn't a month that we knew everybody."

After an Island winter or two, she had decided, "I'm not hanging out dydees in this northwest wind," Perry recalled with a chuckle.

Jane's maiden name, Birdsall, goes back about as far in Barnegat as the name Inman does in Surf City, the two say. Her dad, John, was an expert cabinetmaker, carpenter and boat builder, and a kind person "who never turned his back on anyone," she described.

Perry, a carpenter, had joined Burlington County Local 1489 with his brothers, Marvin and Bill, Milt Cranmer, and Paul and Joe Lafferty. At Fort Dix, he helped build some of the same barracks that he later lived in for two weeks.

"When it came to June the 4th of 1940, I was 24 years old, and Uncle Sam pointed a finger at me, and said, 'I want you.' They accepted me right away; nothing wrong with me." Tour of duty was Australia with the 19 and 10th Ordinance Outfit, putting bombs and ammunition on B-24s, B-17s, P-40s, P-39s and a number of other planes. Perry's discharge came September 28, 1944.

Perry was making 50 cents an hour in his early days as a carpenter with house builders Gardner and Olonwich in Surf City. He and Janie bought the lot for their modest home on Broadway in Manahawkin, just south of the intersection of present-day routes 9 and 72, for $350 from Eddie Lang, Sr.

"We moved in here in '48 and we had no walls up or anything. We slept in the middle of this room, just to get here, you know, and stop paying rent," said Janie. "And, being that the house was unfinished, we didn't even have to pay taxes until it was finished."

"I want to tell you how good people were in those days," said Perry.

He went to family friend Charlie Conrad in Ship Bottom, who owned a lumber, hardware and furniture enterprise. "I said, 'Charlie, I've gotten married, I've got a lot in Manahawkin, I've got no money and I want to build a house.' I said, 'Can you back me up for it?'

" 'Perry,' he says, 'you go ahead and make out your lumber list and tell me when you want it delivered,' and he says, 'Yes, I'll carry you. Only get what you want at a certain time and then get more.'

"Well, he carried us for two years while we were building this mansion. No bank loan, no interest or any of that kind of stuff."

Perry transferred to a different union local based in Lakewood and, as a shop steward, worked on projects that included the Oyster Creek Nuclear Generating Station and the long-anticipated Southern Ocean County Hospital.

"You don't know how they had to fight Toms River and Lakewood hospitals, who tried to get the money that had already been laid aside for this hospital," Perry said.

Perry belonged to the first aid squad in Stafford Township when there were only seven members. "We had two old Chrysler ambulances that usually ran."

He remembered one accident call in particular. It was in 1955, long before Southern Ocean County Hospital was built.

"My brother Bill was a (squad) lieutenant. He called me one night at 2 o'clock and says, 'Come on, we have a hell of a mess on Route 72.'

"What that mess was, they used to collect the garbage from town and they used to burn it not too far from Route 72. They used to let it burn all night, but the dampness had come in, and all of the smoke had settled on 72."

The smoke was so thick, the rescue crew had to leave their ambulance and walk to the scene.

"Here was a baker truck, I forget what, upside down, two or three cars that came in there and they had all run together." The first aid squad from Tuckerton took their patients to the hospital in Mount Holly, but the Manahawkin vehicle had to go to Lakewood. At 3:30 in the morning, there was no doctor in attendance at Lakewood Hospital. "They had to call in and get a doctor out of bed even to take care of our patients. Thank God nobody was seriously injured."

In his 80s at the time he was sharing these recollections, Perry was spry enough to leap into a leprechaun-like hop, just to prove that he could. People tell him he'll probably live to be 100. His wife, expediter when certain stories ramble, joked, "And you'll be talking all the way."

His reply: "Well, as long as I can talk, you know I'm alive."

— *Maria Scandale*

Lookouts such as this, pictured in The Lure of Long Beach, *gave whalers like the 18th-century Inmans a first alert of the leviathans.*

Blacky's Clams

"People think this place has been here for a thousand years."

An outpost of shore tradition, Blacky's Clams stands on the strength of its simplicity.

"Clams — fresh daily" is all the sign has to say to capture attention amid the tall grasses of Bay Avenue. First-time vacationers, as they head down this shore road shortcut, crane their necks, slow down and turn in.

"People think this place has been here for a thousand years," said owner Charles "Chill" Paul with a grin.

The Pauls took the business over from the Blacks in 1977, moving from their base at the Duck Inn Marina. Blacky's has huddled along East Bay Avenue since 1950. It only seems older.

"People come here and say, 'My dad used to bring me here.' I say, yeah, it's been here a long time."

A noticeable sag not disturbing its pride, the place dispenses its luscious cargo from beaten bins and wooden pallets stacked with bags and bags of fresh clams and mussels.

Business is good enough to keep the stand open during the hours that the Pauls announce on a cardboard sign tacked outside — they don't have to invest much overhead.

The green-painted building is a welcome sight that passersby want to keep in the landscape. Not long ago, some mistook a construction sign for a real estate banner and stopped in a panic.

"It's ridiculous," Chill laughed. "The roof was leaking, so a friend of mine put a roof on, and he stuck a sign out in front with his name, Kitson Roofers. And people — I mean not just one, but dozens of people — said, 'Don't sell this, you can't sell this!' We're not going to sell it; we just had a new roof put on."

The Paul family has been here, not a thousand years, but for as long as Stafford has been a township. Chill guesses that the family does have what might be called "bragging rights way back."

Sometime between 1735 and 1743, Benjamin Paul was one of the first men to buy tracts of land in the area that became

Blacky's as it looked in 1987. The east half of the building holds an apartment, but the Pauls reside on Beach Avenue.

Stafford Township. He was born in Massachusetts and descended from William Paul, an Englishman who settled in America in 1635, according to *Salter's History of Monmouth and Ocean Counties, N.J.* One local historical account also listed a Perry Paul as one of the first six men to buy land in Stafford, but the modern-day Paul family can find no written record of his arrival.

"When I was a kid there were Pauls on every street," Chill noted. "Years ago, you had to be careful what you said to somebody because everybody was related in some way."

Charles L. Paul, of Beach Avenue, is the son of George Birdsall Paul and Sadie Stevens Paul — and, by the way, has "no idea in the world" how he got the nickname Chill.

Chill Paul keeps the clam shack tradition alive in his spare time. In his retirement, he still clams three or four days a week. After retirement from the military in 1972, he worked in the bay for about 15 years until bursitis in his shoulder forced him to quit. He took jobs as a personnel officer with Ocean County and in the cabinet department at a local plumbing company, but "came back to the bay."

Other than their past hobby of racing sled dogs, Chill and his wife, Barbara, have found the clamming business the most enjoyable, and they have stuck with it.

"I don't think we're crazy enough to do it if we're not making money," he said. "For a seasonal business three or four months out of the year, it's fine."

To hang on for three decades, a clam retailer has to have a hard shell.

"We've seen a lot of people come and go who were going to get rich in the clam business," Chill said, reflecting back. When clam stands dotted the bayside in proliferation, there were more clams to be found, and more men making a living by the water.

"Back then, in the early '70s, there were just clams everywhere. You'd figure if you didn't catch 500 an hour, it was bad clamming, and you'd move to another spot. An average day's catch then was like, 2,500 for a decent clammer. When I go now in the wintertime, when I'd catch 500 clams, that's a lot."

Quality control at the clam stand for all these years has been achieved by knowing where the clams come from.

"We basically buy from the same guys all the time. We know where they clam, we know that they clam in good water, and so our basic philosophy is, we won't sell something we wouldn't eat ourselves," Chill said in an interview in 1988. A decade later, the Pauls were buying from a dealer whose goods are monitored by state regulations.

The only tools required have been some baskets and a sturdy scale for the mussels (the clams are sold by the dozen). They used to use a primitive-looking machine to sort the clams by size; it stretched the length of a garage in the back of the property. Built by Dave Wright of Surf City, the machine was modeled after potato-sorting devices in Maine. Rolling the clams downhill along two slanted rollers that merge at one end, it sorted the chowders from the cherries.

Nowadays, the Pauls order only the sizes they want, and so the sorter has rolled off into antiquity.

"Years ago we would have 12 or 15 clammers we bought from every day. We didn't sell them all at the stand; we wholesaled a lot of them to Philadelphia and different places," Chill said. "Now we don't even deal with any clammers. We buy them from certified dealers. In a way it's a lot easier, because when you buy from the clammers you buy everything they have, and the big clams, there's very little demand for them. So we tell the dealer how many of what size, and that's what we get." Most of the clams come from Great Bay.

Low prices allowed clams to be more of a mainstay of the diet in the '50s when Chill was a young clammer selling to the dealers.

"We got a penny apiece for them when we sold them to these guys. And I can remember at that time, they were selling three dozen for a dollar. Think about it. Three dozen for a dollar, and we're getting, for littlenecks, more than $3 for a dozen

now. Back then, the bay was loaded with littlenecks."

Chill remembers a particular bounty in Little Egg Harbor.

"I retired from the Army in 1972; I started working the day as soon as I got out of the Army. At that point there was a growth of clams in an area called the Goose Bar between Beach Haven and Tuckerton, and it was unlike anything that anybody I ever met had encountered before. The baby clams were by the millions; they were in a huge area.

"Normally you couldn't sell clams under an inch and a half, but the state let us take these up," Chill continued. "We were selling them to a fellow who was transporting them and replanting them in Virginia, which was a shame, because in retrospect probably what should have been done, they should have planted them by the open bay here."

A clammer could still make a decent living when he got out of the service, from 1972 to as late as 1985, Chill said. "As a matter of fact, our son clammed full-time about then. He finally reached the point where he couldn't do it anymore; he couldn't make a living. Just not enough clams."

As the 1990s have turned into the new millenium, the Pauls keep on keeping on — as much for something to do as for any other reason.

"We've pretty much analyzed it that it's so congested and crowded here in the summer, there's nothing much else for us to do, anyway."

That fact hit home one Fourth of July after Chill and Barbara sold out of clams.

"We came home, and we were sitting there looking at each other like, what are we going to do now. So we went down to the bathing beach in Barnegat and the greenheads were eating us up. Barbara said, 'I hope nobody goes by that knows us.' So we went home."

In the last four decades, the owners of many other clam stands have closed up shop, and they remain only in the memories of long-timers on the bay. A culture is disappearing.

"Gosh, yeah, there used to be, let me think how many ..." Paul began mentally counting clam stand after clam stand from his to Ship Bottom.

"You know where the Old Causeway Inn burned down," he began, referring to a spot just down the road. "There used to be one there — this was back in the '50s. That was Wimpy's place. His name was Paulsworth. Wimpy was the first original hippie, I think. He used to go surfing, and he would leave a sign on there saying just take the clams and put the money in the jar."

"Can you imagine doing that today?" Barbara laughed.

The Ashtons owned a clam stand near where Margo's Marina is now located, Chill recalled. "They were there all through the '60s and '70s. That was a big operation. They used to buy 75,000 or 100,000 clams a day.

"Going further back, on the island where the Dutchman's is, there used to be another place there. In the '40s and '50s, there was a place there owned by a fellow named Burrel Adams."

There were more still; the string of clam shacks marched right on across the bridge. On Long Beach Island, "the place is still there, by Hochstrasser's; it was called Chippy's. Then, where the Italian restaurant (La Spiaggia) is was Joe's Clam

"Chill" Paul manning the roadside stand.

Bar. Then if you go over to where Causeway Glass is now, that was a seafood place in the '40s and the '50s. The original people were named Middleton. Then, if you go to where Oskar Huber's is now, that was another clam stand and a restaurant; my aunt and uncle had that. His name was Ernie Stiles."

Heirs to Blacky's may be the Pauls' oldest daughter, Susan, and her husband, Walter. "Hopefully it'll stay there and they can have it one of these days. They're real interested in it, and he's a clammer; he can sell his clams there."

So, from their open-air window on the world, the Pauls continue the bayside tradition.

"People will come, and then they'll be back and they'll have a friend with them, and they'll be amused and the one guy will be pointing out different things to the other because we're 'primitive,' but it works," summed up Barbara.

Nodding from the metal stool he pulled up beside his wife, Chill added, "If it ain't broke, don't fix it. We complain about it, but we must like it, or we'd be out of here."

— *Maria Scandale*

Phil Hart

"We could talk about how the draggers were ruining the fishing in near shore. Whatever it was, we didn't get any fish, and after the war, nets were hard to get; rope was hard to get. It just died out."

"It's too bad the fishing died off. I never would have done anything else for the rest of my life." Phil Hart is one of the last of the pound fishermen who clambered aboard the open skiffs, shoved off the beachfront with six other men and faced the sea before dawn.

It's the people he likes to talk about, more than the unique mechanics of the vanished system that snared fish with a stationary curtain of nets and poles.

From a heyday in the 1920s and '30s to 1956, the men motored out the mile or two to the traps, or pounds, and lifted the nets to find what the Old Man of the Sea shared with them.

"I thought that was just part of the day's work. It was the social end of it and the fellows themselves that are such wonderful memories," Phil said, allowing the recollections to light his face with an ever-present smile. "It seemed like each one of them was almost your dad."

Phil's dad, Bergen Amundsen, worked at the Beach Haven Fishery within the same block as their home; so did his brothers Gurney and Shorty.

"There are only so many other people and we're going to fade away." A momentary shade of wistfulness crossed Phil's face as he sat flanked by nautical memorabilia on his Manahawkin porch. "And once we go, we're the end, because we fished the last years in the fishery."

Men like Hart were born for the sea. "Our mother had a great love for fishing. She loved Beach Haven; she loved the water. So we just lived on it."

Their father came to Beach Haven in 1923 with the sea in his veins. "He was a sailor in Norway since he was 14 years old. It was automatic; everybody went to sea. That's where the livelihood was at."

As the story goes, Norwegian men in Bergen Amundsen's time were forced to come to grips with seasickness. "He said they used to put you on a sailing ship, sail you from Norway to England. And if you didn't get better by the time you got to England, they'd put you on a ship and send you home. That's the way they cured you of seasickness; they'd tie you up in the mast and let you hang up there."

Phil can't name many parts of the world that his dad didn't sail. Then Amundsen went to New York City, looking for a job. "They told him, 'Down on Long Beach Island they're hiring fishermen.' He came down here and got a job in the fishery and that's where he stayed."

Beach Haven Fishery stretched along 12th Street the width of Beach Haven. Kids like the Hart boys grew up as eager hangabouts, endured by the men who saw themselves 20 years earlier, and who were friends of the boys' fathers.

"They worked hard and had their enjoyment, too, but the important thing, they never hollered at us. They always treated us nice; they never swore and used foul language around us," Phil said.

Little kids around the fishery in the 1930s were treated well, but they did take their chances like everybody else at suffering from the practical jokes that were the men's pastime on land.

A narrow path ran next to the fishery's three buildings. The fishermen's socks soaked in buckets upstairs. The boys came riding by on their bicycles. "They'd wait till we got right underneath and they'd throw that water down and stand there and laugh." At jokes directed toward each other, the men might find their shoes nailed to the floor, or fishery owner

Phil Hart has led an active life on land and sea, and helped to found several of Stafford Township's community organizations.

Clifford Morris might find the underneath of his car tied to a telephone pole.

The good times followed the men home at night, and the family worked together to prepare for lobstering, which some men substituted for pound fishing, or used to supplement it. "My mother's door was always open. My mother loved to have people come to the house. In the wintertime, they'd be sitting there talking, and they'd be making nets for the lobster pots."

Phil pulled up a wooden kitchen chair, grabbed some twine, and found a four-inch, oval-shaped "needle" that happened to be lying on the desk.

"They'd each have two chairs, one to sit in, and on the back of the other chair, they'd fasten the net to it."

With a couple of knots to secure it to the chair, and a deft series of threadings in and around, a length of twine became the beginnings of a net in the fisherman's hands. "They're just half-hitches," he dismissed.

"There were a lot of things we didn't have, but, I tell people, we had lobster to eat during the Depression," Phil said, as he found a picture of his mother while leafing through a photo album. "She used to go out and lift the lobster pots with my dad."

Even Habitual Work Was Exciting

A few precautionary measures were in order to keep things flowing safely. The men were told to take their rings off and never to wear them, because if the ring would catch in a dropping net, the momentum would tear the whole finger off.

Occasionally, a hammerhead shark would come along and threaten to tear the net to pieces. The skipper, Willie Bordwick, had a unique way of getting a handle on the hammerhead.

"He'd get them over next to the boat and he'd get them by the tail and give them a flip right into the pound boat."

The feat involved grabbing "just where you wanted to grab," Hart tried to explain, quickly adding, "I never did that." He laughed. "I always thought that was pretty good."

The fishery didn't operate in the coldest winter months, but that still left plenty of frigid air. "We'd put the new poles in in February, and it'd be so cold that your hands would freeze right around that jet rod," he said, referring to the metal rod through which sea water was pumped, or jetted, to flush a hole in the ocean floor where the pole would sit.

Poles could be set in calm seas, or in a slight swell.

"It was nice if you had just a little bit of sea," Phil said, "because every time the boat would go up in the air, you'd tighten the chain. Then when the wave would wash under you, the weight of both of those boats on that pole would push the pole down in the hole."

Work was usually finished around noon. "You had to be in and have the fish ready for the train so the train could turn around and make it to the Fulton Fish Market and put the fish on sale."

When the nets were too "dirty" with growths of sea grass, the men took a new net out while the old one was cleaned and dipped in tar pots. The tarring process took place in an open field. Tar kept down the growth and protected the nets against rot.

Phil, born in 1924, recalled that he was in his late 20s when it all came to an end.

"It wasn't making money. There were no fish."

Asked why, he answered, "We had our reasons, we thought. We could talk about how the draggers were ruining the fishing in near shore. Whatever it was, we didn't get any fish, and after the war, nets were hard to get; rope was hard to get. It just died out. That was the end of it."

He went to work with electrician Ronald Cox and later became a self-employed electrical contractor and active community member. There are many recreational opportunities for young people that weren't there before Phil helped organize them after the family moved to Stafford Township in 1950. The sandlot baseball that later developed into Stafford Township Little League is one. Phil was also a member of the committee to charter the first Cub Scout organization in the township.

He sat on the committee that organized Southern Regional High School in 1957 and was a president of the Board of Education. His time also went into membership on the township elementary school board. He was there during the chartering of the Stafford Township Municipal Utilities Authority, and he made decisions as a member of the township Board of Adjustment. He also belonged to the Stafford Township First Aid Squad and the Lions Club.

Folks still present him with model boats from all over the world.

— *Maria Scandale*

Aerial from 1947, showing (left, center) Remson Meadows. Notice the old railroad bed crossing Bay Avenue.

Beach Haven West

No longer would that place on the south side of Bay Avenue be referred to as Remson Meadows. Then and for all time it would be known as Beach Haven West, where, by 1986, some 3,000 families would own a house down by the shore.

Once upon a time there was a place called Remson Meadows on the south side of Bay Avenue in a sleepy town called Manahawkin.

"Ah, yes, we remember it well," sang a trio of former mayors. Jack Cervetto recalled that some of those little ditches in the meadows were big enough for a skiff to get through for some good duck hunting. "But I can still smell the mud in the meadows.

"It was a musty, grassy muck kind of smell came out of there, like salt hay that had died off and rotted. Some of the water was stagnant, too, and there were mosquitoes galore."

Milt Cranmer would walk across the marshes in search of table food, he said, boasting that he never came home empty-handed.

And Charlie Boltner, well, he liked to talk about the duck hunting lodges along Mill Creek. Charlie spun a pretty good Babe Ruth yarn, too.

Joe Oliphant, who along with his wife, Liv, shared the honor of being named grand marshal in the township's 1988 Founder's Day parade, recalled walking across the fields to Manahawkin Bay with a fishing pole across his shoulder and coming back with a string of fresh weakfish and some more fish stories.

And then one day a little boy came down from northern New Jersey with his dad, and his dad used to say as they crossed the old wooden drawbridge that some day they ought to buy that land over there on the right-hand side of the road.

The boy's father, Milton L. Shapiro, a developer of seashore communities in Ocean County from 1926, died in 1949, but the fairy tale did not end there. His sons, Herbert and Jerome, bought that land called Remson Meadows from Stafford Township in 1950, and later on, after extensive negotiations, those properties south of Mill Creek down to the creek at Cedar Run.

The brothers knew they'd need a dredge to get things started, so they hired Reynold Thomas, owner of the Barnegat Bay Dredg-

Miss Stafford Linda Seekell and contestants at the Beach Haven West Civic Association club in 1964.

ing Co. in Harvey Cedars, and Charlie Strickland, an expert in hand machinery, who owned the Strickland Boat Yard in Beach Haven.

According to the surviving brother, Herbert (Jerome passed away in 1969), the group traveled to Elizabeth City, N.C., to look at a dredge being advertised there for sale.

"Reynold and Charlie gave us the go-ahead, and so we bought that dredge and had it towed up the inland waterway. And we were in business."

Manahawkin was a sleepy little village in those days, Herbert described, with little work to be found. A craftsman had to travel north or over to Long Beach Island for work, or else he retired. For the Shapiros, seeking out competent and dependable tradesmen to develop the project was not a dif-

ficult task then because these fellows needed work.

John Jakielaszek and Jim Coates worked the dredge; Milt Cranmer and Ed Hazelton hammered the nails; Phil Hart handled electric wiring. Joe Cranmer did the plumbing, and Billy Penn painted. They and dozens of others got things moving for the developers.

No longer would that place on the south side of Bay Avenue be referred to as Remson Meadows. Then and for all time it would be known as Beach Haven West, where, by 1986, some 3,000 families would own a house down by the shore — along with 1,300 others in Village Harbour and 175 more in Colony Lakes, the last two adjoining sections having been built by Lincoln Properties.

The Shapiro brothers, each a qualified attorney,

had devised a method of financing to enable people of all incomes to afford their houses.

When the first model went up on Selma Drive, a down payment of $390, and sometimes even less, would ensure the buyer a vacation home along the water. "It took some of them a year or so to pay off that $390," Herbert Shapiro said, "but as soon as they did, they could move right in."

As a comparison one could look in the local paper and see that in the spring of 1957, $3.98 at the Hand Store was good for a pair of Levis to wear by the bay. The Great Bay Motor Company in Tuckerton offered top quality used cars for 15 cents a pound, "perfect for running around in the summertime," the ad promised.

Loveladies Harbor sold houses back then for $7,000, with 100-by-100-foot lots *extra*, from $3,570 up "if purchased with a house." M. L. Shapiro Co., "Ocean County's largest builder," proclaimed in a full-page ad in *The Beachcomber's* Easter issue that it had the greatest home buys ever offered:

"Visit our model home on Selma Drive in Beach Haven West, a two-bedroom Cape Cod with expansion for two more. Knotty pine paneling and knotty pine cabinets in an all natural kitchen, two picture windows, screens and an outside shower. On 60' X 80' waterfront lots *included* in the $6,990 purchase price. A down payment of $990 will guarantee delivery by June."

The ad continued: "For those interested in occupancy *next* year ... join the increasing numbers enjoying our layaway plans as an easy way to meet our low down payment ... and as the only way to protect yourself against future price increases. Just $100 now and $100 a month until occupancy in early spring, then only $66.62 per month for 10 years."

This, then, would be the answer for the average guy who dreamed of one day owning a house down by the shore. An economical house-and-lot package deal, with financing terms too good to be true for those families who for 51 weeks out of a year had to pinch their pennies to pay for a one-week vacation in an apartment on Long Beach Island.

The lagoonfront community of Beach Haven West, about 30 years after its inception in 1957.

John and Alice Jakielaszek of Irvington, who bought that first model home on Selma Drive in 1957, still lived there 30 years later. When they first moved in, there were 411 houses, and out of those 411, only 14 were occupied year-round.

For 11 years, John Jakielaszek worked for the Shapiros as a crane operator by day, and house salesman by night and on weekends. "They had built a model of the Sea House on the seventh floor of Bamberger's in Newark," he recalled, "and I averaged 125 sales a year.

"People used to think we made an awful lot of money selling these houses, but depending on the model, we'd get from $25 to $100 commission on a sale." He was quick to add, however, that with those commissions he was able to pay off his own house.

Herbert Shapiro remembered John Jakielaszek as one of his top salesmen. "We had a lot of customers from Jersey City then, and John could talk to them; he had a feel for them. Of course, I'm not sure it was a question of selling in those days, or just order taking, but I'd say it was probably a combination of both."

Innovative Marketing Perfect

Even the Shapiros themselves did not visualize the extent to which Beach Haven West would grow, or how fast.

"For that we have to thank the Garden State Parkway," the developer said. "It opened up the whole area of Southern Ocean County to people from northern New Jersey and New York. Prior to that time, most people coming to the shore area were from Camden or Cherry Hill and Pennsylvania."

Water flowed to Beach Haven West initially from a pressure tank on the corner of Morris Boulevard and East Bay Avenue. At a cost of $250,000, a water tower was constructed in 1957 on Mill Creek Road to the right of Paul Boulevard. Later, a new pumping station was built on the corner of Mill Creek Road and Beach Haven West Boulevard.

Houses in the original section of the development used septic tanks for sewerage disposal. As the number of year-round residents increased and construction continued on a upswing, it became obvious that these systems were inadequate to handle the extended usage.

According to Robert Sheppard, executive director of Stafford Township's Municipal Utilities Authority, "It became generally known that the septic tanks were being operated by the tides."

The MUA was formed in 1960 to correct that problem and to begin planning for the township's growth. Then-chairman Philip W. Hart scooped out the first shovelful of earth for the sewage treatment plant ground-breaking ceremonies that year, as Freeholder Director A. Paul King and 100 others looked on. Informal ceremonies were followed by a luncheon at Carroll's mainland tavern on Route 9 .

The treatment plant became operational the following year with an estimated 500 households connected to the system. In 1975, Stafford was directed to connect to the Ocean County Utilities Authority's regional treatment facility in Cedar Run.

By 1970, the Shapiros had added six new home styles, ranging in price from $11,990 for the Sandpiper to $22,990 for the Riviera Continental. Closing costs for each model were consistent at $490, and a mandatory $300 fee was paid by each homeowner for connection to the township's MUA facility, this charge payable over a four-year period.

The Beach Haven West Civic Association, formed in the late '50s, continued to thrive. Membership dues were only $3 a year, and when the swimming pool complex was built as a private venture in 1965, a family could join the club for $50 a year. This fee entitled members to unlimited use of the pool, adjoining tennis courts and the club house.

"The Beach Haven West Yacht Club," as early members liked to call it, became the gathering place for children and their mothers who were generally here only for the summer. Fathers joined them after they returned from work in the early evening hours and on weekends.

Many social functions took place at the clubhouse — holiday dances, Miss Stafford Pageants, "Hi, Neighbor" parties in the spring and the unforgettable "So Long" gatherings on Labor Day.

In 1986, the owners of pontoon boats in Beach Haven West revived the Labor Day festivities when they organized a 16-boat parade on the water. The number of participating boats swelled to 26 in 1987, and the captains were thrilled to see their audience waiting for them.

Betty Simon of Jeri-Ann Drive said that when

she first came down in 1964, neighbors would decorate their boats — rowboats, garveys, sailboats, all kinds — on Labor Day weekend, and cruise the lagoons, waving and shouting goodbye to their neighbors. "It's great to see the people getting together again," she said 24 years later when the tradition revived.

Shortly after the Shapiro organization sold its remaining holdings to Lincoln Properties in 1973, the pool facilities were offered to the civic association.

Dream, Economy Go Different Ways

As the economy changed, enthusiasm began to wane, and it was agreed by the voting members of the association that mounting liability insurance and maintenance costs were beyond its reach. The pool and its facilities fell into disrepair and eventually became victim to vandalism.

The property was sold later to a private investor, and today, on the site where the pool once stood, there are a number of private homes. The original charter for the association, however, remained open, and the association later was revived.

The Shapiro family expressed the hope in a 1988 interview in *The SandPaper* that they would be remembered fondly in Stafford Township for their generosity. "We considered ourselves part of the community in which we were making a living, and we gave then because we wanted to give," Herbert Shapiro said.

"Today, giving is compulsory," he added. "You can't build anything, anywhere now without first giving, but in those days the concept was different. The concept was that the people wanted us to build. They needed us to build. And by giving employment to its people and establishing new ratables for the town, we became a part of that concept and gave willingly and freely on our own accord."

As early as 1957, the developers had donated to the township a bathing beach and children's playground for the exclusive use of its residents. The beach is located off the bayfront of Jennifer Lane and was later refurbished by the town's recreation department with new playground equipment and permanent benches.

Their donation to Stafford Township of its first municipal building in 1959 was unprecedented at the time. In an article appearing in the *New York Times* on Sunday, August 30, the $45,000 gift was credited with ending the threat of a local property tax rise that had persisted for many months.

With the opening of the Garden State Parkway, this area adjacent to Long Beach Island has grown rapidly, stated the newspaper, making a local municipal building an absolute necessity.

The *Asbury Park Press* described the dedication as a gift stemming from the Shapiro family's desire to show appreciation to the township committeemen for "good government and a reasonable tax rate" in Stafford Township.

The Shapiros turned over the deed to the building and adjoining five-acre plot to Mayor William S. Burnham with a request that the edifice be a memorial to their father, M. L. Shapiro, who had founded the firm.

"Originally there was a plaque to that effect inside town hall," Herbert Shapiro said, "but somewhere down the line it disappeared."

Much like the one that disappeared from the lobby of the hospital, he added. "We had given the ground for Southern Ocean County Hospital anticipating that the lobby would be named after my father, but that plaque, too, is gone.

"Sad," he said, "but then that's the way things go."

Additionally, the Shapiros had given the town a deed for some 20 acres of property where Southern Regional Middle School stands today, and a building in Beach Haven West to house an ambulance.

Shapiro said in 1988 that with state regulations as they were by that time, Beach Haven West could not have been built.

"And wouldn't that have been a shame? Think of all the families living there now, and think about all the enjoyment they've been getting over the past 30 years there. Wouldn't it have been a shame?"

Shapiro, who maintained a summer home on Long Beach Island, served as chairman of Bay State Bank.

"I suppose we'll all look back 20 years from now and say, 'Boy, back in the 1980s it was easy, wasn't it?'"

— *Irene Higgins*

Southern Ocean County Hospital

There was much to celebrate as the hospital opened where none existed before.

Adapted in part from an article in A Brief History of the Southern Ocean County Hospital, *titled "Southern Ocean County Golden Book of Founders," first published in the* Tuckerton Chronicle.

In 1954 a group of residents, pointing out that the area had been inhabited for several hundred years, decided it was high time Southern Ocean County had a hospital. It took 18 years for the doors to fully open, but the $2 million investment came entirely from people in the community.

More than 5,000 local people participated and persisted in the effort that brought Southern Ocean County Hospital to fruition in 1972.

In 1956, the first step was to "write to several doctors to inquire as to how to plan for a hospital."

The earliest written record of the group's deliberations lists the participants: Louise Curran, Ann Wheeler, Margaret Kelman, Frank Neubaum, Clifford Sherman, Antoinette Fackler and Jane Barnett.

The years 1956 and 1957 passed with steps to adopt bylaws and to incorporate as a legally chartered body. Proposals at the time were to merge with hospital groups in Toms River and Lakewood. Howard Schifler was hired as president, and fundraising began.

In late 1957, it seemed that the hospital's future address might be Ship Bottom, as the borough council donated a 200-by-200-foot piece of land for the "Long Beach Island Emergency Hospital."

In their eagerness to achieve their goal, Mayor Charles H. Moore and members of the hospital auxiliary held a ceremonious ground-breaking. "Under the circumstances, no hospital was actually begun and on September 30, 1962 the borough asked for the return of its land," noted the SOCH "Golden Book of Founders."

The record shows that the four years from 1958 to 1962 were full of hopeful effort. In 1959, the hospital group traveled to Trenton to interest the Catholic Church in taking over the project. Bishop Ahr of the New Jersey Diocese pointed out that they did not have nearly enough resources, that it cost more than $20,000 a bed to build a hospital, and that the hospital's treasury contained enough to pay for about one bed. "Finally, he stated that the only way the Diocese could take the effort over was, if it were agreed that the membership of the hospital Board of Trustees were to consist exclusively of people of the Catholic faith," the Golden Book of Founders chronicled.

For some time, there was more discussion of turning the assets over to Paul Kimball or Toms River Community hospitals, but those who believed in the project refused to abandon it.

"There were those who said, 'Forget it, take your money and give it to them," recalled James J. Mancini, Long Beach Township mayor, who would become a state assemblyman, Ocean County freeholder, and chairman of the board of directors of Southern Ocean County Hospital.

"When I moved to Long Beach Township, we had to go to Kimball, up in Lakewood, if we needed to go to the hospital," said Mancini, who with wife, Madeline, made the trip to the maternity ward nine times over the years. "The hospital in Toms River opened in 1960. They didn't think we needed another one."

By 1964, funds had accumulated to $69,288.87 and Stafford Township donated a new parcel of land, more than 20 acres. Shifler resigned as president and James J. Nobel was elected in his place.

The years through 1967 were marked by continued efforts to increase the treasury, mostly by the ladies auxiliary and its associated groups, so that by February 1968, Treasurer Elvin Ewald was able to report total assets of $161,279.49.

"Yet these years were also marked by an increasing sense of discouragement and futility," noted the Golden Book. In the 14 years, 1954 to 1968, less than $12,000 per year average had been raised. "The annual increase in the costs of building a hospital was greater than this, so that actually the goal was further away than ever. In 1965 a study by a firm of professional hospital consultants made a finding against building the hospital, as 'non-feasible.'"

The state of New Jersey ruled that if the applicants wanted to build a hospital of fewer than 100 beds, an older hospital of more than 200 beds must act as sponsor. An osteopathic hospital in Cherry Hill at first agreed to assume the role, but on Dec. 1, 1968 expressed doubt about the commitment, finally withdrawing in June 1969.

"Some activists in the hospital effort offered to resign. Some did," reports the hospital's historical record.

"A great deal of time was taken up with sparring with various departments in the New Jersey State government, with the county Medical Society, with the Health Facilities Planning Council, with voluminous application forms that seemed impossible to fill out, and with renewed demand that we yield our assets to the other three hospitals in Ocean County."

The winter of 1968-1969 marked a turning point.

It began with a proposal at the Dec. 10, 1968, meeting of the board of trustees to open a public office so that all the people in the 13-community area would have easy access to the hospital effort.

"Because of evident reluctance, this was not accomplished until 20 months later when a temporary office was opened at 1800 Boulevard, Ship Bottom, and two months later transferred to Old Borough Hall, 11th and Boulevard, allowed rent-free by the Surf City Borough Council." On April 28, 1969, total cash assets reached $198,201.18

The board of trustees then created a new office, that of executive vice president, and elected one of its board members, Sam Darcy, to fill it. He was charged with heading the building fund drive, creating a task force, and serving as chairman of the Negotiations Committee aiming to reach agreement with Burlington County Memorial Hospital for sponsorship of the project.

In September 1969, Connolly Associates, an independent hospital consulting firm, completed a study that showed a need for 83 to 96 beds in the area. Even this study first had to meet approval of the state.

On April 7, 1970, at a meeting in Trenton, state officials agreed that in accordance with the criteria set up for affiliate and satellite hospitals, Burlington County Memorial Hospital and Southern Ocean County Hospital were authorized to reach an agreement for the building of a hospital facility in Manahawkin.

Events then moved rapidly. It had become increasingly clear that little or no funds would be forthcoming from either the federal or state governments or foundations. It would all have to be raised from the people of the 13-community area.

On Aug. 31, 1970, about one month before the annual meeting, 165 people, including 120 delegates from 42 organizations, met in the Long Beach Township Municipal Building to review plans for the hospital. They agreed to bring pledges of money for the building fund to the annual meeting of the Southern Ocean County Hospital Association the next month.

Several auxiliary funds were established — notably the J. Lawrence Entwhistle Fund in Mystic Island, the $100,000-Plus Business Men's Fund under the leadership of Frank Klein and Ray Reynolds, several mainland activities guided by Jack Hendrickson, the gathering of funds previously established by Reynold Thomas of Harvey Cedars, and leadership groups in a number of townships. The women's auxiliary was to function independently.

Another influential supporter, Edmund T. Hume, a past commissioner of the New Jersey Department of Community Affairs who later retired to Surf City and served as chairman of the SOCH Foundation, recalled the momentum of support that the project gained.

"It first started when we needed some facility close to the Island with the summer crowds that we have," Hume said in 1991. "It started out to be more of a first aid center than anything else; then we got involved and got going."

Simultaneously, the arduous work of trying to come to a satisfactory agreement with Burlington County Memorial Hospital was proceeding.

James Mancini, who was elected an assemblyman in 1972, credits a particular neighbor of his, William T. Cahill, for shepherding the hospital plan.

"Governor Cahill had them all working on this, and finally they made a deal that never happened before and has never happened since: They gave us permission to build a hospital, and we had to operate it under another hospital's medical license," Mancini said. "He lived in Brant Beach, and I knew him personally. He probably is the one, if you wanted to pinpoint someone who, if it wasn't for him the hospital wouldn't be there."

An agreement was reached in January 1971. Dr. Thornton M. Stearns, a urologist at Burlington County Memorial Hospital, would prepare and head the medical staff of Southern Ocean County Hospital. The State Health Planning Council approved the plan on June 10, 1971.

The scoreboard on Oct. 29, 1971 showed a total of $906,443.20.

By then, several new difficulties had arisen, the most troublesome of which was the parcel of land on the south side of Route 72 donated by Stafford Township. A former landfill (along, appropriately named, Recovery Road), its condition was what was known as "refill land," but the refill had not fully settled and the engineers were doubtful that it would sustain a heavy building. It could be built on pilings, but the cost would exceed $80,000.

Nearby, on the north side of the road, slightly westward on Route 72, lay a 15-acre parcel owned by the Shapiro family. The Golden Book of Founders reports that after "considerable negotiations," Herbert Shapiro and his associates agreed to donate 9.8 acres of the land for the site. It turned out to be excellent ground with a heavy deposit of gravel, providing a sound foundation.

Construction contracts signed Sept. 8, 1971 gave the job to the Hospital Construction and Equipment Co. of St. Louis. James J. Mancini was designated chairman of the Building-Design Committee. Ground-breaking had already occurred on July 10, 1971.

Burlington County Memorial Hospital, in consultation with Southern Ocean County Hospital Association, appointed Stanley Duncan as assistant administrator for both hospitals with special responsibility for the Manahawkin facility.

On June 19, 1972, the final agreement between Burlington County Memorial Hospital and Southern Ocean County Hospital Association was signed by Burlington County Memorial Hospital President Dominick Ferrelli and James Nobel. William D. Locke and Sam Darcy co-signed as witnesses.

Essentially the agreement, following the direc-

Southern Ocean County Hospital nears completion, top, as workers put finishing touches on the building in 1972. Below, an ambulance pulls up to the emergency room at the new hospital shortly after its opening.

tives of the state of New Jersey, provided that one medical staff (actually an enlarged staff of Burlington County Memorial Hospital) would serve both hospitals, while administrative functions for the Manahawkin facility ultimately rested with the Burlington County Memorial Hospital staff headed by William D. Locke. A joint management board with four representatives from each side would advise in the business dealings of Southern Ocean County Hospital.

The administration would endeavor to make the hospital financially self-sustaining. But all building costs, including paying off the mortgage, would have to be met by the SOCH Association out of money raised outside the hospital's income from its services.

The hospital's two mortgages totaled $700,000, with payments to run for 25 years at 7.5 percent

interest. The annual payment due was approximately $62,000. Should the hospital run at a loss, it would be up to the SOCH Association to cover it with funds raised outside hospital operation. The agreement ran for 10 years, unless either side would find it operationally unsatisfactory, in which case it could be terminated by either party with 12 months' notice.

There was much to celebrate as the hospital opened where none existed before. But another accomplishment could be seen by inspecting the books.

"It is an accepted standard in 1972 that a new hospital should cost to build between $62,000 to $68,000 per bed," hospital officials said in an article in the *Tuckerton Chronicle*. "We have in our files estimates given us by accepted experts in the field that our Hospital should cost upwards to $4,216,000. Actually it came in at less than $2 million. Including contributed services, the cost runs at about $2.2 million, or about $35,000 per bed, that is, about half the expert estimates."

While part of the credit for the achievement goes to "good management," the officials went on to say, "Chiefly it is due to the new concept of building a facility affiliated with another and avoiding unnecessary duplication of equipment, and making maximum use of services."

The hospital opened in 1972 with a skilled staff of doctors and surgeons, an experienced administration, "and the fact that our Hospital is one of those rare institutions which will have no debt obligations ... should insure a very successful and self-sustaining operation," founders hoped.

The 32,000-square-foot hospital had 54 beds, two operating rooms, two X-ray rooms, a "heart room" with electrocardiograph and other equipment, emergency and outpatient sections, and a recovery room. Its facilities held a solarium, a pharmacy, a laboratory, isolation and special observation and care units with monitoring equipment. Plans came complete with a dining room and kitchen, administration offices and a gift shop.

The hospital was self-contained with its own water and sewage system, and a backup emergency power unit. The building was completely air-conditioned. Each patient room had an oxygen supply piped in and vacuum suction power, as well as telephone, radio, television and private toilet facilities.

Into the Future

The most dramatic growth was yet to come, in a shorter time.

In 1980, the James J. Nobel Pavilion, a two-story wing, expanded the hospital to 100 beds, a necessity in the area that had grown in both year-round and summer population. An intensive care unit was added that year.

Community involvement had been the cornerstone that built SOCH, and that interest continued. That effort was officially established in 1985 as the SOCH Foundation, a New Jersey nonprofit corporation that directs philanthropic initiatives on behalf of the hospital.

SOCH obtained a separate operating license from Burlington County Memorial Hospital in 1987, a milestone of independence.

Between 1992 and 1999, hospital outpatient visits increased more than 300 percent. In those years, the hospital invested $47 million in its physical plant and equipment, more than twice the amount invested in the hospital's 20-year prior history.

In 1993, the hospital embarked on a major renovation and expansion project, including construction of a patient bed tower, a four-story building where 102 medical/surgical beds replaced 68 inpatient beds that dated back to 1972. The patient bed tower opened in 1994, housing also two medical/surgical units and the Susan B. Horn Oncology Resource Center.

The opening of the Southern Ocean Center for Health in Forked River also took place that year. The center is an 18,000-square-foot, fully licensed ambulatory care facility. In 1997, a second center opened in Little Egg Harbor Township, 13 miles south of the hospital. Between 1992 and 1999, 40 percent of the people treated through the SOCH system were treated at satellite centers.

Important additions were finished at the main hospital campus in 1997. The 45,000-square-foot Medical Arts Pavilion housed a regional dialysis center and an ambulatory surgical center, as well as centers for physical therapy, wound care, and speech and hearing. Seven medical office suites allowed space for 30 physicians. The pavilion is also home to the Family Resource Center, the center of the hospital's community wellness program and health information resources.

The hospital brought maternity services to Southern Ocean County in 1998 with the opening of the Maternity Pavilion, a service that was long awaited.

In 1999, the hospital broke ground on the last expansion project before the end of the century, which includes a 20-bed, sub-acute unit and an expanded intensive care unit. In 2000, the hospital completed work on the community's first radiation therapy center.

By that time, Southern Ocean County Health System Inc. and SOCH's staff of over 200 physicians were already serving more than 90,000 outpatients a year, with more than 28,000 emergency department visits, 6,200 admissions, and offering many community outreach programs.

Surfing

"I told him it was a surfboard. He said, 'You mean, like in California and Hawaii?' "

Imagine a time with surfing an unknown sport on Long Beach Island, only a rogue boarder here and there. The date wasn't as far back as we might think; it was the early 1960s. And some of the local pioneers weren't beach dwellers; some guys from Manahawkin had as much to do with launching the sport as anybody.

"I was 16 and was living here in Manahawkin, and right next door to me was Ron DiMenna, and next door to him was the Manahawkin Baptist Church," recalled John Spodofora.

Ron and John would become recognizable names in surfing circles and the world over. But not quite yet. They hadn't set foot on a board.

"The new pastor who came to town was the Reverend Earl Comfort. He had just served a ministry in California. He moved to town with a strange-looking object called a surfboard."

"Surfing basically was unknown in the Manahawkin-Long Beach Island area," Earl said, taking over the narrative from his point of view, from a young man 10 or 15 years older. "That is, until some fellows from California came in. One of them, I remember, was a guy named Wimpy Paulsworth. Another fellow used to build some boards over at the Ship Bottom Fishery.

"So I watched them build some boards, and I said, 'Hey, I can do that.' So I came home, bought two big blocks of Styrofoam and a redwood stringer, and shaped my first board. I used the wrong resin the first time I built it. I no sooner applied the resin to the fiberglass than I noticed that the Styrofoam was melting. Fortunately, it didn't go all the way through, and I changed the resin and was able to save the board.

"I was going out of the parking lot one day with this thing on top of my car, I was going to do some surfing, and the fellow at the house next door — his dad owned a meat market in Manahawkin, and his name was Ron DiMenna — he had just

Ron DiMenna and Earl Comfort, second and third from left, during a day on the beach with friends.

gotten out of the Marines, where he was an honor guard. We had become good friends, and he saw me with this on top of my car, and he wanted to know what it was.

"I told him it was a surfboard.

"He said, 'You mean, like in California and Hawaii?'

"I said, 'Yeah.' He said, 'Well, can I come with you?'

"So I said, 'Sure.' So Ron and I went over to the beach and I taught him what I knew, which was not much about surfing, but we used my board. Since it was somewhat of a crippled board, we would ride maybe four or five waves and we'd have to bring the board in and drain it before we went out again. But we basically learned to surf."

John, meanwhile, was a water-skier, a little younger than Ron. "We started talking one day. They wanted to go water-skiing, and the deal I made was if they would teach me how to surf, I'd teach them to water-ski," recounted John.

"We only had one surfboard between the three

of us at that time," John said with a laugh. "Whenever we'd go surfing, I'd watch what they did and I'd go out on the board and try and replicate it. Eventually Ronnie and I decided we needed our own board."

They took measurements off the reverend's board and bought foam. "And looked at pictures from a lot of magazines," according to John.

"You could not buy a surfboard around here because nobody surfed at that time. The closest place to find a surfboard was Abercrombie and Fitch up in New York," John recalled.

"We built our surfboards, which was a lot of fun. We shaped them outside, and when it came to actually doing the fiberglassing, we'd bring them inside the house. At night, I had my mother's kitchen table with a tarp over it and Ron had his wife's kitchen table, and we were doing the resin."

"Ron and I built two surfboards in my living room," Earl's part of the story continued. "My poor wife had to watch the television around the surfboards, because we had to have them in the living room to dry them, because we needed 70 degrees to dry the resin."

"It stunk up the whole house," added John. "But we built our first boards and really started surfing."

Every time they took to the surf, they drew a big crowd, attention which they didn't mind at all.

They didn't really know how to master the waves. "By watching some of the films that came from California, we understood a little bit more about how to do it," Earl said. "At first, we just rode the waves straight in, and then we saw them cutting, riding the waves sideways, and said, 'Hey, that's the better way to do it.'"

The sport was starting to outlast the first home-made equipment.

"We eventually decided that somewhere along the line, somebody's going to have to buy one of these things," Earl recounted. "So I bought one from California, a beautiful board. I had it in my home, and high school kids heard about it. I used to have a flock of kids coming in every day, 'Can I see the surfboard?'

"Well, Ron watched all this, and he figured that this probably would catch on."

"People kept coming up to Ron and I and asking where we could get one," John said. "At first, Ron and I started to build a couple boards and sell them, but we soon realized the demand was much too high."

Besides, it took about a week to make a board, and at the time, the boys were charging about $60.

"The first surfboards we built, you'd have to do them in stages — shape the foam, install the stringers, lay the glass, and then the resin would have to dry.

"So, what we decided to do, we started ordering them from California and selling them," said John, who still had to try and sit patiently through high school classes during the day.

It was 1959. A printed history of the shop that became Ron Jon's lends a view from the perspective of Ron DiMenna, who later moved to Florida: "When his father heard that Ron wanted his own custom surfboard from California, he suggested, 'Buy three, sell two at a profit; then yours will be free.'"

John Spodofora, the "Jon" half of the early business, took up the rest of the story. "Ronnie's father,

Felix, had a grocery store in Manahawkin, and at first he'd put the boards out in front of the grocery shop. It got to the point where it was interfering with the grocery shop business.

"So, Ron and I took them over to Long Beach Island. We rented a trailer. We put it up right on the location of where his current shop is now."

The original Ron Jon Surf Shop opened in Ship Bottom in 1961. Even as the '60s began, surfing hadn't crawled past its infancy stages in New Jersey.

"It was unknown," Earl said. "We went to Ocean City, New Jersey, Ron and I, and surfed off the jetty down there. These people had never seen surfing in their life. They were lined up on the stone jetty, watching us."

Earl also remembers "an older guy down in Surf City by the name of Stretch Pohl who did some surfing — these vets who had been in Hawaii had probably gotten a shot at it there — but it never really took off here until Ron opened his shop.

"And then kids bought surfboards like breathing."

"It just kept building and building," John marveled.

No matter that half the surfing crowd lived on the mainland; they could almost smell when the surf was up.

"We would watch the wind," Earl explained. "If you had a northeast wind and the wind shifted, that was a dead giveaway that there was surf. Or we would just take a chance."

The ones who didn't have cars got there by hitchhiking with boards under their arms. "People would actually pick us up and take us over there, the boards sticking out both sides of the car."

The ones who had cars "customized" them around the longboards. "We'd break the windows out of a regular car — absolutely — and ride up and down the Island that way."

Ron Jon's was off and running. John worked the business after school and all summer, after graduation carrying his board to his dorm room at Drexel, jumping in the car with it to head homeward every weekend. Later, he went on to a career in engineering with the U.S. Navy. Ron DiMenna began supplying former customers with surfboards to open their own shops along the East Coast. He parlayed the business into a worldwide enterprise.

Talent from bigger waters brought the next wave in surfing know-how, when well-known boarders from California and Hawaii checked out the Eastern Seaboard potential.

"People on the West Coast saw it was a great market — Dewey Weber and Greg Noll and all the famous surfers back then came out to the East Coast here to promote their products," John said.

Some of the older local guys, Earl among them, were too busy mastering the waves themselves to become very star-struck.

"We had a couple champions at the East Coast, but we weren't that knowledgeable about them," in Earl's memory. "We were just crazy guys learning a great sport. And I think most of us agreed, it was probably the best sport we had ever tried."

John, meanwhile, made closer friends with some of the new guys. Love of surfing united everybody.

"Dewey Weber was probably my favorite. I surfed with him," John said. "He was a small guy, sort of like me, a really super nice guy." Dewey and Iggy, his shaper, stayed almost the whole summer of '62. "He taught me a lot about shaping boards," John credited. "Back then, I had the shortest board; it was 9 foot 1, a real hot dog board. The average boards were 10 foot, 11-foot, 12-foot; they had some 14-foot boards we would buy. It has changed a lot."

The guys started surfing up and down the coast, looking for the ultimate surf spots. "Up to New York, all the way down to Florida, Cocoa Beach, surfing the ECSC, East Coast Surfing Championship, every year," John recalled.

He considered the local surf challenging, but to some of the traveling boys, it must have been practice. "Ralph Hahn and a group of his friends from Hawaii were stationed at McGuire Air Force Base; they'd spend every spare moment over here. They just blew everybody away."

As surfing caught on, not all onlookers were friendly.

"The surf fishermen didn't like us very well," Earl remembered. "They'd oftentime throw their dipsies at us, cast their lines out and try to hit us."

Conditions on the political front became gnarly. Some town fathers scanning the horizon saw only dangers and inconvenience to other bathers.

"We formed the Long Beach Island Surfing As-

sociation because the five mayors of Long Beach Island were a little bit cautious about surfing," Earl put it delicately.

"In fact, their first reaction to it was not to allow it at all. But we would go to the town meetings, and we would pressure and show them how it could work."

The surfers had begun meeting once a month to plan strategy. "We would hire some hall in Manahawkin or on the Island, fire halls," Comfort said. "We would plan how we would present our case to the mayors, and we actually had jackets and patches, which went like wildfire.

"Finally they granted us the hours before the beach opened and the hours after the beach was closed. So that's when we would surf." Eventually, the governing bodies set aside several beaches for all-day surfing.

The association promoted safety-conciousness for its members' own good, not just to appease the elders.

"It was interesting; we wrote up what we called Rules for Surfing, to keep the guys safe," outlined Earl.

"In those days we didn't have ankle leashes; there was no such thing. So if you lost your board, you lost your board, which was dangerous, because if somebody was bathing inside, and a 9- or 10-foot board came crashing, it would hurt someone."

One of the rules was, never surf alone. Earl broke his own rule one morning when he wanted to go out at 5:30 a.m.

"I fell off the board and it went way up in the air, and as I came up out of the water, the thing came down and creased my forehead. Blood was spurting all over the place."

Standing on shore was a surf fisherman, one of the unsympathetic ones. "Fortunately, I didn't lose consciousness. I thought maybe he'd offer to help, but he just looked at me and cursed, and turned around," said Earl. "So I showed up at Doc Irvin's office over here in Manahawkin — we were real close friends — at 7 in the morning. He just looked at me and said, 'Oh, good night. Get in here.'"

The young minister was wearing a white patch on his forehead the next Sunday. "I stood up in the pulpit and said, 'I don't want anyone to say a word about this ...'"

In the early days, equipment for the sport was nonexistent or primitive. Not only were there no leashes, "they didn't have wetsuits for surfers back then."

"The only wetsuits that were out there were for divers," said John, a diver himself. "They would rip real easy, because they didn't have nylon. The flap went between your legs and fastened around your abdomen and, well, you lay on the surfboard and got huge welts from the metal fasteners. It was a sign of somebody who had been out there surfing."

The diver's suits were constantly ripping under the arms, letting water flow in. John and the guys tried smearing heat-rub all over their bodies in a naive attempt at keeping the cold ocean out. The first good wave or two would wash it right off.

"It's funny; I still remember coming in from surfing and trying to start the car, and my hands would be so frozen I couldn't turn the car key. Your feet would get so numb you couldn't feel them on the board," said Earl. "But we'd go out."

Some of the best times of a lot of kids' lives were spent surfing. John recalls the time a whole school of porpoises swam with the surfers, bumping their noses into the boards. He never had a problem with sharks; jellyfish, yes. "Since the wetsuits would let a lot of water in, your chest would be one solid welt."

Surfing association meetings weren't all business. "We bought films from *Surfer Magazine* to show at the meetings," said Earl. "They'd pull huge crowds," added John.

Between the movies, like "Endless Summer," and the California surfers themselves, a lot of Manahawkin boys began running around in baggier shorts, talking about "shooting the curl" and "wiping out."

"And there was one we heard from California called 'Cowabunga!'"

In Retrospect

John surfed the Great Lakes, California, Puerto Rico, Africa, different places all over the world. Surfing gave him an affinity for the ocean, a devotion to keeping it clean.

"I want this to be there for our kids."

As a minister in his early 30s, Earl Comfort didn't mind the chance for evangelizing among the young boys who followed the older surfers into the waves. "I tell my son, I've introduced you to two things, Jesus Christ and surfing," he said, smiling, "and sometimes I'm not sure which one takes precedence."

All three of Earl's boys are avid surfers — Chris and Greg, who followed him at Dallas Theological Seminary, and Geoffrey, of Florida, who lost one leg in a motorcycle accident on Long Beach Island. "He still surfs to this day."

In retirement, Earl returned to Manahawkin, but his eyes still reflect the sparkle of the ocean.

"I was living in Florida, and one day I got home and there was a message on my answering machine, and it was Ron. He had been in Australia for 20 years, and heard that I was in Florida. He contacted me and asked me to come up to his complex in Cocoa Beach. We kept in contact, and we still do."

Like surfing itself, Ron Jon's reached around the world. And beyond. High above the Earth, on space station Mir, clings its logo.

— *Maria Scandale*

Crossroads

The contrast of scenes shows the change in character of the community from the turn of the 20th century to 1964.

As a measure of changing times in Stafford Township, the year 1964 marks a good vantage point. That year registered as New Jersey's Tercentenary celebration of 300 years of growth and change, so Stafford Township took the chance to document its own turning points.

The following pictures from that document, *Stafford Township: A Pictorial Review*, were published by the Stafford Township Tercentenary Committee. They contrast what had become a "rural suburban" view in 1964, at bottom, with an earlier time around the turn of the 20th century when the scene was of a self-sustaining farming and fishing village.

Some sturdy landmarks remained as the town built upon its past, and other structures had already taken their place in history.

Bay Avenue looking west from Letts Avenue, circa 1900, above, and in 1964, below, in Manahawkin's business district.

Bay Avenue facing east from a point near Route 9 in 1920, above, and 1964.

Main Road ~ Manahawken, N. J.

Main Street looking south toward Bay Avenue about 1930, above, contrasted by the 1964 view. The National Hotel is in the center of both photographs. It was torn down shortly after the bottom photograph was taken, and is now the parking lot for Carroll's Restaurant (then Carroll's Tavern), which was an ice cream parlor known as the Lake House in the 1930s.

Main Street looking north from Beach Avenue about 1900, above, and the structures that remained in 1964. The building at right center of the top photograph is the former Cranmer Meeting Hall, and once housed the first telephone office, located on the second floor. The building was later moved across the street and later became Johnson's Luncheonette. Below, left, is the Cranmer Store, which was at one time a Quaker Foods store operated by Charley Farley.

Standing on Main Street in front of the Baptist church, this was the view looking south in 1903, above, and in 1964.

Stafford Avenue around 1900, eastward from Main Street, when streetside trees stood, above, and in 1964, below. At the far left a corner of the National Hotel porch is visible.

Beach Avenue east of Main Street in 1905 (above) and some of the residences as their exteriors had been remodeled in 1964. The school can be seen in the center of both photographs, and a barely discernible horse and buggy head down the street in the top photograph.

The scene on picket-fenced Beach Avenue, east from the old railroad right-of-way, about 1915 (above), and in 1964.

Excepting the road surface and utility poles, Beach Avenue looking west toward Main Street in 1905 (above) hadn't changed much by 1964. The former home of Althea Fredrickson can be seen at the end of the road. It was later torn down to expand Manahawkin Lake Park.

A Picture of Growth

The Parkway afforded easy commuting for people who found they could work in Middlesex or Monmouth County and live at the quieter, more affordable shorefront.

"**B**oom!" in a word most aptly describes the status of Stafford Township from the 1960s to the year 2001.

At the turn of the 21st century, Stafford was ranked one of the fastest-growing townships in the fastest-growing county of New Jersey.

The population of Stafford Township decupled from 2,000 in 1960 to 20,000 40 years later. Some 7,100 moved here between 1992 and 1999. Several attractions beckoned.

First, where the road led, travelers followed, and the Garden State Parkway paved the way to the beach. They followed and came back to stay. If an observer could have watched the township's growth through a time-lapse view from today's satellites, he would have seen the picture develop via the Parkway and Route 72. The roadways positioned the township geographically in the path of migration.

In 1954, the Parkway opened a straight and clear route for visitors to fly south in the summer and back to northern New Jersey in September. Three years later, bungalows in the new Beach Haven West development sold at a price that almost anyone could afford. Fast forward a generation, and some of those families decided to spend year-round retirement in their former summer retreat. The Parkway also afforded easy commuting for younger people who found they could work in Middlesex or Monmouth County and live at the quieter, more affordable shorefront. People began developing the Ocean Acres lots that they had bought for as little as $500 in the 1970s.

Where Stafford Township's population had grown by only 100 to 200 people in the decades between 1930 to 1940 and 1940 to 1950, a new trend began. Between 1950 and 1960, the count jumped by almost 600 residents. Then between 1960 and 1970, the population almost doubled, from 1,930 to 3,684. The increase in the next decade expanded by 7,000 people, to 10,385.

The transition to year-round living would bring permanent changes. Anticipating this in 1980, the Pinelands Commission released its landmark Comprehensive Management Plan, limiting growth.

The plan made predictions that the "conversion of seasonal housing to year-round occupancy will significantly change the character of these communities." What would result, the plan said, would be "a sharp increase in demand for public services in communities where services today are largely rudimentary in nature."

That prediction came true, for better or worse. Back up a generation to 1964, when Stafford was ready to celebrate the 300th anniversary of the state's founding. It was more than 200 years since the first landowners made their home in the township. The town did not have a full-time police force, and Police Chief Frank Carletto was urging the township commission of the need for a night patrol. He was joined by businessmen and civic organizations who were worried about break-ins at the bowling alley and skating rink, and at Beach Haven West homes that were vacant during the week. Another issue of growing pains concerned Southern Regional High School. School taxes were up $61,486 to run the school, including the cost to operate the district's own school buses for the first time. By contrast, the previous year, school taxes had been reduced by $9,000.

The changing face of Southern Ocean County, and with it, Stafford Township, was forecast in another statement made by the Pinelands Commission in its November 21, 1980 management plan. This remark foretold displacement of lower-income residents. "On the mainland, many of the modest developments in Southern Ocean County are occupied by retirees and other moderate income households," it said. Although these homes were "among the least expensive housing units available anywhere in the region," demographics would change that. The Pinelands Commission predicted that during the next decade, initial occupants would be "increasingly replaced by more affluent, younger households."

In many quarters, growth had been anticipated. Inevitably, the northern and western metropolis would extend its urban reach closer to the shore. Also, the first half of the 1980s was marked by a building boom that paralleled economic trends throughout the country.

"The economy locally started to grow a little bit, allowing people to live and work here," explained Carl W. Block, mayor from 1984 through the turn of the 21st century. "First the growth occurred more in the northern end of the county, and today the hospital is a large employer, and there is a lot more retail business here year-round, as well as service-oriented businesses like accountants, doctors, lawyers."

The township generally followed national trends in the real estate market, slumping in the late 1980s and rebounding in the 1990s. Stafford Township's housing starts in the 1990s exceeded those in other areas for a reason — pent-up demand.

Development from the northern metropolis keeps moving south, Mayor Block pointed out; to Monmouth County, then into Ocean County, "and sooner or later, it's going to meet coming north from Atlantic City."

However, the extent of the growth in Stafford Township was not as dramatic as some had expected. Although Stafford grew by 13 times its size from 1930 to 1990, Dover Township grew by 19 times, to a population of 76,000 versus Stafford's 1990 count of 13,325.

"Had the 1976 master plan been 'built out' the way it was projected then, we would be a town of over 75,000 people," Block, who is also deputy Ocean County clerk, said in the year 2000. "As the plan is today, the population will peak at less than 38,000 by design when every buildable lot is built upon. And we would like to lower it even more."

If the difference between 75,000 and 38,000 is planning, the greatest part of it was imposed by an outside force when, in 1980, the Pinelands Comprehensive Management Plan stepped in front of the trees and firmly curbed growth west of the Parkway.

The larger acreages of housing in the township already lay on the drawing board in previous decades. Lots in Beach Haven West were approved in the late 1950s and early 1960s when brothers and developers Jerome and Herbert Shapiro added lagoon-front shore bungalows to the bayfront landscape. The development extended to three miles inland.

Lots in Ocean Acres, which by contrast were sold by thousands of different landowners, were approved in the late 1960s through about 1972.

"An Ocean Acres developer used to bring bus trips of people down here and sell them lots on time," said Block. "You could buy a lot for $500 with $10 down and $10 a week."

Some owners had kept the lots but did not build on them until the township Municipal Utilities Authority sewered Ocean Acres in 1990. About that time, a study had attributed the main cause of pollution in Manahawkin Lake to stormwater runoff, with a secondary cause as the need to run sewer lines in the upper watershed, where the Ocean Acres development was served by 1,500 septic tanks.

The houses were sprinkled here and there on the map, so to reach septic tanks that weren't working, the sewer lines had to run down entire unoccupied streets. That paved the way for later infill.

"Had they applied under current standards, we would have forced the developer to put all that in," Block said in the year 2000. "So the MUA went in and cured an environmental problem, but it did allow the lots to become buildable, so that's when you started to see some of the infill in Ocean Acres."

There are 5,500 lots in the Stafford side of Ocean Acres alone, with more in adjoining Barnegat Township.

With population influx came commercial growth, and in all, the character of the town has changed.

The censuses of 1970 and 1980 showed that 75 percent of the people lived east of Route 9. At the end of the 1990s, the case was exactly the opposite: 75 percent lived west of Route 9. Meanwhile, Route 72 became the primary corridor of commercial activity as businesses located there along the new road to the beach only five to 10 minutes away.

With Long Beach Island hosting 100,000 to 120,000 visitors on a given summer day, there are economic spin-offs for the mainland as well, Block noted. "On a rainy Sunday, you see people drive off the Island to shop or partake of restaurants. At the same time, Beach Haven West, Colony Lakes, Village Harbour and Ocean Acres have developed. Even if half are vacation homes, half are year-round, so that leads to more demand for more stores and restaurants."

In an attempt to strike a balance between the old and the new, the township council moved to revitalize the old downtown, and to plan parks in the other areas that have grown.

Through the Neighborhood Preservation Program, Stafford Township obtained state grants totaling $500,000 to revitalize Bay Avenue in the 1990s. "We pumped that into upgrades to businesses," said Block, "and that's one of the reasons we built the new town hall in that location."

The multimillion-dollar, 42,000 square-foot facility at 260 East Bay Avenue was dedicated in 1998.

More commercial development — buffered by strict environmental standards — has been sought to stabilize the tax base. In 1999, the township saw $50 million more in ratables, but $45 million of that was residential, as compared to $5 million commercial. Residential ratables translate into service demands — trash pickup, educating students.

Future commercial growth in the township is designated along the Route 72 corridor, with some additional growth along Bay Avenue and some minor growth along the Route 9 corridor, under a plan submitted to the State Planning Commission. According to the Pinelands Comprehensive Management Plan, another regional growth center includes Ocean Acres, Fawn Lakes and the 200-acre business park on Recovery Road at the site of the old township landfill.

The community is proud of its environmental achievements in the face of its growth. Its ordinances and standards are being utilized throughout the world. Initiatives in stormwater management, groundwater protection and preservation of trees and open space have put Stafford Township on the map. The township has won more national recognition than any other single community in the United States, said Council President John Spodofora.

State and federal regulations control what can be built in more than half of the township's 47 square miles, through either the Pinelands Commission, the Coastal Area Facilities Review Act density rules, or the Edwin B. Forsythe National Wildlife Refuge.

The mayor assessed in the year 2000 that "although Stafford is booming now, we really have almost seen the end of the boom."

September 1990: The old Manahawkin Railroad Station takes to the highway enroute to its current location by the Old Stone Store. The trip on Route 72 was not its first move; the station had been relocated in the 1960s from Stafford Avenue to a spot next to the old Town Hall on East Bay Avenue.

ACKNOWLEDGMENTS

The genesis of this book was the work of Louis A. and Lillias F. Brescia, who devoted years of research and a true passion to preserving the history of Stafford Township.

The Brescias compiled and edited *Stafford Township, 1749-1964: A Pictorial Review* for the Stafford Township Tercentenary Committee in 1964, which is the basis for many sections of this book. The volume is the source of photographs as well as several historical essays that were adapted slightly for publication in *Stafford Chronicles.* Those essays focused on transportation, government, religion, education, businesses gone but not forgotten, and Manahawkin Lake. The Brescias' research that appeared in annual Founder's Day booklets also encompassed information on notable places such as Lane's Pharmacy, Cavalry Cottage, the Old Stone Store, and stagecoach stops that served seashore travelers.

At the time it was published, the pictorial review was dedicated to "the residents of Stafford Township, past and present, who have contributed so much to its growth and development." That recognition still applies today.

Those people whom the Brescias acknowledged in 1964 for information and access to pictures, maps and reference material from personal collections should be mentioned first in this book, also.

They were: Mrs. Elmer Aker; Mary Aller; Eben Berry; Mr. and Mrs. George Bowen; William Burnham; Jack Cervetto; the Rev. Earl Comfort; Mary E. Corliss; Minnie Courtney; Irene Cramer; Carrie Cranmer; Margaret Cranmer; Barbara Eismann; Grace Elley, curator, Hilliard Museum; Evelyn Hansen, curator, Barnegat Light Historical Society Museum; Ed Hazelton; Edna Hazelton; the Rev. William Hodgdon; Mr. and Mrs. Clarence Holloway; Perry Inman; Norman Levison, trustee, Beach Haven Library and Museum; Sonja Mesterton; Natalie Miller; Mr. and Mrs. Joseph Oliphant; Milton Paul; Sadie Paul; Howard Peer; Albert Scully; Thomas Shinn; Mr. and Mrs. John Wozar; Lynn Wozar.

The following were the published works which were cited in the bibliography of the original Stafford Township pictorial review: Alfred Heston's *South Jersey, A History, 1664-1923*; the Rev. E. Horace Mathis and Anniversary Committee's *160th Anniversary Booklet of the Methodist Church*; Ocean County Principal's Council's *Tide of Time in Ocean County*; T. F. Rose, T. T. Price and H. C. Woolman's *Historical and Biographical Atlas of the New Jersey Coast*; Edwin Salter's *History of Monmouth and Ocean Counties*; Frank R. Stockton's *Stories of New Jersey*; and Harold Wilson's *The Jersey Shore, Volume I.*

To this list, Down The Shore Publishing would like to thank others who provided help and information.

First are the subjects of the profiles in this book. Thank you for taking the time to share your stories with us all.

For their trust and patience, we are especially grateful to members of the Stafford Township Historical Society: Lil Brescia, Tim Hart, Phyllis Buford, Ed Hazelton and others. They placed the photographic repository in our hands, and paved the way for many of the profile interviews.

For an overview of Stafford Township growth into this new century, Mayor Carl W. Block and Councilwoman Jeanne DiPaola lent enthusiastic cooperation. So did Councilman John Spodofora, who also looked over an initial draft and suggested additions. Southern Ocean County Hospital Public Relations Manager Joe Guzzardo sent us a healthy stack of material on that facility's development.

For the segment "A Picture of Growth," The Times-Beacon granted access to its microfilm archives, which we perused for information on the year 1964.

Letters, cranberry business reports, newspaper clippings and personal papers shedding light on the life of Nathaniel Holmes Bishop III were found in the Ocean County Library Bishop Building, New Jersey Reference Collection. Around the corner, the folks at the Ocean County Historical Society Museum are always glad to look up information.

Several books provided helpful reference, notably John Brinckmann's *The Tuckerton Railroad*, and the Ocean County Historical Society's *Downshore from Manahawkin to New Gretna*. Mayor Block's office lent its copy of *New Jersey Historic Sites Inventory, Ocean County*, published in 1981 by the Ocean County Cultural and Heritage Commission. The essay by Joseph R. Steelman was found in the Stafford Branch of the Ocean County Library. Elizabeth Morgan, always an encouraging friend to fellow history lovers, had much to do with that essay's publication.

Ray Fisk knows a worthwhile project even before the words fall in order, and he devotes to it the resources of a first-class publishing house, with a Down The Shore touch. Leslee Ganss wore many hats: in addition to designing and structuring the book, she prodded us all to check locations and historical details. She handed the baton to Anita Josephson for computer layout and copy editing — Anita is the binding of any project she touches. Thanks also to Doris Horensky, our favorite typesetter; Jay Mann, for direction and encouragement; and before all of them, there was Curt Travers. Travers, The Sand-Paper publisher, lent editor Maria Scandale and his other employees to help with this project. Photographers Patti Kelly, David Gard, Ryan Morrill, Jonathan Cohen and Danielle DesFosses worked darkroom magic, part of which involved conjuring up photos from piles of files. The Beachcomber publisher Margaret "Pooch" Buchholz loaned archival material and advice.

Burrel Adams, in addition to his role as one of our profile subjects, showed that his journalism skills were still fresh after retirement as he aided with proofreading and tracking down information on several photographs. Fred Kerr, a longtime managing editor with the Asbury Park Press, was gracious enough to review a galley of the book.

No book can contain every facet of a community's history, but we thank our sources for their help in compiling the collection that became *Stafford Chronicles*.

PHOTOGRAPH CREDITS

INDEX

Down The Shore Publishing specializes in books,
calendars, cards and videos about Long Beach Island
and the Jersey Shore. For a free catalog, or to be included
on our mailing list, just send us a request:

Down The Shore Publishing
Box 3100
Harvey Cedars, NJ 08008

or visit our website at:
www.down-the-shore.com